Nine Lives  Alaska Bush Pilot

by Ken Eichner

Edited by Robin Taylor
and Suzanne Eichner

First Printing, May 2002
Second Printing, Jan. 2003
Third Printing, April 2007

Published by: Taylor Press
a division of Taylor Freelance, LLC
2559 Woodbine Place, Bellingham, WA 98229

Copyright 2002, Ken Eichner

ISBN: 0-9662517-1-7

Library of Congress Control Number: 2002103615

Manufactured in North America

Cover Photo by Bucky Dawson, Aviation Arts Unlimited

Map Art by Douglas and Terri Bennion

Dedicated to the memory of:
Stan Maplesden
Kenny Swaim
Ralph Yetka

CONTENTS

Nine Lives of an Alaska Bush Pilot	1
Introduction, My "Nine Lives" As A Pilot	7
Chapter 1, Early Life	11
Chapter 2, Flight Training	39
Chapter 3, Piper Cruisers	66
Chapter 4, Early Prospecting	95
Chapter 5, The Bradfield Claims	109
Chapter 6, First Helicopters	121
Chapter 7, Avalanche at the Granduc	145
Chapter 8, TEMSCO's Early Work	165
Chapter 9, Mountaintop Repeaters	199
Chapter 10, The Wolper Era	209
Chapter 11, Groundhog Basin	219
Chapter 12, Cargo Lessons	243
Chapter 13, Turbine Helicopters	253
Chapter 14, TEMSCO's Growth Years	288
Chapter 15, Savoonga	313
Chapter 16, Last Years with TEMSCO	327
About The Author	349

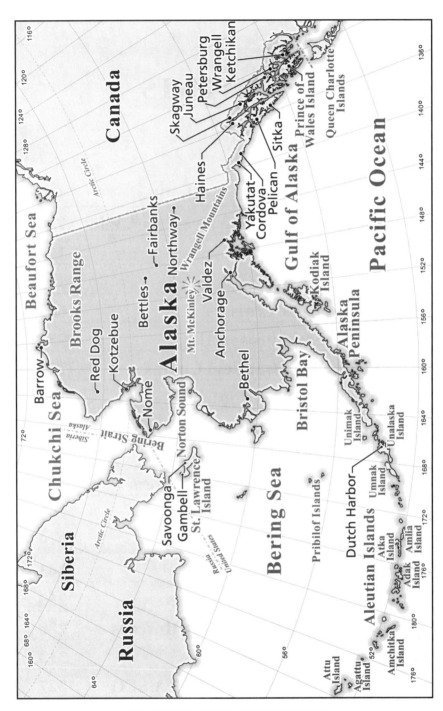

ALASKA AND VICINITY

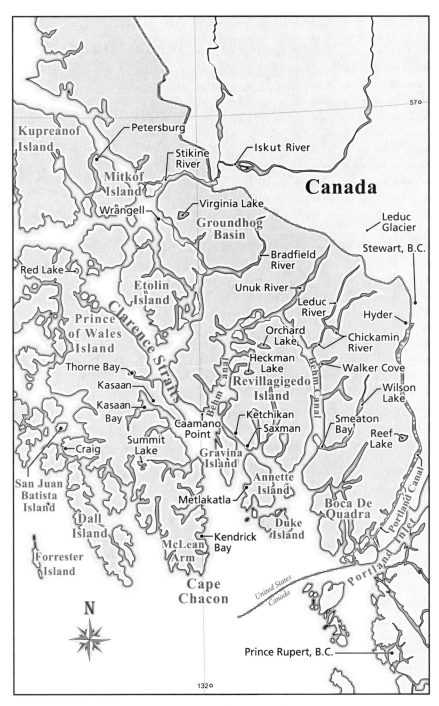

SOUTHERN SOUTHEAST ALASKA

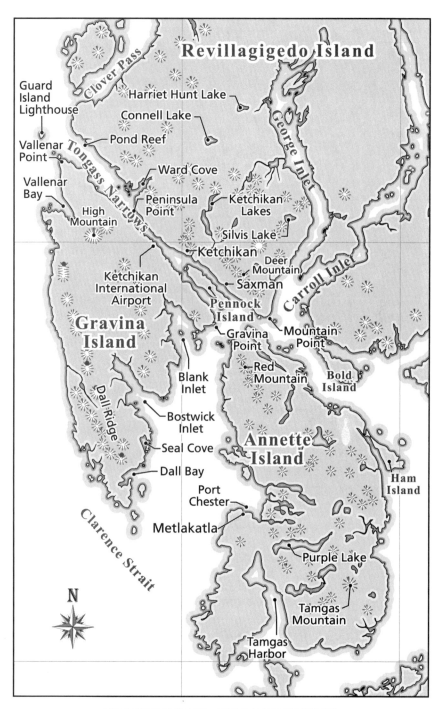

KETCHIKAN AND VICINITY

Introduction,
My "Nine Lives" As A Pilot

A number of years ago, the most respected pioneer pilot I have ever known, Bob Ellis, urged me to write a book. With his encouragement I decided to put down some of my life experiences into a book that would share what Alaska was like when I first came here and also record some of the many lessons learned through my misadventures. With luck my grandchildren, and the others who read this book won't have to learn those lessons the way I did.

Most of this book comes from my own archives, notes from my log books, and from memory. My memory isn't perfect so I apologize for any discrepancies. Of 53 years of flying experiences, I could only tell half of them in this book. I chose the ones with the most intrigue from a pilot's perspective, along with a few historical things.

Looking back over the years, I count myself lucky. By rights I should have been killed many times. I know now that I was blessed with having the "nine lives" of a bush pilot, even before I knew I would fly.

Early Rescues

On a couple of occasions when I was young, things happened that demonstrated that when the chips were down I was able to make the right move. In the early 30s, we had moved to little old house in Lebanon, Oregon at 315 East Ash Street. There I built myself a little shop in the attic so I could make model airplanes. On one occasion I was up in the attic working on airplanes when Mother ran by the hallway door and screamed, "Run for your life; the house is on fire!" I dashed downstairs, and as I came down the stairs, I was looking right into the kitchen where the fire had started on the stove. Mother had been rendering some lard, and the lard had spilled over and caught fire. The flames shot right up to the ceiling, and smoke and flames were spreading all over the kitchen except at low level. Right across from the doorway was the sink which was close to the back door.

Mother had gone out the front door, taking our valuable papers—she always remembered to do that. She set them on the porch of the house and ran out in the street to get away from the fire. (We teased her about that afterward.) I ducked down underneath the flames, dashed to the sink, grabbed the dishpan full of water, and threw it up to the ceiling. It turned out to be the right move because the water vaporized with the heat and put the flame out. It had just started to burn the paper on the ceiling. Everything was wallpaper in those days. The fireman said if I hadn't done it, the house would have been a total loss in a

very few minutes more. Throwing the water was something I did instictively, but it worked.

On another occasion, I was playing in an old creamery with a boy by the name of Leon Lafonne who came from a family where the kids were tough and kind of crude. The creamery had a cement floor, and there was a light cord hanging down from the ceiling. While we were standing around talking, Leon was handling the light cord, not realizing that the electricity was still on in the building. Why it had been left on in an abandoned building, I don't know. Leon started wrapping the wire around his arm, and all of a sudden he hit a bare spot, and he was being electrocuted. I made a diving tackle at him and knocked him off his feet, breaking the electrical connection. Everybody thought I saved his life; maybe I did. From then on, Leon was my good friend. He would do anything for me. He was a good football player and one of the toughest ones, so it all ended well.

My sister, Miriam, liked to tell the story about a close call my friends and I had on a hiking trip. Late in the fall, six of us high school boys set out on an overnight camping trip on one of the Three Sisters Mountains near Lebanon. As we progressed up the mountain, we ran into a snowstorm with winds high enough to blow trees over. We started to get rummy and wander off the trail—early signs of hypothermia. I realized the predicament we were in and rounded the boys up and got them headed back down the trail. After we descended for 30 minutes, they started to warm up and to realize we had been in trouble.

That ability has served me well, particularly in my career as a pilot. I wish I could say it was something I had developed, but when you come down to it, it's not much more than keeping a level head, combined with plain dumb luck.

My sister Miriam and I peer into the biplane that took us for our first airplane ride.

Chapter 1,
Early Life

There was a total eclipse of the sun on June 8, 1918, the day I was born in South Bend, Washington, to Loleta May and Kenneth B. Eichner. My parents named me Kenneth Charles, and I joined two sisters, Evelyn and Miriam.

When I was about five years old, my dad bought a grocery store in Lebam, Washington, which was six or eight miles from South Bend. We lived in a little tarpaper shack on a knoll north of downtown. South Bend was a logging community, and things were booming for a while in the early 20s. I went to the first, second, and third grades in Lebam, and I recall a few childhood memories.

I was very excited when my father built a crystal radio set. I can remember him with that little wire probing the crystal, and over a little dinky headset, we heard music coming from some far-off place. The next big excitement came when my dad built a super heterodyne radio. This was a radio with tubes and coils and all kinds of things. It took him quite a while to hand-build everything, and finally the day of trial came. Using two batteries to operate the super heterodyne, we had a headset for everybody in the family. We all sat around the table, the radio was turned on, and we actually heard New York on the radio. It was astounding. We would sit around the radio and listen to various programs. The one I can remember was Amos 'n Andy which was a very comical program; it was the hit program of the day.

Playing marbles for keeps was a serious matter, and around the house we played some cards and did a few things like that to keep ourselves busy. There were occasions when we would take a trip a short distance from town and camp overnight in a tent near a trout stream. This was always a great thrill for me. We would wake up early in the morning and go fishing for trout; once in a while we even caught one.

We used to like to go to the silent movies. This didn't happen very often, but once a month or so there would be a silent movie in town. Whenever there was a silent movie there was always a little sideshow. On one occasion the sideshow featured a big white mule and a prize for whoever could ride the mule. Several big tough loggers tried to hop on that mule, and it would immediately buck them off. I volunteered to be the next one to ride the mule, and sure enough they put me on the mule, and it walked around the area in a very mild manner. I thought I was quite the thing. I had done what the big loggers couldn't do. Obviously it was a very well-trained mule.

Moving On

In 1927 the Great Depression was on, and I believe it was the cause of my father's business going on the bum. He had a partner who took over, and my family had to go look for work.

As luck would have it, there had been a bank robbery, and the bank robbers had been caught. Their practically brand-new Model T Ford touring car went up for sale by the Sheriff's Department, and my dad was able to buy it. He paid around $300 for it, which was a lot of money then, but it was practically a new car. Pop made some sideboards for the car so we could put all of our cooking utensils and food in side boxes that sat on the running boards between the two fenders. The touring car had a canvas top on it, and in those days it was quite a car, really. We loaded up everything we owned, which included the three kids and mother and father and the dog, and we headed down the highway looking for a job.

We stayed in campgrounds along the way. They were usually located in a tall grove of trees with an area big enough for tents, a regular outhouse, and a little food concession.

In our travels, we found that many of the rivers had no bridges, but there were little barges used as ferries. The barges were pulled back and forth by horses or by men pulling on a rope. Often times the ferry only held two or three cars, which meant everyone had to be patient and wait for their turn.

Model T touring car similar to the one that carried the Eichner family to Lebanon, Ore., in search of work. (Photo courtesy of Glen L. Whiteley.)

We headed on south to the big city of Portland, Oregon, with all of the confusion of clanging streetcars and traffic going every which way. Since my dad had been in the grocery business, he went to a grocery store to inquire about a job. They told him of a job managing a store in Lebanon, Oregon, 90 miles south of Portland. When we arrived in Lebanon, my father went in to see about his new job. It turned out to be shelf stocking and general clerking duties. He was a little displeased, but he was getting a small wage that we could live on which was most important.

That first summer in Lebanon we lived in the tent. The place is now a grade school, but it was a little campground at that time. When winter approached, my dad rented a house for $5 a month. It was a big, old house with five rooms and big black-walnut trees all around it. To be inside a real house was quite a thrill to us then.

Introduction to Flight

In 1927 Charles Lindbergh had just flown the Atlantic Ocean in the "Spirit of St. Louis" which aroused our thoughts of flying. One day my sister Miriam decided that she might be able to fly. So after a lengthy process, she built a pair of wings that looked like a couple of kites, and the date of the flight was set. On that day, the flight was to take off from a six-foot-high fir stump in the back yard. Miriam, realizing she would probably get to some pretty high altitude in this flight of hers, dressed up in everything we had in the house for clothing so that she would be protected against the elements. We managed to get her up on the stump, and after an inaugural speech, she started flapping her wings and then launched. She was airborne for a split second, but ended up at the bottom of the stump with a sprained ankle and a sore behind. I guess that was my first introduction to flight.

The next one occurred when my uncle Roy, who was a veteran of World War I (rumor had it that he'd shot down a couple of balloons) and some World War I buddy pilots got together and bought an old Curtiss Jenny. At that time you could buy a Jenny right out of the factory. The planes were still in crates built for overseas shipping. Roy and his buddies put this Jenny together in their spare time. One day they were enjoying a flight over Lebam when the engine quit. My school was located in the bottom of the valley. In front of the schoolhouse was a yard, and adjacent to it was a cow pasture. The cow pasture had a wire fence with a couple of strands of wire to keep the cows from wandering into the schoolyard. Roy touched down in the schoolyard and rolled right through the fence, ripping some of the fab-

Uncle Roy crash-landed his Jenny in the field next to my grade school. (Photo by The Jay Miller Aviation History Collection, Central Arkansas Library System.)

ric from the bottom of the lower wing of the Jenny. This event made me quite a hero because my uncle had done the daring feat of making a dead-stick landing in the schoolyard. Roy and his friends repaired the Jenny, and one day when school was not in session, away went the Jenny. That was the last we saw of it.

On another occasion I remember going to Raymond for what I believe was the Fourth of July. A pilot in a Jenny on pontoons was taking people for rides, and my aunt Isabelle, uncle Roy's wife, was one of the lucky ones who got to go for a ride. We watched the airplane as it slowly took off, got airborne, and flew around a little bit. Then it sailed in for a safe landing. The pilot had a little dock he maneuvered up to, and with a lot of people grabbing wings, he was able to dock the airplane and unload his passenger. This was awesome.

Living in Lebanon

In my spare time I used to fish in the millrace. I had a piece of grocery store twine and a bent pin, but I wasn't having much luck catching fish. One day one of the workers at the powerhouse saw me fishing there, as he'd seen me fishing numerous days, and he gave me a real fishhook. That was one of the real prizes of the day.

Later my dad found a cream receiving station that was for sale. (A cream receiving station would buy cream for daily pick up by one of the big dairies.) I believe my dad paid about $50 to take over the concession. I remember the fellow who sold it to him was an archer because I was so impressed that he could actually shoot an arrow through a Montgomery Ward catalogue.

Pop then quit his job at the grocery store and started working the cream receiving business, which he later expanded to selling feed to the farmers. It became my part-time job to help in the feed store. You had to be approved by the state to test cream, and I was the youngest cream tester in the state of Oregon. I could sign the checks and everything else for the farmers. We always retained a little sample of every batch of cream that was tested so that if the farmer complained the next day, we could run the test again to make sure that he got the proper payment for his cream. Because the family was in such dire straits, we would save those cream samples, shake them up, and make butter out of them.

When you think of having to be that frugal nowadays, it doesn't seem possible. We got along fine, but we had to make every little turn count. At the age of twelve, I was able to drive the Model T touring car, and I could deliver the feed. That was always my biggest pleasure. It was a big help to my dad, and I had a great time doing it.

There were a lot of little covered bridges around Lebanon. Invariably the covered bridge came across the river from the higher side. The bridge would be level across the river, and on the down side there would generally be a pretty good drop. We used to get the car full of kids, go through the covered bridge, take a flying leap with the Model T, and jump off the other end, which would invariably throw all the kids in the back seat into the front seat. We thought that was great sport, especially if we had some unsuspecting kid along on the ride.

Early Aviation

Through my teenage years, aviation became more and more interesting to me. We had heard stories about the Langmacs who were a couple of farm boys who bought a Jenny and taught themselves how to fly. They would taxi around the field until they got up enough nerve to jump over a fence. Finally they got to where they were actually flying the plane. I never saw them doing this, but I heard the stories.

There was a little field right behind Lebanon that was called the Landing Field, and on big occasions like the Fourth of July, there would be three or four airplanes doing stunts. They would do snap rolls, loops, tailspins, and on one occasion they let people parachute-jump out of the airplane. They took volunteers, and of course I volunteered, but they thought I was too young.

We could never afford one of those rides at that time, but on another occasion Tom Medley and I rode our bicycles 13 miles to the Albany Airport to see a big air show. We watched those guys making spot landings. Now that I look back on it, they were really clever. They came in almost to a stall and landed those planes within inches of a line that had been drawn. They were really good.

While we were there, a big Ford Tri-motor came in to the Albany Airport dedication. Tickets were being sold for a trip over the Three Sisters Mountain behind Lebanon. This would be a real trip for us, but we didn't have the fare. We hung around and asked about it anyway, and the pilot said, "Sure, you guys clean the airplane up, and you can have a ride over the Sisters." To do the cleaning they gave us some rags and a gallon of gas in an open can. Tom and I worked all day long wiping that corrugated metal down. We cleaned off all the residue from the engines and made the airplane look pretty good.

When the time came for the flight in the evening, the pilot said, "Well, sorry, Sonny, the flight's all filled up today," and he gave us 50¢ each. That was the biggest disappointment of my life. When I got home the folks felt kind of bad about what had happened so the next day Miriam volunteered to go to Albany with me, and Father gave each of us a dollar so we could pay for our airplane ride. We drove over to the air show and took a ride in a biplane. There was room in the front seat for two of us, and for a dollar they took off and flew over Albany and back. I think it was a five-minute ride. That was my first airplane ride, and it was the thrill of a lifetime, something I really wanted to do.

Every evening and sometimes through the fog, you could hear the drone of the mail planes. In those days searchlights were strung all down the valley and through the mountains into California. The lights served as navigation aids for the mail planes following those searchlights all the way to their destination. The mail planes then were Boeing biplanes. The pilot sat in the open, and I think there was room for a couple of passengers in the lower part of the airplane, plus mail.

Lindbergh had flown over the ocean, and of course he was the world's hero. When his airplane was brought back to the United States, he made a trip all around the United States with the "Spirit of St. Louis" to show people. I couldn't go to Portland to see the plane where he had landed, but we did see him flying the "Spirit of St. Louis" up the Willamette Valley.

During the time when Lindbergh was trying to get across the ocean, there were numerous other people trying it, and there were news stories in the paper every day. Some of them crashed on takeoff, some of them got nearly across the ocean and crashed, and others were never heard from again. It was high adventure.

On another occasion, coming down the valley was the Macon, the Navy's big dirigible. I can see it yet. It looked like it was just hanging there, hardly moving. It had several little engines on it, and it was chugging away. It was an enormous thing, and I can see what a terrible time they must have had when they got in the winds. One of them even had a little airplane they could launch from a hook underneath. On its return the airplane would clip onto the hook and be pulled up inside the dirigible. Of course dirigibles didn't last too long—they had accidents.

We saw the first mass flight of Army pursuit planes flying from San Francisco to Portland. There must have been fifty of them. They were all bunched up in a big gaggle, no formation, just like a swarm of bees and making a terrible noise. They were short, stubby biplanes with large motors flying two or three thousand feet high. They all landed safely in Portland.

Around this time, the Russians were making a nonstop flight from Moscow to Los Angeles or San Francisco. They flew an enormous low-wing airplane which I believe had only one engine on it, but it had an extremely large wing. They got as far as the Vancouver, Washington airport before they had to land for fuel. The airport was just a grass field with a couple of small hangars near Highway 99E. We drove up to see the airplane, and I didn't realize it at the time, but it was important that a big airplane had made that long trip without stopping.

Dorothy Hester and Tex Ranken were famous stunt pilots. They used Great Lakes Sports Trainers to do all kinds of stunts including outside loops. I think they did 40 or 50 outside loops in a row, and when they came down, their noses and ears would be bleeding. They put themselves through terrible punishment, but that seemed to be the thing to do. Every pilot wanted to do something more often or greater than anyone else.

Endurance flights were also going on. Two guys would fly around Portland in a Belanca, Fairchild, or Stinson. When their fuel got low, another airplane with a can or two of gas would fly above them and lower it down on a rope so they could catch it and pour it into their tanks. They passed oil, food, and messages the same way, and they were able to keep flying for a whole month at a time. It was in the newspaper every day, of course, tracking the days, the minutes, and the hours that these guys were still up in the air.

One day our neighbors, Dr. Irvine and his wife, took me to Swan Island Airport near Portland because they knew I was drooling over airplanes. I saw the Ford Tri-motor, Boeing mail plane there. We also saw a small, all-metal airplane some people had built. They planned to set a transcontinental record from west to east with it. I remember the airplane taking off from Swan Island. It was heavily loaded and just barely cleared the end of the field, laboring to get altitude. Unfortunately, the plane didn't get to its destination. It crashed in the mountains in Colorado.

College Days

After high school I went to the University of Oregon as a pre-med student with plans to become a doctor. In Lebanon I had been in a National Guard hospital company, so when I went to the University of Oregon, I joined an infantry division of the Guards to keep my Guard status going. I also joined the ROTC and tried out for the rifle team. I shot a perfect score in the try-outs, which made the college newspaper. I can still see the headline "Eichner Shoots 100!" Needless to say I made the rifle team, which I enjoyed very much. While I was in the ROTC, we served as the honor guard in a parade for the governor. We were just college kids, but we thought we were pretty important.

During my second year of college, I played intramural basketball and got hurt. I bumped my shin, and it got infected. It became a bone infection, and I ended up in the infirmary. When I got well enough, they sent me home. I went back to school later, but I couldn't make it. I was just too run down. I'd been working in the hospital, going to school, and trying to keep up. Things just weren't working out for me.

In the spring, while recouping from my leg injury, which didn't fully heal at that time, I heard stories about my uncles Victor and Firman Lovelace who owned fish traps in Alaska. They were single for many years, and they did a lot of hunting and fishing and trapping. Alaska was always the great dream for me.

Alaska

Firman and Victor owned the *Estella*, a 50-foot seine boat which they used as a cannery tender. In the spring they took the boat to Alaska, and in the winter they returned to Seattle. My friend, Bruce Parton, and I decided it was worth a chance to go see my uncles and find out if we could ride to Alaska with them. They agreed to take us so we helped them get the boat ready and made the trip to Alaska in April of 1938—early spring.

We helped get the fish trap ready for the season, and when we finished Firman and Victor took us to Ketchikan and said, "You are on your own now." This was a new experience for us. I had saved $28, the price of a steerage fare to Seattle. I figured if I couldn't make it, I would use my last dollar to make the trip back home.

As I recall, Ketchikan at that time was a town of about 2500 people, which was one of the larger cities in Alaska. I think Anchorage had about 1500 people and Fairbanks probably had 1000. Juneau was about the same size as Ketchikan.

Ketchikan was built along the waterfront with fairly steep

The *Estella*, owned by Firman and Victor Lovelace. I rode north to Alaska aboard the *Estella* to work on Firman and Victor's fish traps.

wooded hills behind it. Deer Mountain stood 3300 feet high and was the big landmark. The west side of the mountain was the lee side and held snow all year long. Cannery workers and fishermen came to Ketchikan in the summer doing what they could to make a living during the salmon runs. This was before the war so Ketchikan was very much what people today would have called a "frontier town."

The streets of downtown Ketchikan were built out over the water or ran up steep hillsides to the homes overlooking the town. Almost every road was built on pilings with the road surface made out of spruce lumber. When it was wet, the streets got quite slippery; and when they got worn down, the knots and nails would stick up. Those 4x12 planks had to be replaced every three or four years because the cars simply wore them out.

White Cab and Bus Company

I did odd jobs, built rock fences and rock walls, and cleaned chicken coops. I did everything I didn't like to do just to make a living. I finally got a job driving a taxicab with White Cab and Bus Company. After about six months I was promoted to bus driver, but I drove cabs in my off hours to make a little extra money.

We cab drivers were of the age where we were kind of frisky, and the cabs we had were a lot of fun to drive compared to the old Model As and Ts we were used to. At that time we were driving '36 Plymouths and some '37 Hudson Terraplanes which were a little soupier, but I liked the Plymouth best.

The cab company office sat on one of the spruce-and-piling streets that overhung the water downtown. Today most of that

White Cab and Bus gave me my first "real job" in Alaska. This is Oral Bundy standing next to one of our Hudson Terraplanes.

The '36 Plymouth didn't go in the bay, but it was close. This put a damper on any "squirrely" driving by the cabbies.

area has been filled in, but back then a lot of Ketchikan hung out over the water. The spruce streets were always slick, and a little rain combined with oil leaked from the cab engines made the area around the cab company even slicker than usual. We were used to it so we developed a technique for parking our cars late at night after the boss had gone home. We would goose it as we came around the corner to our cab office and make a hard turn. The car would break loose, do a 360° spin, and end up ready to park. We would back the car up against the fence railing overhanging the water and call it a night. We did this pretty regularly until one of the drivers spun too late and hit the fence railing. The car didn't go in the bay but came very close to it. The car was damaged, and that was the end of that kind of maneuver.

The cab drivers' biggest business was to meet the boats that came in to Ketchikan. The boats were a combination of a freighter and a passenger ship. They generally tied up at one of the cannery docks so they could bring supplies in and load canned fish to take south. Of course the passengers on board all wanted to take a tour of Ketchikan or go downtown. We delivered people to and from the ships at Ward Cove Cannery, Sunny Point Cannery, and New England Fish Cannery. At that time there were seven salmon canneries in Ketchikan so it was a pretty busy place in the fishing season.

Marriage to Peggy

Our regular bus route ran from downtown Grant Street to Smiley's Cannery, a three-mile run. We made the trip every 30 minutes, then sat for 30 minutes at the bus stop on Main Street by the Heckman Building. We passed our spare time across the street at a confectionary called the Peter Pan.

One of my favorite bus customers was an English girl named Peggy Barton. Peggy was living with Alice and Bert Houghtaling on Austin Street and Second Avenue. Her dad was the skipper of the lighthouse tender *Hemlock* before I got to Ketchikan. By the time I got there, the Lighthouse Service had been taken into the Coast Guard, and he was transferred to Alameda, California, and then to San Juan, Puerto Rico. Occasionally Peggy would ride the round trip with me. She was the high school principal's secretary, and she also moonlighted at the Revilla Theater as an usher. She always gave me a seat in the back so she could sit with me. (There was segregation at that time. Natives sat on the left, the rest on the right.)

Things got pretty serious, and we wanted to get married. Her father, Captain Barton, insisted that she come to Puerto Rico for six months. If she was still inclined after six months, she could get married. After three miserable months, she talked her parents into allowing her to return Ketchikan.

The wedding date was set for August 31, 1939, at 4:00 p.m. Of course we had to go to the courthouse and get a $10 marriage license. I pulled out my checkbook, but the clerk said, "No, it has to be cash." I didn't have it so Peggy came to the rescue with the cash. I hoped this wasn't going to be a pattern.

When the big day came, Peggy's sister Helen and her husband were going to stand up for us at the Episcopal Church. I went to the Lutheran Church, and not a soul was there. In despera-

A happy couple. White Cab and Bus not only gave me a place in the community, it introduced me to Peggy Barton.

Asked by her father not to marry until she had spent six months in Puerto Rico, Peggy dutifully shipped out. Thankfully, her parents relented soon thereafter.

tion I figured it must be that church down by the Alaska Sportsman building. Having no car I took off on the run and arrived just a few minutes late. The ceremony was short and sweet but legal. We went out to the Prices' house (friends of Helen) just past Buggy Beach for a short reception. There were no other guests. Later they delivered us to the Foss Apartments. Our apartment was No. 3 in the lower level looking out over the channel. Friends had everything fixed for us. They short-sheeted the bed, tied cans with rocks in them under the bed, and put Limburger cheese in the electric heaters. Every day for a week I brought home a cab or bus driver to show off Peggy's ability to cook Spam and eggs. It was an exciting start in our married life, and it has lasted 60-odd years.

Territorial Guard

I had been involved with the Oregon National Guard in college so when I moved to Alaska, I joined the Territorial Guard. We were supplied with Enfield rifles, some wire to string for communications, a few medical supplies, and a few flags for signaling. It would have been a feeble effort if we had ever had to fight a battle.

The National Guard was formed just prior to Pearl Harbor, and some of my bus drivers, Vic Madsen mainly, joined the National Guard and wanted to know why I didn't join. I was a sergeant in the Territorial Guard, and I didn't know the difference between the National Guard and the Territorial Guard. I was lucky that I had not joined the National Guard because after Pearl Harbor, members of the National Guard were immediately shipped out to the north country to be trained for the regular U.S. Army and were later shipped off to wherever they were needed.

Pearl Harbor

One terrible morning we were having coffee in the Stedman Café about nine o'clock in the morning, and we got the news that Pearl Harbor had been attacked. We did not know what to make of it. We were all astounded. This was the start of World War II for us. We had been hearing lots of stories about England, and it sounded pretty bad. One local boy, Lt. Irving Thompson, was lost on one of the battleships that was sunk in Pearl Harbor.

About this time the Japanese bombed Dutch Harbor, and the next day they bombed it again. In my lack of knowledge of Alaska, I had no idea how far Dutch Harbor was from Ketchikan, but we were all concerned that our Territorial Guards would have to defend Ketchikan. We figured the Japanese would send in a ship and take over the town, and we would sit up in the mountains and snipe at them. We had caches of food in the hills, and we were ready. Thank goodness nothing like that ever happened.

Relocations

With Pearl Harbor, a lot of changes were made in my life. I was classified as 3A, which meant I was physically fit but had a family. Also I had a transportation job that was considered essential. The night after Pearl Harbor, the cabin on top of Deer Mountain mysteriously burned down. Everybody in town thought the Japanese were signaling their air force to come in and bomb us, but that was kind of ridiculous. Nevertheless all of the local Japanese people, who were very nice people, were rapidly gathered up and shipped out, leaving their homes and businesses behind. We never heard any more from them until after the war. A few of the families came back, and a number of the boys were decorated for their bravery in the Italian campaign. According to Valerie Tatsuda, her family was interned in the Minidoka internment camp in Hunt, Idaho. After being there a while, her parents were allowed to go to Chicago because her mom's sister lived there, but the rest of the Tatsudas remained in camp. George and Irene Inman moved into the apartment above Tatsuda's grocery store and looked after the property until the

Tatsudas were allowed to return home.

About this same time, the federal government moved a number of Aleuts from the northern war zone to a CCC camp near Ward Lake. Many of them died there due to the change in climate and diet. Jonnie Dyakanoff, a long-time Ellis Air Lines employee, was one of the Aleuts who survived and stayed in Ketchikan.

Liberty Ships

With the war on, we sometimes had blackouts. We rigged up the buses with little tiny lights and cut our night schedules down. It was tough in the wintertime because the days were so short, but there was no way around it. Liberty Ships came through the channel continuously. Some would stop in Ketchikan for various reasons, but most would plow right by headed north. All were single-screw ships rapidly built to transport materials for the war effort. The ships did not handle very well so occasionally one would ram the dock and do some damage. I can remember standing on the dock when a ship hit and being knocked off my feet. There were no bad accidents because of it, just a little damage to property.

Airplane Traffic

Driving the 1935 Ford bus up and down the waterfront, I could keep my eye on the airplane activity. Every time I drove by

Bill Boeing's Douglas Dolphin, flown by C. Scott. As seen in Ketchikan in 1939.

Munter's hanger, I would look over to see what aircraft were in town. If something new had arrived, I would run down after work and try to get a picture of it. I knew who owned the planes that came in frequently, and who their regular pilots were. Bob Ellis came in regularly in his Waco. He had a new young pilot about my age, Bud Bodding. Herb Munter owned a Bellanca, and Tony Schaumn from Petersburg came in occasionally. Periodically a Lockheed Vega came in from Juneau with Shell Simmons or Lon Cope, and every once in a while some stranger would tie up. I had heard there was a private Stenson flying around, but it soon came to town on a boat all smashed to pieces. (Evidently, the pilot buzzed some people at Kasaan and then zoomed up and stalled.) Three big Navy flying boats anchored over by Pennock Island, and later the first Pan American Clipper, a two-engine flying boat, landed and tied up at City Float. If that wasn't enough of a thrill, the next year the four-engine Clipper came in to Ward Cove and tied up.

Sometimes the Blenheim bombers (the Bristol 149 IVW "Bolingbroke"), flown by war-weary British pilots, would come in and buzz the town. The planes would come over so low we could see the grinning faces of the machine gunners in the forward greenhouse of the Blenheim. Six bombers made a low pass into Deer Mountain Valley, over the ball field, down Ketchikan Creek, and out over the Federal Building. The last one was about ten feet lower than the others, and he knocked the antenna off of

I snapped this picture of Norm Gerde working on CAA's Fleetwing in August, 1939.

Nine Lives of an Alaska Bush Pilot

the Federal Building as they came across. The mayor did not like that at all so the pilots were restricted and were no longer allowed to do low maneuvering in the channel.

Annette Island

Construction of Annette Island airfield started in 1940. This construction created a lot of jobs, and at the same time the port of Prince Rupert, B.C. was being expanded. The CCC boys were taken out to Annette Island first to start preparing to build the airfield, and the Army took over in 1941. When that happened, they brought in a number of people from the Deep South.

When Annette Island airfield was completed late in 1941, it was immediately very active. The American Army and the Canadian Air Force ran Annette Island. All of the airplanes that were ferrying north for the war effort stopped at Annette for fuel, under the protection of Annette's P-40s and some P-39s. I can still hear the P-40s doing dogfight practice. I was often out near Guard Island in my little 8-foot punt with a 1-horse outboard, and the scream of those engines as they wound up into a dive was something else. They were dog-fighting and trying to sharpen up their tactics. One time I saw a P-40 dive at a ship in the harbor, and he was so close it looked like he dipped his wing into the fantail of the ship.

We were not kept informed on the goings-on over at Annette Island airfield, but things did happen that became public knowledge in Ketchikan. One snowy day in '43 the Army Air

Mishaps and engine failures were pretty common for early flyers in Alaska. Here Bob Ellis' Waco had a valve failure. He's being towed in by Light House Service rowboats from the tender *Hemlock*.

Pan American's twin-engine Clipper docked at City Float in 1938.

Force came to town in a Nordune Norseman (a floatplane about the size of an 8- to 10-passenger Dehaviland Otter) to pick up a group of USO entertainers and take them back to Annette Island. It was about a ten-minute flight into Port Chester and Metlakatla to reach the road leading to the base at the airfield. With extremely poor visibility, the pilot entered Port Chester either at a high-speed taxi on the water or flying very close to the water. Just inside the harbor the seaplane hit a group of protruding rocks, killing everyone on impact. A few days later a formal service was held at the base with a fly-by of fighter planes—one of which did a low-level roll, miscued, and flew into the ground causing another fatality.

Submarine Scare

After Pearl Harbor, everyone worried about incursions by the Japanese. I had seen a Japanese submarine scouting near Ketchikan before the war, and occasionally others would see one. The U.S. Air Force stationed anti-sub units along the coast in hopes of keeping the shipping lanes safe, and they caught a few subs along the way.

In the summer of 1943 we had a big submarine scare. One of the Hudson bombers, a Ventura bomber with a load of depth charges, headed out to help find the reported enemy submarine.

The weather was bad, and the ceiling was very low. In the meantime some Navy ships were in position to challenge the submarine. One of the ships was the old *Foremost*, a halibut schooner that had been inducted into the military. The *Foremost* was a wooden vessel with depth charges on it. Nobody ever thought about what would happen to a wooden boat when they dropped depth charges. The *Foremost* and a Coast Guard boat dropped depth charges on the submarine and sank it. Unfortunately, the shock from the depth charges hit the *Foremost* so hard it started to leak, and they were barely able to get back to town.

Depth Charges

Meanwhile the Ventura bomber had disappeared. An alert went out urging us to keep our eyes open, trying to find out if anybody had seen or heard the airplane or if anyone had any idea where it might have gone. We searched for days but came up with nothing.

Fifteen years after the war, a local martin trapper named Stack discovered the wreckage. Apparently the plane was flying outbound on an ADF heading. The pilot was trying to sneak out to catch the submarine by flying in and out of the overcast, but he drifted off course a little and slammed into Cape Chacon at an altitude of about 700 feet. The federal marshal went out and recovered the bones of the five men aboard.

Many years later, out of curiosity, we rediscovered the wreck. Bucky Dawson wanted to find it so I took him and his

Dangerous artifact. One of several live, 40-year-old depth charges found among the wreckage.

party in the helicopter and showed them approximately where I thought it was. I let them off on the beach so they could hike up and look for the wreck. They found it, so the next weekend my son Dan and I and his son Eric went out to see if we could find it too. We found the wreck complete with machine guns, hundreds of rounds of ammunition, and four 40-year-old depth charges. Two of them were broken open, but two of them were intact and looked like they were still live. Concerned that they might explode if bumped or dropped, we gave them a wide berth.

Later while riding on an Alaska Airlines flight, I met a man who was in the Ordnance Division of the Coast Guard. We discussed the depth charges, and he said, "Those should be exploded because they're hazardous. I'll call the Army in Anchorage, and they'll come down and do it." Someone from the Army did come to Ketchikan, and I flew him and some other military men to the area by helicopter. We landed on top of the mountain, and I took them down to the site. We piled all the depth charges in one pile, and he put some explosive material on top of it. We lit the fuse and took off up the mountain. We got almost up to the top before there was a tremendous explosion. There was no question that the bombs were still dangerous.

One of the boys had grabbed one of the 30-caliber machine guns and was dragging it up the hill so we brought it back for him so he had a souvenir. My grandson Eric had taken one of the 50-calibers when we visited the wreck earlier. The guns were rusted and frozen shut. Absolutely nothing usable about them, but they were machine guns off of the lower turret. We had displayed them at one time in the TEMSCO Airline lobby along with all the pictures of the wreck.

Later Eric and some of his friends made a little mount for the 50-caliber and stuck it in the window of their apartment in the Deermount area. A policeman saw the gun and confiscated it. Eric also had a bandoleer of bullets, which were officially disarmed and legal to own, that we'd bought from a surplus store. However, the boys couldn't convince the policeman that this was just an artifact from World War II and not a usable machine gun. He was too bull-headed for that so he confiscated the gun. When we finally got a release, they wouldn't return the machine gun because now it's contraband. We said, "Please, won't you at least give it to the museum?" I don't think they ever did. I think it got taken to the garbage dump. It was a little disturbing because common sense didn't enter into their thinking.

Gillam Crash

The winter of '43 was the coldest winter in a long time. My Territorial Guard unit was alerted that a twin-engine Lockheed Electra was missing on a flight from Seattle to Annette Island. We should be on the lookout for any signs of it or its six passengers. After a couple of weeks, we forgot all about it. Much to our surprise twenty-eight days later, we learned that a Coast Guard patrol boat had picked up two survivors of the airplane in Boca de Quadra.

No one had reported a fire or seen hide nor hair of these survivors for almost a month so everyone presumed they were dead. Believe you me, when survivors turned up on the beach that day in the middle of winter, everyone jumped.

The two who had been rescued were in pretty bad shape, but they said there were more survivors still in the woods. Two were injured, and a girl had died in the accident. The pilot, Harold Gillam, had gone off looking for help a few days after the accident but disappeared. Next we were told that Bos'n Art Hook had taken a group of men on foot to the crash site. A hard-hat diver who came in to the Coast Guard base along with one of the survivors led the way for nineteen enlisted Coast Guard men in an effort to get the injured.

Shortly after that we Territorial Guardsmen were requested to report to the Coast Guard ship *Cedar*, a lighthouse tender. Captain Burns was the ship's captain. About twelve of us showed up including Captain Dick Hogben and me. We set out for Smeaton Bay and anchored up behind Short Point where a stream came out of the Weasel Cove valley.

Soon there was a lot of excitement on deck—some guys were spotted on the beach. The crew of the *Cedar* launched a boat and were back very soon with three men who looked pretty tired. One was a survivor of the plane crash, and two were Coast Guard men. They got together with the brass and told their

Gillam's aircraft slammed into a tree, tearing off one of the wings. Note the massive cavity in the wing fragment discovered years later.

story. Art Hook and all but the three who had just arrived were stuck at the campsite with the injured survivors. Some of the Coast Guard men had frostbitten feet and could no longer travel. They pointed out the location of the camp which, at the time Gillam left, had been moved to the bottom of the Weasel Cove valley to a warmer spot at a lower altitude.

The two healthy survivors had kept the injured ones alive for almost 30 days. They had foraged for food. Going to Smeaton Bay for clams had been easy when the ground was frozen even though Badger Bay was closer. The ice was solid all the way to the entrance. Now the snow was softening, and the Smeaton Bay route was bad.

About this time two seaplanes arrived. One was Pros Ganty in an Aeronica Chief and Gill Joint in a Kingfisher, a single-float Navy plane. It was decided that Gill Joint would take Bruce Johnstone in the Kingfisher and make a decision on how to proceed with the rescue. When Bruce and Gill climbed into the Navy Kingfisher, Bruce had an ax with a streamer tied on it. Gill hollered as he boarded the Kingfisher, "If I'm not back in five minutes, come looking for me." The ceiling was very low, only a couple hundred feet above the trees. In five minutes Gill was back. He had let Bruce off on the ice in Badger Bay after Bruce had dropped his ax near the camp. Bos'n Hook had stamped in the snow the words "Send a blimp." Bruce sent a message to us that the Badger Bay side was much closer. We all agreed with the decision to enter from Badger Bay. I had been hunting in the area they showed us on the map, and the route Bruce took was the one I had used to hunt the area.

The *Cedar* then pulled anchor and headed for Quadra. I put myself in the bow of the *Cedar* to look for any signs of Gillam. We had gone just a few miles into Quadra when I spotted an orange streamer hanging from a bare yellow cedar tree. I sounded the alarm, and the ship came to a stop. Captain Burns sent Jack Johnson and a Fish and Game warden ashore. They soon found Harold Gillam's frozen body. He had made the nearly impossible trip from the wreck to this point. He apparently had over-extended himself in his weakened condition from the crash. But with great presence of mind, he hung up the streamer and rolled himself up in his parachute. Unfortunately it was not nearly enough protection from the near-zero temperatures that time of year. He had some emergency gear with him but not enough. The memory still haunts me of the black beard of the first victim I had ever seen.

The *Cedar* then proceeded into Boca De Quadra only to find ice all the way out to the front of the bay. Captain Burns said he would ram the ice and see how far he could go. I'll never forget it. The ship penetrated about 50 feet into the ice. As the ice peeled back, all the sea growth from the bottom of the boat was left on the ice. What a great way to clean a steel boat.

Gill Joint (later my favorite FAA man) was flying around watching the turn of events. He let the Captain know he would try his two 50-pound bombs on the ice. He dive-bombed the ice in front of the *Cedar*, but it was ineffective. We were left with no alternative but to walk the Badger Bay ice to the head of the bay and then go cross-country following Bruce Johnstone's tracks into the camp.

Darkness was approaching when we reached the camp. We had only one toboggan so we told the least injured man we might have to come back for him the next day. He said, "Shoot me, but don't leave me here another night!" With a makeshift toboggan and lots of help, everyone made it to the *Cedar* that night. The two victims had a long stay in the hospital, but they survived.

The two healthy survivors had quite a story to tell. They could find very little to eat in that frozen country and finally in desperation crossed the ice in Badger Bay to the old Quadra Cannery. They wanted to burn it to attract some attention, but there was a sign on it that said, "Do not burn. Private property." They found an old skiff and filled the cracks with strips of their clothing. Then they launched the skiff, and with a couple of boards for paddles, headed out into the inlet. It started to get rough when they got to the point between Badger Bay and Weasel Cove. They headed for shore, but the skiff went under. They lost their gun but managed to reach the beach and get a fire going with their last bit of strength.

It was getting dark when the Coast Guard vessel *Salvor* came into the area and anchored up by the cannery they had just come from. They jumped up and down making all the noise they could, but the men on the *Salvor* thought they must be some crazy trappers jumping around their fire. The next morning the trappers were still there waving so the men on the *Salvor* decided to go see who they were. The survivors were saved at last, but what an ordeal.

In the summer of '43 Jack Sherman, Ellis Air's chief mechanic, needed parts for a 450 HP Pratt and Whitney engine like the ones on Gillum's Lockheed. Sherman planned a trip to the Gillam crash site and started getting some guys together. He needed someone to guide him in, and I was happy to do it. Jack Sherman, his mechanic Kelly Adams, my pal Al Hansberry, and I met at Ellis Air and boarded a Belanca with Hugh Ramsdale as the pilot. I enjoyed my first ride in a seaplane.

I led the group toward the old campsite and set off up the hill toward the area where the wreck was supposed to be. Earlier that year Ray Renshaw and another Fish and Wildlife agent had gone to the sight to recover Susan Batzer's body. Her arm had been severed in the crash. Ray felt bad because she was such a pretty girl going to her first job with the CAA in Fairbanks. As I climbed, I realized more than ever the hardship those injured victims went through. Halfway up the hill we found a door from

Some of the pieces of Gillum's aircraft recovered during a 1980s salvage effort. (Photo by Bucky Dawson, Aviation Arts Unlimited.)

the plane that the survivors had used to slide the injured down the steep slope. When we arrived at the wreck, we realized how lucky they were to have survived. The plane had come in parallel to the ridge, and the right wing hit a hemlock tree turning the plane right into the hill. From the pilot's seat you could reach out and touch solid rock.

Jack Sherman was happy. With the war on, parts like this were hard to get. We packed out starters, generators, carburetors, a T30 Lear radio, and other things.

Ironically, in the 90s the sons of one of the survivors wanted to visit the site of the wreck. Bucky Dawson arranged the trip, with me flying the helicopter and Dale Clark the seaplane. Dale's job was to take the visitors plus the two Hassel boys as helpers to the lake not far from the valley campsite. It took a couple trips to get everyone to the site, and more time to shuttle them up to the camp by helicopter.

The fog rolled in just before dark. We were stuck. People were getting a little panicky. One said, "My father said there was no way you could build a fire up here." I had lots of manpower so I sent the boys out to collect all the dead upright snags in the muskeg.

Outdoor Survival

Survival in Southeast Alaska is primarily being able to keep yourself dry and warm. Hypothermia is the ever-present thing you have to contend with in survival so building a fire is critical. I was always so proud of my son Dan because whenever we hit the beach, he always had a fire going whether he needed it or not. It is one of the best virtues an outdoorsman in Alaska can have because if you find yourself having to start a fire after dark, you could be into a lot of trouble.

We never hesitated to start a fire at the base of a big spruce tree or a big cedar tree because they were generally the driest places, and in our wet weather you could never set the tree on fire. There are many trees along the beaches in certain areas that have burns on them. This was one of the tricks we learned from the natives of Alaska. They would build their fires time and time again at the base of the same tree because that was the spot where they might end up for survival. On a wet night with a fire going at the base of the tree, all the heat would reflect out. That was a very good trick to know.

The other good things to know were that a lot of dead trees are dry, and that the little dead limbs sticking out on a spruce tree are all loaded with pitch. (The hemlock is the worst tree; the only good thing about a hemlock is that the needles have pitch in them.)

Armed with that knowledge, the Hassel boys and the visitors gathered a bunch of good firewood, and it wasn't long before we had a rip-roaring fire going. The warmth helped calm everyone down a bit as we contemplated spending a cold night on the mountain. We had survival gear with us, but this was not going to be fun.

Then the fog lifted.

One quick trip to the lake, and the next load was homebound just at dark. Now these visitors really had a taste of what their father had gone through. It was a good lesson for all.

A few days later Dan and I flew to the site and got the engine ready to lift out. Bill Gale came in with a 204 Bell and a long line, and we hooked the engine to it and took it to town. We also recovered a tail fin, and a few other related parts which appear in some of the pictures in this chapter. After the hoopla died down a bit, Bucky had the engine fixed up and mounted on a section of a spruce tree that must be 300+ years old. It's a beautiful presentation piece, ready for a museum. I hope it will turn into a memorial to poor Gillum, and the people who crashed with him that day.

Ketchikan Air's Standard Waco, with Howard Beamer (left) and Cliff Hogue alongside.

and demonstrate spins in front of the inspector. Doing a spin solo was probably the most difficult thing to accomplish the first time. Howard rode with me on all the maneuvers except the spin. For the spin, he landed and said, "Now, take off, get up to 3000 feet, come in front of the hangar, do a one-turn spin to the right, and pull out within 10 degrees of your headed direction. Then recover, get back to 3000 feet, do a one-turn spin to the left, and pull out within 10 degrees of your direction. If you fail you are allowed to take one extra spin." I took off and got to 3000 feet, and I flew in front of the hangar. I knew all eyes were on me. If I did not spin, it would appear that I had lost my nerve. The pressure was on. I entered the right-hand spin first and pulled out right on the nose. That was not so bad. I climbed back up to 3000 feet and flew in front of the inspector and did another good spin to the left. Now I was all smiles. A few days later Burly Putman, the CAA inspector, came to town and signed my license.

Soon after I got my license, the draft board called me and said they were sending a group of sixteen men over to Annette Island, but they did not have a leader in the group. I was 3A, but I was going to be classified 1A very shortly. They wanted to know if I would go over as the leader of this group. I agreed to go, and we were taken over to Annette Island to go through the induction process. The first thing was a physical exam. The Army doctor started giving me a physical exam, and he said, "How long have you been 1A?" I said, "Well, I'm not yet, but the draft board thought I would be next week." He said, "Those people think I have nothing to do over here. If I give you a physical exam today and you're 3A, and tomorrow you are 1A, I have to give you the same exam tomorrow because I can't induct you when you're 3A." So he sent me back to town and bawled out the draft board. Before long the war was over in Germany, and the draft board did not know what to do with me. I thought I would be going into the occupational forces, but as it turned out the draft board did not react, and I never was drafted into the Army.

Learning The Easy Way . . . And The Hard Way

During my flight training we rotated back and forth between the Chief and the T-Craft, whichever was available. The T-Craft was probably a little easier to fly, but it was almost the same as the Chief. I continued practicing and doing a little cross-country, which meant now I could go fishing. My instructor would oftentimes go fishing with me, which would give me a little additional training. Better yet, Ketchikan Air Service would

That first log book. What a treasure it was!

Flying lessons had to be worked in around work time. As a result, I ended up doing my first solo wearing my cabbie's uniform.

occasionally call on me to take a trip if they didn't have another pilot available. Any time I got a chance to fly, I was happy to do it. I did not expect to get paid for it because I was not a commercial pilot, but that did not matter in those days—nobody paid much attention.

Quite often I took people out to look at log rafts or fish traps or took them to their logging camps. I made trips to Duke Island, Long Island, Dall Island, Craig, Etolin Island and a few times as far as Juneau. I was getting around pretty well and started learning more country all the time.

Milton Dailey, the owner of Ketchikan Spruce Mills, always liked to fly with me, and he frequently called on me to take special trips. On one occasion I flew Milton to Juneau. As we were taking off from the harbor, a humpback whale surfaced right in front of us. Fortunately, I was going fast enough that I was able to haul the plane off the water and clear the whale by a very small margin. It was an unusual experience. On the trip back from Juneau, about a 230-mile trip, we were within about 15 miles of Ketchikan, which meant we had been flying for about three hours; and I was getting kind of lackadaisical, I guess. Instead of heading for Guard Island, I kept going down the straits, and Milton turned to me and said, "Aren't we going to Ketchikan?" What a shock to realize I was heading down the outside shore of Gravina Island and right past Ketchikan. He certainly woke me up. It probably was not the only time I did that.

One day my partner Duey Barber and I decided to go into a lake to go trout fishing. We rented Ketchikan Air Service's Aeronica Chief, loaded up, and took off. The motor was acting up a little bit so I turned around and went right back. I think we were gone 15 minutes. The mechanic changed some spark plugs, and said, "Now you're okay. You can go ahead."

The little Chief was pretty crowded. Duey had fishing poles between his legs and a life raft in his lap. We started to take off, and I got about 200 feet in the air when all of a sudden the engine blew. Oil sprayed up on the windshield, and smoke was coming in through the floorboards. All I could think of was a story I had heard about an airplane that crashed and burned in Saxman (just south of Ketchikan) killing the pilot and his passenger. The pilot stalled the airplane in the same predicament I was in. He was having engine trouble, and he turned back over land and stalled. So that was the one thing I did not want to do. I turned the engine off and set up for a dead-stick landing straight ahead and told Duey to open the doors so the minute we got to the water we could jump. I was sure the plane was going to burn. As soon as I touched down, we both started to get out. I hung on to the wheel of the airplane, and we got out on the pontoons just far enough to get the splash of the water as we came off the step. The plane did not burn. No more smoke. It was all right except the engine was shot. The people from the

Getting a private license meant great back-country fishing trips. This photo comes from a fishing trip with my father, making a special visit from Oregon. I borrowed Russ Simpson's Aeronica Chief for the occasion.

hangar had seen the smoke and had already launched a boat. They reached us in very short order and towed us back in. It was my first forced landing.

Every spare minute I had, of course, I hung around the hangar at Ketchikan Air Service and got to sneak in trips here and there. I remember Howard Beamer had just finished rebuilding a T-Craft, and he was getting ready to test fly it. He asked, "Do you want to come along and go for a ride? We'll test fly it." We took off and flew around a little bit. Everything in the airplane worked fine. Howard said, "Did you ever do a loop?" We were about 300 or 400 feet high. I said, "No, I've never done a loop." Howard said, "Would you like to?" and I said, "Sure, go ahead." So Howard put the little T-Craft in a dive, built up a little extra speed, and pulled up in the loop. Right in the top of the loop, the gas cap came off.

The little gas cap sat right in front of the Plexiglas windshield on the airplane. It had a little wire with a bent top on it, which indicated how much gas there was by how high it was floating. All the gasoline came rushing down right across the windshield. I thought we were going to blow up right then. Howard completed the loop and with much chagrin headed back to the hangar, put the gas cap on, and parked the airplane. Nothing more was said.

When the mechanics at Ketchikan Air Service overhauled an engine or something, and they wanted someone to put a little easy time on it, Stan Oaksmith would always call me to do it for them. It would save their pilots going out when they could be earning money doing other things. I was ready and willing to do any little job that came along. Besides, every time I could scrape up enough money, I would go trout fishing and take a passenger along with me.

One day Ketchikan Air Service bought a brand new plane, a nice yellow Piper Cub on floats. And it had a stick. I had never flown an airplane with a stick—I had always flown one with a wheel. Not that it made any difference, but it seemed like it might. By now I had a little over one hundred hours of flight time so I was beginning to feel pretty frisky. When they said, "We got a brand new Cub. Take it out and fly it," I was happy to do so. That little Cub really performed well. I can smell it yet, fresh airplane, brand new everything, the smell of the fabric and dope and the little interior odors that come with it. It was a real thrill for me.

Carburetor Ice

I got acquainted with Russ Simpson, and we started doing a few things together. I would fly trips for Russ, and in return he would let me take his airplane out so I could go hunting and fishing. Russ had a full-time job at Northern Commercial so he did all his commercial flying early or late in the day.

I flew his Aeronica Chief 36774 quite a lot. One day I took some people up to Mesa Lakes. I made a couple of trips from the beach to the lake, and we spent the night up there fishing. There were small fish in the lake, and the fishing was pretty good. In the morning there was moisture hanging in the air. I got the airplane warmed up and took off on the first trip. I was able to get on the step before I came to a Y in the narrow part of the lake. The left leg of the Y was the preferred takeoff run, but it had a bigger turn. The right leg of the Y was too short. I started the take off and just barely got in the air near the Y when the engine quit. I was able to duck into the short end of the lake and get it down. Then I realized the engine was running at an idle so I pulled on the carburetor heat, and the power came back on. I turned around, taxied back, and took off using the proper carburetor heat procedure. It was a close scrape, but it taught me a lesson on carburetor icing on take off.

Overloaded?

Among other things, I used to fly dynamite in to Silvis Lake for Russ. We would load the Aeronica up to the maximum with cases of dynamite and make as many trips as time would allow. George Roberts was the powder man who was doing the drilling and blasting for the tunnel between the two lakes.

One time I recall going in there, and George said his wife and two girls wanted to ride back to town with me. I put one of the girls in the baggage box behind my seat since there really was not much room in that Aeronica Chief, and the other girl sat in her mother's lap. The lake was not very big, but I had learned to use the whole lake and take advantage of the turn to get out of there. We made it with no problem at all. As I look back on it, that maneuver would certainly be frowned on today. We had four people in a two-place plane. It was a good thing the girls were small.

Out of Gas

One day one of the pursers on the *SS Prince George* mentioned that he would like to go on an airplane ride. We were doing sightseeing bus tours for the *Prince George*, so I said, "Sure, right after I get back from this trip to haul in the dynamite, you meet me at Russ's hangar, and I'll take you for a ride around the pattern." We got in the airplane, flew around the channel a bit, and turned around to come back for a landing. Another airplane was coming in a little close from the side so I decided to go around once more. I firewalled it, and we went down the channel and started to turn over Pennock Island when the engine quit. I had just enough altitude to glide to the water. I did not tell Bob, my passenger, anything. I managed to reach the water and make a good landing. I called on the radio and asked Russ to bring five gallons of gas to me. Bob asked me, "How come you landed here?" and I said, "Well, in case you don't know it, you just made your first emergency landing. We ran out of gas." That was another rude lesson of things you just do not do. I was very fortunate to have been in a position where I could get to salt water. Never again did I run completely out of gas. If you're running low, you're much better off to land and call for help.

Close Call with a Grumman Goose

Duey and I took off one day in Ketchikan Air's Piper Cub with a front and rear stick in it. I was letting Duey fly it from the back seat. I was sitting in the front seat. We were flying along Caamano Shore, and we had about a 100-foot ceiling. Visibility wasn't too bad underneath it—in fact it was pretty good. But a 100-foot ceiling is pretty low. And for some reason, I thought I had a vision. Now that I think about it, I wonder if my vision hadn't picked up slightly before my mental capacity grabbed the fact that I was looking at a Grumman Goose coming right at me. I grabbed the controls away from Duey, turned the airplane on her side, and pushed it into a dive. Mind you at 100 feet you don't have far to go. It felt like somebody had a hold of my tail, and I couldn't get down. I couldn't move. I did get below the Grumman, and just as the Grumman got abreast of me, he flared wildly because he hadn't seen me until the last second.

First Airplane

In April of 1947 Duey Barber and I bought Taylor Craft N36210 from Ketchikan Air Service for $1200. It was a big thrill for us to own an airplane, and I was able to get more flying in than I had in the past. Because Duey was an equal partner in the T-Craft, I taught him how to fly. Duey's daughter Sherry also wanted to learn to fly. I gave her quite a bit of dual training, but she never went any further with it.

After buying our first airplane, we used a hangar at Ketchikan Air Service. It was not much good, and one day we decided not to leave the airplane in there. We left the airplane somewhere else, and the hangar collapsed that day. We were thankful our little T-Craft was not in it. Somebody else's was though, and that was too bad.

With the airplane we could hunt in a lot of different places that just weren't feasible to hunt any other way. It's a wonderful feeling to be able to reach those relatively untouched, wild places, but there's a downside. If you get in trouble, only another person with an aircraft can come out to help you, and they won't come until you're reported overdue. If you get lost in the aircraft or go down someplace unexpected, you're in serious, serious trouble. I remember one hunting trip to Summit Lake when Art Pengra took one of Ketchikan Air Service's Aeronica Chiefs, and I flew the T-Craft Duey and I had purchased. We climbed up the steep side of the mountain and shot a couple of great big deer. By the time we got them down, the weather had gone to pot.

Art took off first and ducked out through the Cholmondeley Sound entrance. It did not look good to me so I went out the back way. I went down through Summit Lakes into Hetta Inlet and finally found my way across Twelve-Mile Inlet into Kasaan Bay. I realized this was all new country to me in addition to the weather being bad. I went around the corner thinking I would turn to the right, which put me out into Clarence Straits. The waves got bigger, and it was obvious I was going the wrong way into the open sea. I turned to my left and went downwind staying close to the land and soon came to a little harbor, which turned out to be Hadley. I landed at Hadley and waited. It was a nice little beach—a nice place to keep the airplane. I sat back in there checking the map and just before dark the ceiling lifted a little bit. I could see across to the Caamano shore and to Ship Island so I knew where I was. I took off and hit the Caamano shore and followed it until I could see Guard Island light, the entrance to Tongass Narrows and home. I flew into town just after dark. That was one of my first experiences handling the bad weather in Ketchikan.

On another hunting trip Art Pengra and I decided that we would go early in the morning up to Harriet Hunt Lake. It was about ten miles from town beyond the end of the road, and it was a nice hunting area. Art had his pilot's license, but he didn't get much time to fly so I thought the proper thing to do was to let Art fly our Taylor Craft N36210. I hand-cranked it, and we taxied out. I crawled in the right-hand seat and let Art fly the left-hand seat. I had the two guns between my legs because a T-craft is pretty small. We made a normal takeoff and headed up toward Harriet Hunt Lake. It was a beautiful morning, absolutely glassy calm water, and just a few riffs of fog here and there around the lake.

Art swung around and started his approach to the lake, and we hit one of those little riffs of fog. That upset him a little bit, but he kept going. As we got close to the water, he started to level off and about that time, whack! We hit something. Art had been making a normal landing instead of a regular nose-high,

Peggy and I used a war-surplus weapons carrier for plowing snow, and sledding up at Harriet Hunt, among other things.

Nine Lives of an Alaska Bush Pilot

glassy-water, power-on landing, and the glassy water had fooled him. We hit hard, and something broke.

Art immediately added power and got the airplane back in the air. We were just a couple feet in the air, and I hollered, "You better set it back down because something's broken. We're close to the water, and we'd just as well put it down here." So Art very carefully lowered the airplane back down and reduced the power. He touched the water so smoothly with the left float that we couldn't tell the struts were broken on it. As he slowed down, the right wing went up in the air, and the left wing settled down on the water. To me, the airplane appeared to be stalling, and I had one horrible moment. Then the wing hit the water, and Art poured the power back on. We were glued to the water with one wing in the water and only the one float operational. With full power on, we went around in circles in the middle of the lake. Art made a couple revolutions with full power, and then the engine started to quit. We knew we were going to sink and tip over. I hollered at him, "Carburetor ice!" and pulled the carburetor heat on. The carburetor ice melted out, and the roar came back in the engine. The aircraft recovered a little, but we kept dragging the wingtip on the water.

The next alternative was for me to get out on the float.

Art Prengra wrestles with a damaged N36210 on an ill-fated hunting trip to Harriet Hunt Lake.

With full power on the engine and the aircraft leaning hard to the left, trying to get the door open with the guns between my legs and get out on the float of the airplane was a real struggle. Once I managed to get out on the float, I leaned out on the strut as far as I could which put more weight on the high wing and brought the wing that was in the water up to where it just barely touched the water. This allowed us to make larger circles, and we circled and circled and circled until finally one circle brought us real close to the beach. I jumped off into the water about waist deep and grabbed hold of the airplane and turned it around. One wing was in the water and sinking. Art got out of the airplane as fast as he could and between the two of us, we got hold of the wing which had sunk a couple of feet and was taking on water. We lifted the wing and held it and held it, seemed like forever, letting the water drain out of it. When we got the water out, we were able to turn the airplane around and back it up onto the beach where we could secure it. We also made a brace to hold the wing up in a fairly normal position.

This put us in a precarious place. The radios were not doing us any good, and Harriet Hunt Lake is probably ten miles from the main road and another five miles to town. The airplane was secure, and the proper thing to do was for me to go get some help. A blazed trail went out one end of Harriet Hunt Lake and down to the Ward Lake area, and I ran the whole distance. I don't remember how long it took me, but I know I didn't stop when I hit the first road at Second Ward Lake. I kept on running. No cars were around so I ran down the main highway to Ward Cove and kept running toward town.

About that time a fellow I knew, George Kammerzell, recognized me and stopped and gave me a ride. He and his wife were out for a ride, and they were heading back to town so I asked them to drop me off at Russ Simpson's hangar. I told Russ my predicament. He said, "Well, go ahead and take the Aeronica and go pick up Art." I took Russ's Aeronica Chief N31774 up to the lake, landed, and picked up Art and our guns.

By that time Art had the airplane all braced up properly, and it looked like there was nothing wrong with it. We were able to diagnose what parts were necessary to fix the airplane. One strut and a couple of fittings were all it was going to take to put

N36210 braced up and ready for field repairs. Note the lashed poles supporting the port wingtip.

it back in business. The next day we collected the necessary parts, and Russ loaned me 774 again, and we flew back into Harriet Hunt Lake. Art flew the T-craft home, and I followed him with the Aeronica. It was a little incident, but again it taught us a lesson. I had a little too much confidence in Art. He was always physically more coordinated than I was. He was the star basketball player, and he was good at everything he did, but he was not as good at flying the airplane as he should have been.

Hangar Project

Building a hangar was our number one priority. I had been taking Earl Walker out quite a bit in the T-Craft, and he said he would build us a hangar. First he wanted to salvage the sheet metal and some of the sawmill equipment that had been left at an abandoned fish hatchery at Heckman Lake. During the early days if a person owned fish traps and a cannery, he could get a tax break for building a hatchery to put fish back in the ocean. The big companies built these hatcheries.

First they would go in and build a sawmill so they could make their own lumber to build their own buildings. There was quite a little village at Heckman Lake. I imagine at one time it was a dream spot to live because of the beautiful location. The quarters were very good too—they even had a pool table for recreation up there. By this time it was collapsing, but all the old iron sheet metal on the roof was still good.

I took Bill Putvin and Earl Walker up there, and they got the sheet metal ready to go along with some of the heavy metal and some of the gears from the shafts. We devised a method to get it out. We put the sheet metal between the spreader bars on the T-Craft with a piece of canvas over the front of the sheet metal so the sheets would not separate in the wind. We figured out exactly how much weight we could haul out of there. Bill, who was a very efficient worker, made sure everything was secure and tight. We poured just the right amount of gas into the gas tank to make the trip with a little safety margin. I hauled the sheet metal down to Bullhead Cove, about a five-minute flight, landed in the water, taxied to the beach, and unloaded it. Later Earl picked up the sheet metal with a boat. We figured we hauled 12,500 pounds of sheet metal out of the lake, which at 250 pounds a crack, was quite a few trips.

One of the biggest feats that we performed was taking out a 275-pound bull gear for a winch. When I look back on it now, it scares me to think of it. We put a little platform between the floats and set the bull gear on it. I attempted to take off, but all I could do was churn the water up. I came back in, and Bill Putvin, with his good eye for detail, said it looked like the thrust of the propeller was striking the bull gear instead of hitting the water and driving the plane ahead like it should. He said, "What we've got to do is to raise the level of that bull gear so the air can get underneath it." We built the platform up and

Bull gear ready for takeoff—almost.

Me overlooking the hangar. Ellis Air's Bellanca was getting an overhaul that day. Note the Model T Ford at right.

secured it. Sure enough, I was able to get on the step this time.

I maneuvered around until I had the greatest distance for my takeoff. I got the airplane in the air and nursed it very, very carefully until I was going a little over 40 miles an hour. As I recall, 45 to 50 was my absolute top speed. I just could not go any faster with that heavy gear hanging underneath the airplane. I very gingerly turned around the lake, and one of the thoughts running through my mind was, "Well, if you stall this airplane, you'll be history just like that old airplane down there now."

As I circled down the lake I had a vivid memory of Roy Jones and his passenger in his North Bird stalling at that end of Heckman Lake years earlier. They both survived, but the old North Bird bit the dust there. This thought made me even more careful than usual. After circling around a couple of times, I was able to get enough altitude to clear the trees. When I got about 100 feet above the trees, rather than waste any more time and gas circling, I decided to go for it. I got across the ridge and landed on the water. Earl was there to meet me and help get the heavy bull gear unloaded. I often thought if I had stalled with that heavy bull gear and that little light airplane, I would have just disappeared into the muskeg.

We got enough sheet metal for Earl to finish his roof, but

we discovered we did not have quite enough to finish the hangar so we went looking for more sheet metal. The obvious place, of course, was the next abandoned fish hatchery which was Yes Bay. We went up to an old fish hatchery at the head of McDonald Lake. The buildings were in a very bad state of collapse, but we managed to salvage enough sheet metal to do the roof on our hangar. Earl and Bill built us a dandy hangar out of their custom-cut lumber. It lasted quite a while.

Trapping Wolves for Bounty

Taking the sheet metal out of the lake by airplane gave Bill Putvin an idea. His main occupation was bounty hunting—he trapped wolves and shot eagles and seals. He thought an airplane could be used in this work to make a little extra money.

In the spring of 1948, Earl, Bill, and I set a trap line on the back side of Revillagigedo Island. We set the wolf traps in each little river valley at the confluence where the river hit the salt water. Each valley could feasibly have a population of wolves. Our trap line was a hundred miles long so the airplane was the ideal way to run the trap line. We went out with the boat and established all the sets, and then every three or four days we would take the airplane and fly over the sets. We tried to make the sets where we could see them from the air, but most of the

Hunting and trapping wolves for bounty was a favorite activity back then. We killed these two in Smeaton Bay in 1947.

time we had to land and examine them.

To make a wolf set we found a spot where the tide left a little puddle of water, and we put a seal carcass in the center of the puddle. Then we piled rocks on top of the carcass, and in the perimeter around the rocks, we set our traps. The wolves would try to get to the seal, and they would not notice the traps in the water. They would try to sneak in and get the seal out from underneath the rocks. Occasionally they were able to do it successfully, but usually there would be a family of wolves, and one would accidentally get in a trap. Then the others were able to get the seal carcass out. I have never seen them eat the carcass, but they would drag it off.

Cold Swim

We got our trap line pretty well established, and it was going to be a lot of fun. It was still very cold, and the tide was extremely high when we arrived to check our set in Blakewell Arm one day. The high tide allowed us to get the airplane quite close to the set. In the set was a wolverine which created a little excitement, and we didn't tie up the airplane like we should have. As we got the wolverine out of the trap and reset the trap for wolves, we turned around and looked as our airplane was floating off. Well, here we were fifty miles from home with nothing but what was in our hands for survival, and our airplane was floating off.

Since I was a little faster than Earl, I made a run for it but could not catch the airplane. The water was going over my boots so I went back to the beach, peeled off my boots, took off my pants which were already wet, and swam for it. Hitting those cold pontoons when I was cold and wet was quite an experience. I got in the airplane and taxied back to the beach. Now all I had were wet clothes so we tied the pants and shirt and underwear onto the wing struts of the airplane. We got back in the airplane, and I flew it to the next trap about 10 miles away with only my jacket and my wet boots on. We figured the wind would dry those clothes off. We stopped at the next trap, and I was getting pretty cold. Some of the excess water had dried off the clothes, but we realized that it was not going to be a successful move. I put the wet clothes back on, and we headed for home.

High-Speed Taxiing

On one of the first trips out to inspect the traps, we were pretty tickled to get two wolves. We skinned them out with the four legs attached to the hide as required by Fish and Game to earn the $50 bounty. On the way back we got in a heavy snowstorm coming out of Smeaton Bay. We crossed over to Smeaton Island, and the snow got worse and worse. Finally I couldn't see at all so we had to land. I set a compass course to taxi across Princess Bay.

Earl and I were sitting in the airplane talking away as we taxied—we were excited about having trapped the wolves. Soon we noticed a little change in the angle of the airplane. I opened the door, peeked out, and saw the back end of the floats were under water. I immediately added power, which made the floats plane a little better. We still could not see the beach anywhere, but we were on a compass course, and we knew we were in

Earl Walker and I pose with some of that winter's wolf hides and a rare wolverine (in front). Using aircraft to extend the trap line was an entirely new idea at the time.

Princess Bay so we continued our high-speed taxiing to keep the floats above water.

When we were finally able to get to the beach, we shut the airplane down and realized what had happened. We had about six inches of snow piled up on top of the wings and there was so much weight that it was sinking the airplane. This was a pretty good lesson for us not to get caught in that spot again. We pumped the floats and scraped the snow off the wings with our hands and with a rope. Finally, the weather cleared up a little bit, and we were able to take off for town.

That really doesn't sound like too hairy an experience, but it was a pretty critical situation, and we made some right moves at the right time. At that time you couldn't count on help from any source. Every time you went out, you were out on your own. There were not many airplanes around, and the communications were poor. Someone might have known your destination, but that was all they knew. Generally it was a day or two or three before anybody would start looking for you if you were overdue. Sinking into the freezing water as we almost did, hypothermia would have set in almost immediately. We likely would have died inside half an hour.

Successful Season

The wolf trapping was very interesting because every time you visited your traps whether you caught a wolf or not, you could interpret what the wolf had done and what would be a smarter way to try to trap him again. Our traps were all set so the wolves would drown when the tide came in. It worked most of the time, but there were cases when the wolf was strong enough to get away from us. Occasionally they went into the woods, and we had to go after them. We knew what the wolf would do in defense so we had to be very careful as we approached them.

On one occasion we had a live wolf in the trap cornered, and we killed him as he lunged at us. When we realized only one toe was left holding the wolf, we wondered what would have happened if he had made that lunge before we fired the shot. You never know.

We ended our first trapping season with 10 wolves, 2 wolverines, 30 seals, and 8 eagles. Our biggest wolf was trapped in Princess Bay and weighed 124 pounds. We thought we were pretty good. Later on Bill and Earl really concentrated on trapping. Next season I was too busy working, but Earl and Bill got 50 wolves. They stretched their trap line out quite a little bit and worked every flying day they could on it.

Second Taylor-Craft

We just could not pass up a good buy so we got our second T-Craft, an excellent airplane, for $1400. Soon after we bought it, Russ Simpson's Aeronica Chief was laid up, and he had a trip up to Telegraph Creek so he borrowed our old T-Craft 210. Two or three days later, Russ called me on the phone and said, "Say, how much was it you wanted for that aircraft?" I said, "Well, we paid $1200 for it, so I'll take $1200 for it." "Okay," he said, "I'll make you out a check." I said, "You want to buy it, huh?" And he said, "I bought it, all right. I dumped it up at Sawmill Lake in Telegraph Creek."

On his trip to Telegraph Creek, Russ had taken one passenger with him, and he had a gas can in the back of the plane. He took off, went around, and was going to make a turn. He figured

Taylor Craft N36210 down at Telegraph Creek.

he would be turning back into the wind when he completed his turn at the westerly end of the lake, but he misjudged and was turning downwind. He stalled into some birch trees that were kind to him. They were pretty flexible and cushioned his fall. The airplane was ruined, but nobody was badly hurt. Russ's arm was broken, and the gas can he was carrying hit him in the head and knocked him out temporarily. Other than that he was okay.

The Royal Canadian Mounted Police told him, "You have to take the airplane back out of here—you can't leave it in here. That's an import, and you'd have to pay duty on it and all that." They did not even offer a solution; they just said we would have to take it out. So Russ and I went back up to Sawmill Lake in our new Taylor-Craft and cut the wreckage into pieces and dropped it in the lake so nobody could see it. The next season when we were up there, we saw some kids paddling around the lake on the pontoons they had salvaged.

Ketchikan Volunteer Rescue Squad

On October 28, 1947, I was called to go on an aerial search for a missing Pan American DC-4. Captain Alf Monson was on his last flight before retiring, carrying a planeload of 25 or 30 passengers aboard when his plane disappeared near Annette Island. It was obvious it had crashed, but we did not know where. The weather was not very good, but several of us took off to go look for them anyway. My search area was Mirror Lake. It felt kind of strange flying in the mountains looking for this wrecked airplane, and I really didn't know what to expect. When the weather cleared, the airplane was spotted. Somebody had heard it crash on Tamgas Mountain. This was actually my first aerial search, and this event triggered the formation of the Ketchikan Volunteer Rescue Squad.

Once the aircraft was located, a rescue party was formed and sent in to the crash site. Dick Borch, Dick Richner, Rocky Johnson, Del Richardson, and others whom I have forgotten were the ground troops involved. Rodger Elliott flew them into a small lake close to the base of the mountain, and they were able to climb to the wreck from there. It was quite a chore bringing the remains of the people back down the mountain. Everyone felt just terrible about how many people had been killed, and how long it had taken to find them. This made us realize the need to have a search and rescue organization and somebody with the local knowledge to organize it.

From then on Dick Borch and I started working together on searches, and we actually formed a little rescue squad with Terry Myser as secretary. We had some good volunteers: Doug Giles, Don Moore, Earl Mossburg, the Ketah boys, basically all the guys who hunted and fished. We used any aircraft or boat that was available and willing to go on the search. Ellis Air always participated in the searches pretty heavily. It was a very cooperative thing. It was really not an organization, but it was just a bunch of guys who met together whenever the circumstances demanded it, and away we went. Dick was especially dedicated. On some occasions he even left his job to go on a search or to help somebody out. At that time in Ketchikan we had no agency with the ability to do the kind of search and rescues we had to do.

Mama And The Cubs

One of my more memorable bear experiences was on the Bradfield Canal, one of our favorite hunting spots. It was an area with big tide flats and big tides. There were no people for miles around so we always had it to ourselves. A fair number of migratory birds would be there in the fall. On this occasion my partner Duey Barber, his girlfriend's daughter Lois, and I had flown to the flats for some bird hunting. I landed in the tidal area and taxied up the river letting Duey and Lois off on the west side of the river. They could hunt the flats, and when the tide came in there was a big stump they could get on until I could pick them up. I would hunt the east side of the river.

In the tide flats there were a number of sloughs that were nothing when the tide was out, but when the tide came in, it was a different story. All these tributaries were like limbs of a tree reaching out to the river. I taxied up the river a ways and dropped the anchor. Then I moved the plane close to the bank of the river where I tied a shore line and let the plane swing out into the current. I secured the shore line to the nearest high spot hoping I would be back before the tide covered it. I then hiked down river to the biggest slough where the hunting would be the best. The hunting was good, and I got my limit of ducks and a couple Canadian geese. The tide was starting to be a problem so it was time for me to move.

We had cached a collapsible boat in the woods on the east side of the river in case we could not reach the plane. It was a funny boat with quarter-inch plywood sides and a half-inch stern and rubber seams so it could be folded up. It was not much of a boat, but it was enough to paddle out to the plane.

I packed up my birds into two bunches, swung them around my neck, and started for the plane. Ahead of me in the tide flats, a big grizzly stuck her head up. I had no fear of bear. I figured I could handle it with my old Model 97 Winchester hammer pump 12-gauge shotgun. I always carried two shotgun slugs with me which were plenty good for big bear at close range. The bear was right in the way where I wanted to go. I had to cross four little sloughs to get to the plane. Without too much thought, I pumped a shell of bird shot into the gun and fired it knowing it was just going to sprinkle the bear. The bear panicked and started to run in a circle. As she accelerated her front paws threw big patches of mud and grass out behind. She was making a roaring noise, and as she came around two more heads popped up. She had two 2-year-old cubs, not babies but about 200 pounds apiece. After her circle around the cubs, she headed right for me.

There was one pretty big slough between the bear and me; it was 20 yards across and two feet deep. I thought that would slow her down quite a bit. Just as a precaution I pumped the bird shot out of the shotgun and reached in my pocket for my two bear slugs. I got one in the gun but dropped the second one. With my eye on the bear, I pumped the one shell in the barrel. She was coming fast—just a couple splashes and she would be across the slough. I could not reach for the dropped shell now. I had only one shot with three bears facing me! She came within ten feet of me and rose up on her hind legs. Her sides were heaving. She had the cubs on each side and a little behind her.

My instincts told me do not shoot unless she takes the final step. If I shoot and do not kill her, she will get me, and if I kill her, the cubs will get me. I stood my ground for what seemed like forever, and her breathing started to slow down. The two cubs stayed behind the mother. I think that was a big factor in her not finishing me off.

This picture was taken on one of many ice skating parties done by float plane—this one at Purple Lake. I'm standing on the float of Russ Simpson's Aeronica Chief.

As her breathing slowed down, I knew I had gained a little advantage. It seemed like I had to make some kind of a move so I took two steps toward the bear, each one inch long with a little exaggerated body movement. The bear slowly turned and dropped down on her four legs, her eyes still on me, and she moved off toward the woods. The two cubs ran ahead of her. Then I was able to breathe a sigh of relief.

The bear headed for the woods where we had cached the boat, and apparently she smelled something on the boat that triggered a rage. She swatted the boat hitting the transom with one of her paws. All of her claws went clear through the half-inch plywood. She proceeded to tear the sides apart with mouth-sized bites. When she finished the boat was totally destroyed.

There I was in another predicament. I had to get to the plane, and the tide was coming in fast. The weather was cold. As the tide moved in, little pieces of ice that had been in the bottom of the slough started to float. I crossed a couple of the small sloughs successfully and realized that I had to leave my birds. When I reached the last slough, I saw the shore line had been covered by the tide. I would have to leave my gun and my clothes and swim for the stump where we had tied the line. The smartest thing I did was to use my rubber boots tied together upside down as life preservers. It really worked. As I swam bare-naked across the slough, the thought went through my head, "If I should drown, what are people going to think?"

I got to the bank where the shore line was tied. It was covered with two feet of water, but I managed to find it with my feet, which by now were numb. I pulled the plane in and crawled aboard. My feet were on the rudder pedals, but I could not feel them. I pulled in the rope and anchor and put them in the baggage compartment. I started up the engine and taxied over to my clothing and gun, then to my birds. It was hard getting my clothes on my wet body in such limited space in the airplane. Then I taxied across the river to pick up Duey and Lois who were stranded on the big log in the tide flats. Duey wondered why I left them so long and what I was doing taxiing all over the tide flats. My best explanation was to show Duey what was left of our boat.

Later we made a trip out to pick up the pieces of the boat and put them on display at Harry Cowan's sporting goods store. From then on I had great respect for any kind of a bear.

Ice Landings

One January day the ice was nice and slick for ice skating, and we got the bright idea of trying to land a floatplane on the ice on Purple Lake. We had quite a little collection of airplanes. I flew our T-Craft; Pete Cessnun, his Luscombe; Herman Ludwigsen, his Luscombe; and Russ Simpson, his Chief. Herman had a little trouble landing on the ice the first time. A screw in the keel of one of his pontoons was sticking down a little bit which was not a problem when landing on the water, but on the ice it caused the airplane to turn. I can see Herman yet. He was out of his airplane, hanging on to the tail. The engine was shut off, and he was trying to stop it as it slid on the ice and turned into the bank. Fortunately, nothing was hurt when his airplane hit the beach.

After that we had many skating parties arriving by floatplane. The ice is so solid there is no give, and the floatplane is built with no give in the struts so you have to land very gently.

The takeoff was especially easy because there was no friction. You were in the air twice as fast as on the water. A little snow on the ice slowed you down a lot. Wind was a factor for direction and security.

At times it seemed like the airplane would never stop so we developed a method of stopping. We would bottom the left rudder pedal and give the engine a little blast. This turned the plane around so it was sliding backwards. A little blast of power now worked like air brakes.

Lessons Learned

Interesting things happened to us, and we learned lessons as we did things. One example is when I went moose hunting in the old T-Craft, I elected to take the stick out of the right-hand side so the passenger would not be tempted to grab it. Thinking nothing of it, I slipped the first bolt off and pulled the stick right out. Nothing to it.

Well, everything worked fine until one occasion when Russ Simpson had gotten a moose up on the Stikine, and Carl Bradley and I went up to see where he was. We over-flew him before I realized it so I immediately looked for a place to land in the river. I was going downwind for my landing, and I did a Split S, 180-degree turn ending up going almost straight down at the river. It took a hard pull out to get the plane level for landing. Well, much to my surprise, Carl fainted on the way down. I was making a rather rapid move, a little abrupt, a little too much G-force on it for him. As I was trying to pull out, I could not quite get the nose up. The controls had jammed. I did not have time to think about what I was doing; I just reacted. As we got real close to the water, I knew we were going to plow in so I just added a little power to lift the nose up, and I greased on a nice landing. By the time we came off the step and taxied onto the beach, Carl was okay, but he was not in for any more airplane rides right away.

Later we found a universal joint on the control column that I had not taken off, and when I turned the controls quite severely one way and then pulled back on the stick, the universal joint jammed underneath the dashboard. That was the cause of my problem. I will never do that again.

Chapter 3,
Piper Cruisers

Russ Simpson was so convinced the Cruiser was going to be the best airplane to do his work with that he talked me into buying one first. In 1952, Bob Young and I purchased Piper PA-12, 3642 Mike. We put a lot of hours in that airplane and really enjoyed it. At the end of my No. 2 logbook I wrote, "This book has 403 hours of flying in it. They have been some of the most enjoyable hours of my life. Let's hope and pray that they have also taught me respect for flying so that I may enjoy another 400 hours like it."

I went back to Tallahassee, Florida, (where Bob was going to school) to get 3642 Mike. Since it was on wheels, I got checked out on wheels while we were there and headed for Seattle. It was a long flight in the old Cruiser. It was pretty slow, but with the 100-horse motor it had about a six-hour range. Even though we were only doing about 85 miles an hour, we could stay in the air quite a long time and covered quite a little distance.

I landed at the Renton Airport near Seattle where the

Bob Young pauses for a snapshot in Dallas, Texas next to PA-12 number 3642M — our first aircraft.

mechanics slipped floats on for us. We were able to put the plane in the water there because they had access to Lake Washington. Then I flew it over to Henry Riverman's where we split the belly, painted it up, and did the best we could to make it last a little longer as a seaplane. I took off from Seattle for Ketchikan and had a nice trip up the coast.

Surprise Start

As a mechanic I could maintain the buses pretty well, but I was not too smart on airplanes yet, and now we had a new PA-12. One time we had to tow it from Clover Pass back into town with a skiff and outboard. I had trouble starting it, and I pulled into a dock between Russ Simpson's and Pete Cessnun's floats. There were some pretty rotten lines laying on the dock, and I tied the airplane up with them and tried to start it again. I stepped onto the float and cranked the propeller. It wouldn't start so I advanced the throttle a little further, and it still wouldn't start. I advanced the throttle a little further, and it did start. It started and leaped forward breaking the lines, of course.

There I was heading out in the bay at about half throttle. Right in front of me was a little cruiser with a man and his son standing on the back deck with their mouths wide open. I was heading straight at them. With great effort I managed to get the door open against the prop blast, reached over, grabbed the throttle, reduced the power, and jammed on the rudder pedal with my hand. I was lying across the front seat in the airplane, and when I looked up the wing passed over the boat—never touched a thing. That taught me a real good lesson. I won't let that happen again.

Boy Scouts

For quite a few years in the early 50s, I was Scoutmaster of Troop #635. My son Danny was in my troop. All of the Boy Scouts were kids to be proud of. I don't know if we were just lucky or what, but all those kids turned out to be good kids. One became an admiral in the Navy.

We went on all kinds of endeavors. One of our adventures took us on a very long trip on foot from the White River Boy Scout camp. All the boys loaded up their packs and everything they had to carry for their camp, and we started to hike from

White River into Leask Lake. We thought we might make the lake the first night, but we only got halfway there so we spent the night in the muskeg. It started to rain, and we had all the problems you can imagine including kids burning their clothes up and improper camp setups. The next day we still didn't quite make the lake and decided we had better abort because we were scheduled to be back the next day. We made it back safe and sound, and all much wiser for the experience.

We started a little project building a cabin on Scout Lake which sits on the hill just above Ketchikan. We were going to reconstruct the old mine shack up there. We put shingles in gunnysacks, and I rigged up a little chute on the side of the airplane. We would make a run over the lake area and drop the bundles into the snow using a trip device. It worked well and was a lot of fun. We would fly over the area, and when we figured it was just about the right spot, we would jerk the trip, and the shingles would fly off and land safely. We were able to recover all of them and put a roof on the cabin. Later we gave all the Boy Scouts a look from the air to see where the cabin was, and from then on it was their project—hiking up to the lake and putting things together. It was a small cabin, and we had all sixteen guys in there one night.

Dan Eichner and Werner Sund head out on an adventure.

I had wonderful experiences with the kids, and I realize now how important it was for all of us. During this period I was pretty busy. All my spare time from the bus company I was taking trips for Russ Simpson, taking prospectors out, and servicing the Boy Scout camp. It kept me hopping, but the long hours didn't bother me a bit. I loved that.

Rough Water Takeoff

In October of 1952 a bunch of guys from the Red Men Lodge were planning a hunting trip on the back side of the channel near Swedish Meadows. I was too busy to go hunting, but I volunteered to take a couple guys who could not leave on time over to meet the group. When I got over in the back channel, a strong southerly wind was blowing right straight up Behm Canal. It was creating waves that must have been two feet tall—about the absolute limit for that Cruiser or any other small airplane. I landed successfully, but then I had to take off again. The airplane still had the old 100-horsepower engine, and with the pontoons it was pretty much a dog, especially with two people in the back. I hit the waves two or three times pretty hard, and I felt something stick me in the leg. I finally got in the air, got squared away, and saw that a piece of the airplane tubing had broken and was sticking me in the leg.

The Cruiser was built as a land plane with shock absorbers on the landing gear. When you put it on floats, there are no shock absorbers. It needs to be solid from the float fittings through to the wing so there is no give. On the Cruiser, the door side had a solid post that went right up through the wing root. On the other side there was no post because the strength was not needed for the wheel plane. Since it was on floats, landing sent the shock right up there, and it eventually collapsed the members between the wing root and the float strut. The fix we came up with was to weld in a post from the attached fitting in the front up to the wing root. That made a real good seaplane out of the Cruiser.

Patching Pontoons

One of the mining companies had located some iron on the north end of Prince of Wales Island near Sarkar Lake. They set up a camp and were drilling so we flew lots of trips in there. One day Earl Walker radioed that his aircraft, 13 Mike, was in trouble. He had hit a rock in Sarkar Lake and ripped a float open. He managed to get the plane to shallow water, but he was in real trouble. I had the bright idea to put some boards in the bottom of each section of the float, and then put an inner tube in the float and pump it up so it would crowd all the water out. Since just part of the bottom of the float was torn out, we decided to try my idea. The plane was a little slow taking off, but as soon as he got that one float out of the water, away he went. He got the airplane home and did a proper patch job. Later on I was able to help one of the Gildersleeve boys out by telling him this solution to fixing a float. He tried it and saved his airplane on the Unuk River.

Hunter Rescue

One afternoon I got word that Jack Cousins was trying to get into a lake near the head of George Inlet to look for Herby Hert and the pilot Windy Barton who were overdue from a hunting trip in a Super Cub. The weather was so bad Jack was unable to get up George Inlet by going around Mountain Point so I took off in the airplane and went through White River pass into George Inlet. The weather was very low, but I was able to sneak in over the treetops and get into the lake.

Here was the airplane in the middle of the lake, upside down. I feared the worst, but I soon saw a little smoke coming from the corner of the lake. Somebody had gotten out of the plane.

I taxied over to the campfire and saw that both hunters were okay. They had gotten a deer and had attempted to take off with it but wrecked the airplane in the lake. They had been able to swim ashore and get a fire going and had spent an uncomfortable night.

I taxied into the beach and hollered at them, "Let's get out of here. The weather is marginal, but I think I can make it right now." Herby got in the airplane, but Windy was still fooling around camp so I told Herby, "Better hurry him up, or we're all going to spend the night here." Then there was really some fast action. Windy got in the airplane, and we took off and managed to get out over the trees and back to town safely.

Herby was pretty pleased about being rescued. He took Peggy and me out for a steak dinner.

Turnbuckle Problem

I was always taking friends out hunting or fishing in 42 Mike. A couple of friends of mine, Ray and Bill Hendricks, wanted to go over to Smugglers Cove Lake to fix up the cabin and do a little hunting. They arrived with a pretty good load of gear. I managed to get it all in the plane along with the two passengers, and I shoved away from the float. I knew I was pretty aft loaded so I either had to have one of my passengers stand up and lean forward to bring the center of gravity forward or exert full forward pressure on the stick. The passengers weren't familiar with that procedure so I used the full forward stick. After I had full power on and had climbed as far forward as I could, I tried to rock it a little. Then the stick went limp.

Something had broken on the elevator controls. There was nothing to do but cut the power and taxi back to the dock. Upon examination we found the turnbuckle that hooked on to the elevator horn was rusted solid so when I moved the elevator control, the end of the turnbuckle bent instead of turning and finally broke. In the next overhaul we moved the turnbuckle to the other end of the control where it would not get splashed with salt water. Thinking it over, if I had gotten in the air before the turnbuckle broke, I might have been able to control the airplane with the trim control that moves the forward part of the elevators. I'm glad I wasn't put to the test. After that 42 Mike went in for major overhaul.

42 Mike Overhaul

In the upper part of our Northern Bus Garage, we built a room especially so we could work on the airplane. Getting the plane to our Northern Bus garage for overhaul presented a challenge. We wanted to take it apart at our garage so as not to misplace any pieces. At that time there was no mall across the street and on the big tides the water lapped at the edge of Tongass Avenue. So on a day when the wind was not blowing and the tide was high, we pulled the plane up to the edge of the street. With a little extra manpower we dragged the plane onto a wheeled cart and rolled it across the street to the bus garage. We planned to rebuild the fuselage that winter and the wings the following year.

The rebuilding and testing of 42 Mike was a wonderful experience and a lot of fun. Almost every night after work all winter long we worked. Bud Hawkins, Eddie Zaugg, Duey Barber, and Kelly Adams helped us rebuild 42 Mike. Eddie was an excellent mechanic, and Kelly had his inspector's license.

Performance Boost

By springtime we had finished the complete overhaul of 42 Mike. We had installed a 125-horsepower Lycoming to replace the 100-horsepower engine. We thought this would be a real boost in performance. I took it on a test hop and had a little trouble with the trim. It was nose heavy so we added six pounds of lead in the tail, and that took care of the problem. Instead of going through all of the mathematics and really figuring it out correctly, we just went by feel. At that time nobody paid that much attention—if you wanted to do something, you did it. FAA would come down and ride with us on test flights. They were very cooperative in those days.

The airplane performed real well, but we had not taken a long trip yet. Earl Walker wanted to go to Pelican to buy Pros Ganty's Aeronica Chief, so we decided to go in 42 Mike. We took off and soon found out we didn't have enough oil cooling. We had to run the engine slower to keep the temperatures down below the red line. We had a lot of trouble trying to figure out how to cool it. We put on a cooler, but the air ducting wasn't right. We changed things around so it would cool and finally got the right combination to cool the engine properly. Now we were all proud of our rebuild job. We had a much better performing airplane.

Propellers were another thing that affected the performance of the airplane. When we first changed the Piper to a 125-horsepower engine, we had the old 100-horsepower propeller on it—a two-position, wooden propeller with metal tips. We noticed that the tips were starting to get loose so we sent the propeller down to Northwest Propeller and asked them to rebuild it. They asked us what we were using it on, and when we told them, they said, "Well, that's illegal." They sent a legal replacement prop that

42 Mike at the Norhern Bus Garage, awaiting its first major overhaul and refit.

was similar except it was heavy-duty. We put it on the airplane, but it just didn't perform well in any position.

We were also having trouble with the cooling, and the FAA had ridden with us several times and wouldn't pass it. We finally just took the two-position prop off and put on a metal prop. The metal prop performed better on takeoff, better at cruise, better everything. At last we solved that problem.

We were trying to get too fancy with that two-position prop because it had worked well with the 100-horsepower engine.

The next year after putting the 125-horsepower engine in, we laid the airplane up for a few months so Eddie Zaugg could do the wings for us. We wanted the very best. We put Irish linen on the wings, and I think we put on 28 coats of hand-rubbed dope. The wings just shone unbelievably. There was only one drawback: We added more weight to the airplane than we thought, but it was a good job.

We were always doing something with the Cruisers trying to improve their performance one way or another. I got the idea that we could use Super Cub tail feathers which were a bigger assembly than the ones on the present Cruiser and would give us a lot more control. With the bigger elevators on there, Russ Simpson devised a method of putting two vertical fins on the Cruiser, and this would eliminate the necessity of having the sea-fin underneath, which was always getting hung up on the dock and getting damaged, creating all kinds of problems. We flew for quite a while without any sea-fin, and there wasn't any trouble except that the FAA said it wasn't legal, and so we finally had to conform.

My First Stall

Every month of August my logbooks show hunting, hunting, hunting, hunting. I think we practically raised our family on venison. Danny got his first deer, a nice big five-point buck, in September of 1955 near Upper Mahoney Lake. I managed to get a picture of it just before he shot it, and he was pretty proud. Duey and I each got two-points on that trip.

Now we were presented with a problem. The weather was still good, but the wind was acting a little funny. It made me a little nervous because I was pretty much a low-time pilot—just starting to show 1000 hours over a period of ten years from the time I got my license. That wasn't very much flying, but since I acquired my own aircraft, the hours were starting to build a little faster. A hundred hours a year when I didn't own an airplane was pretty good, and now that I owned an airplane, I was going to get 200, maybe 300 in some years.

We had landed at the head of Upper Mahoney—we called it Dogleg Lake because it had a right angle in it. It was big enough to take off from under most conditions. Even the old Cruiser with 125 horsepower performed pretty well. We loaded Danny and two deer on and started takeoff, but I couldn't get anywhere. I couldn't even get on the step so we turned around and brought it back. We had already pumped the floats, but we thought we must have missed something so we looked them over, found a little water in one float, and pumped it out. I said, "Okay, I'll take off with just the deer on board." I tried to take off and still couldn't get on the step. So I said, "Well, let's take the deer off, and I'll try it with just Danny." First I tried it with just myself and that didn't work. I guess I was pretty dumb. All these trials, and something was wrong.

I was nervous about the wind, and because of my lack of experience, I thought perhaps we were getting a downdraft that was just not letting me get on the step. I put Danny in the airplane and got on the step. I couldn't quite get up enough speed to take off, but I thought now I know what I am doing, and I think I can improve that. So we taxied clear back down the lake, and I got on the step and got it in the air. I was now coming toward the head of the lake, and I went up on the side of the hill just as far as I could go and started a nice gentle turn to come around. As we came around the dogleg of the lake, the hill sloped off fairly gradually in front of me, and I started to slow while turning back. I still didn't have enough altitude to clear the ridge, which was probably 200 to 300 feet high, so I had to steepen my turn a little bit.

As I steepened my turn the airplane stalled. It was shaking, and we were going down. I had a little more rudder on than needed to complete the turn because I was trying to miss the rock on the corner of the mountain. Just as I cleared it I straightened the rudder pedals up, and the airplane flew. We were quite close to the water when it came out of the stall. It was more good luck than skill.

I leveled out, kept the coal poured on, flew out of the lake,

Hunting and fishing using the airplane was always the thing for me. Here my partner Duey Barber and I are returning from a trip in our PA12, Number 42 Mike.

and landed at our hangar in town. I slid the airplane up on the float and got out, still perplexed. As I got out I looked down, and here the second compartment of the float was spewing water out like nobody's business. It wasn't a very big hole. It was cut by a sharp little rock when we put it on the beach. I pounded it out a little bit and filled it up with gum. Because it took on water as we built up speed trying to get on the step, it pressurized the thing and put water inside the float. The leaking compartment was forward of center causing heavy back pressure to keep the nose up. With the gum in it, I was able to take off like a million dollars. I went in and picked up the deer and brought them out, then went back and picked up Duey and the last deer. Everything was fine.

I always said, "Well, anybody would know when an airplane stalls." Now that I look back on it, one more dimension that I didn't include in the stall was the weight and balance which have a tremendous effect on the way the airplane stalls. In this case, with all the weight being forward, it wasn't the kind of a stall that was going to flip you over on your back, but it was just a stall where you couldn't hold the airplane's nose up enough to keep it flying. It took more speed to give you enough control with your elevators to hold your nose up. It was a very subtle lesson, but a good lesson.

That was the only time I ever, to my knowledge, came close to a stall. It has always seemed so completely impossible because in stall maneuvers you are always pulling the thing up as hard as you can forcing it into a stall so it will turn over on its back. None of those conditions was present so it was kind of a sneaky fool-it, a good lesson learned. Duey was sitting on the beach and watching, and he couldn't figure out why I was diving for the water like that. He didn't realize the airplane was stalled and was shocked when I told him. But Danny never forgot it. Looking right down at the water as you are heading for it is kind of a spooky feeling.

150 Horsepower

Soon we started hearing stories about somebody putting 150 horsepower in the Cruiser so we got together—there were three airplanes involved: 20 Mike, 13 Mike, and 42 Mike—to get 150-horsepower engines. Bob Monroe at Kenmore on Lake

Washington in Seattle agreed to install all the engines.

One by one we flew the airplanes down to Kenmore and flew them back. We enjoyed the flights between Seattle and Ketchikan in the old Cruisers. The flights sometimes ran up to nine hours, and sometimes we'd make it in seven hours. The planes were so slow that the wind was a critical factor.

The flight from Seattle to Ketchikan had various problems. First of all we had to clear Canadian customs, then if we could fly nonstop all the way to Ketchikan, we didn't have to clear U.S. customs. Some people stopped at logging camps and got fuel and didn't bother to clear customs; but we'd do it the right way. Sometimes we'd stop at Port Hardy on the water where they had a customs officer. Sometimes he was a little hard to get a hold of, but it worked. Other times we would go directly into Vancouver, land on the river in Vancouver, clear customs and head north from there. Actually we needed fuel in the Port Hardy area which was about halfway, and from that point we could make it the rest of the way to Ketchikan.

Autopulse

On one of these trips to the Lower 48, as we called it, a friend of mine, Ray Turek, who ran a Western Auto store right next to our bus garage, wanted to ride down with me. Well, I had the bright idea that I was going to make this nonstop. I rigged up an autopulse, and ran a line down into the main section in the middle of one of the pontoons so we wouldn't have trouble with balancing or center of gravity problems. I ran the hose up to the upper wing tank and in through the cap. The wing tank had a glass sight gauge visible underneath so if we were to get any water showing in it, we could shut that pump off. As we flew we would watch the gauge for the tank we were filling and fly on the other tank until we'd filled the first one up. Then once we'd run it down to a safe margin, we'd switch back to the other tank and pump it full again. It worked pretty slick. We had a good 10 hours of cruise time in it.

We cleaned the floats out real well, absolutely dry, warmed the engine up while we were on dry land, filled up the pontoon with about 50 gallons of fuel, slid it in the water, and took off immediately. The floats really didn't leak. They might seep a bit, but for the short time they were in the water, they acquired no water. Just as a precaution, we had a little standoff pipe and a screen system that prevented us from burning the last few gallons. That way if there was a little water, we wouldn't get any.

This particular trip it took us about nine hours to get as far as Bellingham, Washington. On the way down, we ate our lunch and drank a thermos bottle of coffee. Ray decided it was time to go to the bathroom and wanted to know how we did it. I said, "Well, you've got a thermos bottle, and it's empty now, so go ahead and use it." So Ray initiated the thermos bottle, and he said, "Now what do I do?" I said, "Well, just open a window and throw it out." So Ray opened the window, took the lid off the thermos bottle, shoved it outside and started to pour. It immediately came back in his face. A very sad lesson for Ray to learn, but he never forgot it.

Boat Harbor Landing

When we arrived over Bellingham, it was dark. We talked to Flight Service, and they told us Lake Padden was four or five miles behind town, up toward the mountains. We flew back in there for a few minutes, and it got darker and darker and our fuel was getting down to where I was not too sure how much longer we had to go. It just wasn't a good setup so I turned around and asked the tower if we could land in the bay.

The wind was blowing, and it was very rough, but as we flew over Bellingham Bay, I noticed a boat harbor, and the water inside the breakwater was pretty calm. I asked Flight Service if I could land in the boat harbor. They said, "Well, nobody ever has, but if you think you can do it, that's your business." I knew I could do it, no question about that. As Ray told the story, we were lined up to go into the boat harbor, and I side-slipped it right over the rock wall, right down to the water, touched the water, and came off the step just a few feet from the breakwater on the other end. Well, I don't think it was that close, but I did get it in there in nice shape. The next morning it was calm enough so we could taxi out in the bay outside of the boat harbor to take off. Being the first one to land in the boat harbor, we got a lot of attention, and had to fill up with car gas to make the rest of the trip into Seattle. Ray was pretty impressed with the trip.

We made a handful of takeoffs using wheeled dollies, including this one in St. Louis. That's me at right.

Grass Landing and Takeoff

We made many flights to the Lower 48. Probably one of the more interesting ones was when we took 42 Mike down to McMinnville, Oregon. Ross Zeller, a mechanic who worked there, was going to put flaps on it for us. Flaps would help us slow down a little better for landing and would also help us a bit on takeoff too.

When we arrived in McMinnville, we landed our floatplane on the grass at the airport. We made sure we had a smooth area, and there were no rocks that would roll up and damage the floats, but landing on the grass the first time was quite a thrill. Actually it took us longer to stop on the grass than it did in the water. When we landed on the grass, we just sailed along as nice as could be, but we didn't stop very quickly.

When the time came to take off, we had devised a two-wheel dolly that worked real well. We'd start down the runway and as soon as we got enough speed, we pulled it off. The two-wheel dolly sometimes flipped behind us, but most of the time it just ran its course with no damage to the runway.

Cross-Country from St. Louis

Russ Simpson lined up a Cruiser owned by Art Vogler in St. Louis, Missouri and made arrangements to buy N3905 Mike. At that time in June of '53 Russ was too busy running his little operation to go get his airplane, but I was able to get away and go get it for him. The fact is I would stretch a point to be able to fly an airplane, and it sounded like a lot of fun to fly a float-plane cross-country all the way from St. Louis, Missouri to Ketchikan, Alaska.

Danny, who was 12 years old, and I took off for St Louis. We flew from Annette Island aboard Pan American to Seattle, then by United Airlines to Chicago's O'Hare airport and on to St. Louis. Art Vogel picked us up, and we spent the night at his

Refueling on the way home from St. Louis.

house. He took us out to look at the airplane—it was a good-looking airplane. It was sitting on a three-wheel dolly with one crazy wheel on it. I said, "How do you get it out of here?" He said, "Well, you just run down the runway, and when you're ready to fly, you haul it off. That's all there is to it. Want me to do it for you?" I said, "No, if you can do it, I should be able to do it." So I did. I rolled down the runway and got plenty of speed. The dolly was leading off sideways so I turned a little more, and then I hauled it off. The dolly went off the runway flipping end over end behind me. It didn't tear up the runway, and the guys were pretty pleased about that. They thought I did it on purpose.

I just barely got airborne and started to climb, when I started getting flecks of oil on the windshield. I had a short distance to go, just a matter of three or four minutes to the Merrimac River that ran alongside the airstrip. By the time I landed I had a fair amount of fresh oil on the windshield. We looked the plane over, and Art said, "Well, that plug must be leaking at the end of the prop." So he got a new plug and installed it. We cleaned the windshield, and I took off again. Same results: oil all over the airplane. I got it back down with no damage done except I was getting a little apprehensive about taking this airplane to Alaska. Finally we contacted a mechanic and told him about the problem. He asked Art what he had done. All Art had done was change the prop from an Aeromatic to a fixed prop. "Well, then," the mechanic said, "did you put the plug in the oil orifice? The oil pressure is what caused the Aeromatic to change positions." Art didn't know about that. So the mechanic got the plug and put it in, and I made a successful test flight.

Danny and I started on our trip from the Merrimac River to the Mississippi River, then followed the Missouri River to its source, and then on down the Columbia to the West Coast.

It had always been my dream to land an airplane on the Santiam River at Lebanon so the dream finally came true. We traded passengers then. Danny stayed in Lebanon with my parents for a while and Suzy, my daughter, came down to ride back with me. The first stop she wanted to make was at Jansen Beach in Portland. We landed in the river right beside it and enjoyed the entertainment, all of the rides, and the roller coaster.

Finally we took off for Alaska with a stop in Port Hardy for customs. It took 52 hours total time from St. Louis to Ketchikan.

Ed Zaugg

It was just about the Fourth of July and Russ was pretty busy. A guy named George wanted to come in from the cannery in Kasaan so Russ said, "Why don't you take the Cruiser over and pick up George for me. Eddie Zaugg was hanging around the hangar and heard the conversation. Eddie said, "You only have one passenger, so can I ride along?" I agreed to take him with me. When I got there, George and Art were waiting. That was one too many for the airplane. One of the guys said, "Well, why don't we try it and see if it will work?" So I got all three guys in. One of them had to sit on a lap, and it ended up being Eddie. To assist the take off Eddie leaned way forward over my shoulder as we tried to get on the step. This old trick worked, and I got the airplane in the air and flew home and landed in front of Russ's hangar. Just as we were coming off of the step, Eddie popped the door open and stepped out of the airplane onto the pontoon. Russ was standing in front of the hangar with his hands on his hips. As I came off of the step I turned to the left, shut the engine off, and glided into the hangar. By the time the airplane got turned toward Russ, Eddie was riding on the float. As Eddie approached, he informed Russ that was the last G.D. time he was going to ride with Eichner if he had to ride on the float of his airplane. Russ for a moment thought that Eddie had actually been riding on the outside because there were two passengers still in the plane. Russ's mouth dropped open a foot—his eyes wide.

Fate is a funny thing the next day Russ started out with his new plane and just barely got in the air when the fabric on the back peeled off and dropped him back in the water. Had it happened higher in the air, it could have been very bad. The plane was seven years old and the southern climate had destroyed the fabric. Russ then laid up 05 Mike and completely rebuilt it making a lot of the modifications that Russ was so good at.

Beaver Trapping

I guess I always was a hunter-trader-trapper because I loved the out-of-doors, and I always wanted to trap enough beaver to get my mother a fur coat. After my first experience with Earl trapping beaver, I thought I was a pretty good beaver trapper so Danny and I took off for Orchard Lake to go beaver trapping. This was in April of '53. Danny was still in school, but he got to skip school for a week while we went beaver trapping.

The lake was still partially frozen, and it was cold. We lived in an open shelter and would get up each morning, get a fire going, get something to eat, and then take off hiking. We kept ourselves physically active so we were warm. When we got back at night we would get something to eat and crawl in our sleeping bags. We were getting pretty well acclimated to it when I had to take Danny back to town. I picked up Eddie Zaugg who came out and trapped the rest of the time with me.

Nadia Johnston Search

Not long after Eddie joined me, we were surprised to see Joe Diamond land on the lake in an Ellis Air Aeronica Sedan. He came to get us to help search for Nadia and Bill Johnston and Bill Johnson who were overdue from a fishing trip to Heckman Lake. Both men were Ellis Air mechanics. Eddie and I took off right away. When we arrived at Heckman Lake there were a half

Joe Diamond lands on Orchard Lake in one of Ellis Air's Aeronica Sedans.

dozen airplanes there, and Martin Hansen had located the crash. We helped some rescuers bring Nadia down on a stretcher.

Apparently Nadia and the two men had gone to Heckman Lake to go trout fishing one evening. On the way home their Seabee crashed on the outlet end of the lake at the top of a little knoll covered with spruce trees. The two men in the front seat died on impact. Nadia in the back seat was badly broken but survived the long night until help arrived. Martin found the wreck by flying a couple thousand feet high so he could see down through the tall spruce trees.

After Nadia was rescued, we returned to our trapping and got our limit of beavers. I finally was able to have that beaver coat made for my mother.

Weather and Darkness

In '53 hunting, fishing, and a little prospecting were still the main things we did with the airplane. On this particular occasion we wanted to go duck hunting on the Bradfield Canal. It is a neat place to hunt ducks, but with the airplane you had to be real careful with the tide so you would have enough water to take off when you got ready to leave. Where to leave the airplane was always a problem. Oftentimes we had to nursemaid the airplane while we were hunting. This time Art Pengra and Duey took our Cruiser 42 Mike. Duey was not checked out in it yet so Art flew it. Earl and I were in his Aeronica Chief N4470E. We had just started Earl's training program so I was flying it.

The hunting was really good on the Bradfield that day, but when the hunting is good you tend to stay late, and we pushed it right up to the last minute. The weather was starting to go to pot, and it was getting dark. With the failing light we managed to get through the MacDonald Lake pass to the Behm Canal side which gave us nothing but water between us and Ketchikan. By the time we got through the pass it was dark, and we were having trouble keeping track of each other. Four-two Mike at that time did not have the lights hooked up on it, and Earl's 90 Easy had some very dim lights that were not working very well. Duey shined a flashlight out of the back window of 42 Mike so we could keep track of each other. It was getting rough and raining—it was a miserable time.

Shortly after we passed Yes Bay we got separated and had to go our own way and just forget the other guy. Duey and Art took off on the left side. Earl and I went down the Cleveland Peninsula side which turned out to be the wrong choice. We got as far as Port Stewart where we saw the anchor light of a boat in the harbor. It was raining so hard and was so black we couldn't see anything but the light. I circled for about twenty minutes on that light. Earl thought I ought to land, but I said, "No, I think it's best to keep circling here because landing near that boat could present some problems. It's so stormy they might not even know we're circling around here, and what could they do to help us if we got into trouble?" So we circled and circled and circled.

Finally the weather let up a little bit, and we could see a faint shoreline. We headed for it, and sure enough I was able to see Guard Island and head on into town. It was pretty black in town so we landed a little short of our hangar where there were some lights we could see to land by. The wind was so strong it took us another twenty or thirty minutes to taxi to the hangar. In the meantime, Peggy and Duey and Art and everybody were jumping up and down thinking something had happened to us, and there was nothing they could do about it. We were criticized pretty severely for flying after dark, especially when we had such bad weather.

Highway Takeoff

Some guys in Ketchikan rebuilt a Cruiser on wheels, N2352 Mike. It was all ready to go, and they wanted me to take off on the highway near Lighthouse Grocery out on North Tongass Highway. I hadn't had a lot of time on wheels, but I was familiar with the airplane and felt confident about taking it off.

I read the manual again, and it told exactly how many feet were needed to take off the old Piper on wheels. Of course I pooh-poohed that because I knew it took longer than that. On floats it was so much slower, and I just forgot how quick a wheel plane can get off the ground. We put in eight gallons of fuel to get me from Ketchikan over to Annette Island airport where they planned to pick the airplane up and go on their way.

I paced the distance. There was a little downhill slope in the road. At that time the area was not developed very much, but there were three sets of wires across the road. The first ones, I figured would be no sweat at all. I would be underneath them while still on the ground and would have enough room to take off between the first and second set of wires and climb out over the second set.

I got it warmed up early, checked everything out, got the trim set, got everything ready to go, and off I went. The airplane was so light it jumped in the air too soon, and immediately I was looking right at the wires I had planned to go under. All I could do was shove the nose down, go back down, almost touch the ground, and pull it up on the other side. Well, by the time I came up on the other side, I had speed. I went right straight up in the air and cleared the No. 2 wires with no problem, except for a little sweat on my brow. I cruised over to Annette Island and landed the airplane. Duey came over to pick me up with our airplane and gave me a ride back home. Looking at it now, it looks like it would be impossible to take off on that stretch of road. The trees have grown up in the area, and the overhanging brush really would make it impossible.

Forced Landing

In June of 1956 I was going to take my brother-in-law Bud Steffen and my son Danny for a little airplane ride. We were flying over Gravina Point when all of a sudden we heard a terrible noise, and the engine flew apart. I shut the engine down completely and headed for a kelp patch so I wouldn't go anywhere after we got stopped. It was a thrill for Bud Steffen to experience his first forced landing.

In those days everybody was concerned about you. I was able to pass the message on that I'd had an engine failure, and soon two Goose pilots, Leon Snodderly and Max Anderes, came by and checked on me. Bob Whitten was coming by in a boat, and he picked us up and started towing the plane back home for repair. The Coast Guard arrived about half an hour after everything was over, which was kind of typical at that time.

Stuck on the Bradfield with Suzy

In October of 1956, my daughter Suzy wanted to go hunting with me so we headed up to the Bradfield Canal. We landed on the Bradfield, taxied up the river, tied the airplane up to the bank, and proceeded to hunt ducks. We shot six ducks, but we got trapped on the tide flats. The tide had gone out, and we didn't have enough water in the river to take off.

It was a beautiful moonlit night, and as it got dark we were sitting there pondering what to do when we heard a great flock of cranes. We could hear their faint voices as they circled above us. As soon as it got completely dark, they descended and landed on the tide flats. It was quite a thrill to see that.

The temperature dropped, but we had enough clothes so we weren't cold. We sat around watching the tide until finally, just after midnight, the tide had gotten in far enough and there was enough moonlight that I felt it was safe to try a takeoff. We took off in the dark and scared all the cranes, but we got airborne and headed down Bradfield Canal. The wind was starting to blow as I sneaked across the treetops and got into Yes Bay, which was cutting it a little close now that I look back on it. Once we got into Yes Bay, it was a simple matter to follow the shorelines and head for Ketchikan. We landed in the dark in Ketchikan, which seemed to be something I did quite often.

Everybody was relieved to find us home. In those days you couldn't start a search until the next day so nobody ever expected that. You always waited till daylight to give the person a couple hours to get in—just in case he was trapped by the tide or some other delay.

Night Landings

It seems like just about half the time we went out hunting, we came back after dark. I guess after enough of those after-dark flights I got to where I really wasn't too anxious to take them any more.

We often came home after dark from the north end of Revilla Island. When we got to Indian Point and picked up Grant Island light even though it was weak, it was almost like you were home. As soon as you got to Grant Island, you would be in protected water. That was always a good feeling.

Another great feeling was coming around the corner from the Mountain Point area and seeing the lights of Ketchikan. It was always such a satisfying thing to know that you were getting home. When you flew after dark, the flying was bad enough, but if you had an emergency, you would be really hard pressed to make a success out of it.

I remember one night I was coming in from the west side of Prince of Wales, and it was pure dark. I got on the radio to report in, and I remember the relief I felt when Susie Edenso's voice came over the air. Susie worked for Ellis Air as a radio operator. She was one of the most wonderful girls, and she babysat all of us pilots. It wasn't her job to stay on the radio until the last plane was in, but if anybody was out after dark Susie would sit there on the radio until we all got in. When you were coming in late, Susie's voice meant someone was looking out for you. Susie was highly respected by all the pilots.

Rescue at Big Goat Lake

I had just gone to bed with a touch of the flu when Margie Ross called and asked me to fly in to Big Goat Lake and help her find a lost hunter. It was getting close to dark and the weather was setting in, and they couldn't get anybody to go. Margie said I could take her airplane and go in.

Margie had taken David Anniskett and Harry Eli up to Big Goat Lake to go goat hunting. They landed at Big Goat Lake and hiked up to the top of the mountain. They shot a couple of goats near the top of the mountain. It was too far to bring them back to Big Goat Lake so they decided to take them to Little Goat Lake instead. Harry and Margie went back down to the lake to the airplane, and left David Anniskett to drag the goats down to Little Goat Lake.

David got the goats halfway down to Little Goat Lake and couldn't go any farther. In the meantime Margie and David had flown into Little Goat Lake. David wasn't there, and the weather was starting to go bad so they got desperate and flew back into town. Now they wanted some help to find David.

So I got dressed and headed down to the hangar. Harry Eli was going to go with me to show me where they'd left David off. We took a little tent and some sleeping bags and some food. Since I was a lot more familiar with my own plane, and it was better equipped with a radio and lights, I decided to take it instead of Margie's airplane. We fueled it up and took off into the fading light.

It was about a 35-minute trip to Big Goat Lake, and by the time we arrived it was pitch black with the wind blowing southeast. We could vaguely see the outline of the mountains. The huge waterfall at the entrance to Big Goat Lake was visible. I knew if we went right straight through Big Goat Lake from Punchbowl, we would come out over Wilson Lake which was 1000 feet lower but would give us plenty of room to turn around.

We couldn't see a thing as I made a big turn out over Wilson Lake and turned back into Goat Lake. I came in as low as I dared over the entrance. Goat Lake is a little over a mile long so I had time to make a power descent. I got close to the lake holding it a little nose-high, and finally I touched down. When I heard the staccato sound of the waves rattling on the bottom of the floats I realized I had landed downwind. Harry pointed out the spot where they had left David off. We looked through the dark and saw some little flicks of light, just the tiniest flicks, so we taxied over to them. David Anniskett was there. All he had on was a T-shirt and pants because he'd left his coat with Margie and Harry, and he was so cold he could hardly move. He was trying to light a cigarette lighter, and the light we had seen was only the flick of the flint.

We got David into the airplane, and Harry and I hugged him to warm him up. He told us that he had abandoned the goats on the mountain and come back to where he had started. He thought he was having a dream when the lights of my airplane sailed through the valley. It was pitch black now, and we needed a place to stay for the night.

I had hunted goats on Big Goat Lake, and knew of a cave over on the northwest side of the lake. I was able to find this cave in the dark and tie the airplane up where it was safe from the storm. We crawled into the cave, got out our sleeping bags, and pitched the little tent. Then we settled in for the night.

The next morning, the ceilings were so low I didn't think we could get out of there. I stretched out the trailing antenna on the airplane and tied it to a tree. I was able to contact Ellis Air on the radio and passed the word on that everybody was safe, but we were weathered in on Big Goat Lake and would get out as soon as we could.

Everybody had been worried about us and wanted to try and get in to the area to look for us, but Pete Cessnun told them, "No. If he got in there he will be able to take care of himself, and everything will be okay." It proved out that everything was okay. David spread the word around that I had saved his life, and for many years after that David's wife sent me a Christmas card thanking me for saving David's life. It's kind of nice to be rewarded for something like that.

Ice Breakthrough

Looking at the logbook, it seems like I had an awful lot of adventures. I was supposed to be experienced, but now it seemed like I was getting into more predicaments than I was at lower flight time. Hunting, of course, was the biggest problem because we were always going out to hunt in the fall of the year when the weather never stayed with you.

This time there was ice on the lakes when Danny and I went into Lake Bay to go deer hunting. The Lake Bay area is a sweet water lake, and it was glare ice. We planned to land on the ice and go hunting. It would be great.

I touched down on the lake, and as I started to slow down, Danny hit me on the back and said, "It's breaking!" Out of the corner of my eye, I could see the ice shattering out. It started in very short streaks, and as I slowed down the streaks reached further and further out. Before I broke through the ice, I poured on the coal. The acceleration of the airplane kept it on top of the broken ice. Soon the fractures started shortening, and we were back in the air. That was a thrill. I don't know what would have happened if we had broken all the way through the ice.

Dual Instruction

As small as the community was, everybody knew everything that was going on so any pilot who had a little airplane and wanted a little extra training or a little advice or whatever it might be, why yours truly was happy to do it for them. A lot of guys got dual from me and appreciated it. I gave them dual in getting into small lakes and the techniques and basic things that

I felt were vital in my flying. Since then I have been thanked many times for it. My log book shows lots of little notes like "Checked out Sherman Williams' Champ," "Checked out Irwin McKinley in his Cruiser," "Checked Earl in N4490E." For nearly every little airplane that came into town, I was doing a little dual instruction and helping the pilots enjoy the country more—and do it safer. We took our flying very seriously.

Earl Walker's Flying Lessons

One of my students who ended up playing a major role in my professional life was Earl Walker. Earl bought Aeronica Chief N4490E from Pros Ganty and I got the job of teaching Earl how to fly. On one of Earl's first lessons I took advantage of a search to familiarize Earl with flying. We were out looking for a DeHavilland Dove, the Ellis Hall airplane that was lost on a flight from Ketchikan to Prince George. The pilot was a Texas millionaire with his wife, daughter, and her boyfriend on board. We were given areas to search, and we searched and searched and searched to no avail. Apparently the initial search hadn't been well organized, and the millionaire's estate came up and started it again. Someone we knew found the wreck right off, nabbing what I believe was a $20,000 reward!

Earl's lessons continued; he was really anxious to get going. Mart Hansen had agreed to sign Earl off on the dual that I had given him, and I worked on Earl real hard. I had soloed Earl, and he was improving right along. One day Earl came to me and said, "I need a little help on my turns. I just scared myself half to death." I took Earl out over Guard Island, and we worked on turns for over an hour. Earl finally said he had enough. He was getting woozy, but he had gained confidence in his turns.

I felt that Earl was ready to take his test so I went down to see Mart Hansen at Ketchikan Air and asked him to give Earl a check ride. Mart said, "If you think he's ready, that's good enough for me. I'll sign him off." The FAA inspector came down and gave Earl his final check ride and said to Mart Hansen, "That's the best student you ever turned out." So I guess Earl had learned his lessons all right.

New Piper PA-12

By 1967 our beloved 42M was showing the signs of time on

saltwater. Dan and I thought we had better get a dry-land airplane and rebuild it to our saltwater specifications. We located a PA-12 in Colorado, and I called the owner on the phone and made a commitment to purchase it for $2500 based on an inspection.

We traveled to the owner's place about 90 miles east of Denver, where he had an open field in his back yard which was his private airfield. The PA-12 looked good. The owner took me up for a few takeoffs and landings to refresh me in wheel landings. We topped off with fuel and headed homeward in N92582.

When we were almost to Smithers, B.C., and in country we were familiar with, I decided to deviate from the normal route down the highway and go directly to Stewart. The direct route took us up the Cambria snowfield where we made a climb up to 10,000 feet to safely clear the terrain. It was quite a surprise to come over the end of the snowfield and look straight down 10,000 feet below us, to the town of Stewart. I went into a circling glide. It seemed like it took forever to get down to sea level and the airport at Stewart.

After fueling up we took a direct route toward Ketchikan. With no airport closer than Annette Island, we planned to leave the plane at Annette until we could figure out a way to get it to Ketchikan.

Landing in Wingren's Lot

Paul Wingren was clearing and filling a lot right across from our bus garage, and it looked big enough to land on so I talked to Paul about it. Paul liked the idea. He thought it would be a good thing for me to land on his future mall site.

I waited for the next nice day, and Danny took me over to Tamgas Harbor on Annette Island in 42 Mike. I got a ride from the Coast Guard living quarters to the airfield where I, not being very good on wheels, decided the best thing to do was to practice short field landings on the short east-west runway before I tried landing on Wingren's lot. After six or eight landings, I was feeling confident about landing on the lot so I headed for Ketchikan.

When I arrived in Ketchikan, much to my surprise, we had a

pretty stiff wind blowing across my landing area. I made one pass by to check the lot. There were a few puddles of water which at that moment didn't mean anything to me. On my first pass I came over the Bar Harbor breakwater, and I got upset a bit by the winds. I did another go-around working harder on getting a good low approach but with the same results. I took a wide turn around trying to figure out how to avoid that bad air over the breakwater.

It looked like I could come in low, turn inside of the breakwater, and get level quick enough to make it work. I tried this, and it worked pretty well. I did a quick touch-and-go and came around again.

I made the same approach, and as I squared up for the touchdown everything was just right until I hit the mud puddles. It was like someone had put the brakes on hard, and the tail started to come up. I instinctively pulled back on the stick, and with a little touch of power the tail came down, and we rolled to a stop.

Quite a crowd of people had been watching, and Paul Wingren was one of the first to come over to the plane. We wheeled the plane across Tongass Avenue to our Northern Bus Company garage where we took the plane apart and carried it upstairs to our workshop. Danny ended up having to do the rebuilding with a lot of help from Stan Oaksmith and Jerry Castle. Sid Hosier rebuilt a set of Edo 2000 floats, and Jerry Wielder in Port Angeles recovered the wings and flaps. With all of our duties making a living, it would be almost 10 years before N92582 was rebuilt, making its first flight on December 12, 1977.

We later sold our old PA-12, 42 Mike, to Bob DeWitt.

Servicing the prospectors on the Leduc Glacier taught me a lot of lessons, including some rough ones. I learned right away that landing on snow (and getting off again) takes some thought.

Chapter 4,
Early Prospecting

Russ Simpson and I were always swapping things. Russ had gotten hold of a beautiful compass out of a Jap Zero, and I was having trouble with the compass in my airplane. Somehow we had wound some wires around 42 Mike's tubing, and they had given the airframe some magnetic problems. The standard compass just wouldn't work properly so we stuck this beautiful, big Zero compass on my airplane—it was really a nice compass. I can see it yet. Russ and I bolted it into place, and I was so relieved to see the needle swing smoothly around to point north up the channel. What a great tool!

Not long afterwards, I started out on a trip to take Wendell Dawson and Paul Piper into the Leduc Glacier. Right then, Leduc was a pretty hot issue. Everybody was excited about it because of the big Granduc copper deposit just across the Canadian border near Hyder. This was a big find, and there was a big mining camp on the ground already. Wendell Dawson and Paul Piper's trip came about because Wendell Dawson and Don Ross had been prospecting up there, competing with the Granduc stakers. Don had made a trip or two into Leduc Glacier and landed on the snow—without clearing customs. The Canadian prospectors apparently took a dim view of this, and reported him. Someone from customs came out to observe the goings on at the glacier, and sure enough, their Webber Air bush plane landed on the ice of the Leduc when it wasn't supposed to. The next time Don landed in Stewart, B.C. for supplies, the Mounties confiscated his airplane. No one could prove Don was flying the plane when it violated customs, so they released Don, but the plane (belonging to Don Ross and Pete Cessnun) stayed behind. It would take two years of legal battles to get it back.

So now Paul and Wendell were stuck, with some hot claims

halfway prospected, and no way to get to them. When you fly into the Leduc area, you can see big patches of color staining the rocks where copper ore comes close to the surface. Granduc was a huge deposit, but who knew if that was the main lode? If there was another big deposit up there, it could be a very lucrative claim, and Paul and Wendell were just itching to get back on the glacier.

Pete Cessnun contacted me and explained the problem. He asked me to go to Stewart, B.C., clear customs, and then fly Paul and Wendell and their supplies into the North Fork of Leduc Glacier. I agreed to do it.

I took off with this brand-new Zero compass in my airplane. When I arrived in Stewart, Paul and Wendell were waiting for me at the dock with all their supplies. The first trip was to be with a load of supplies and with Wendell to show me where to go. I took off and headed up the Salmon River by Hyder. We followed the Salmon River up to Disappearing Lake. (The outlet of the lake is normally blocked by a glacier, creating an ice dam. Every once in a while that glacier gives way and lets a flood of water come crashing down, which makes a mess of the whole valley. One year it washed out the steel bridge across the Salmon River.)

We flew up past Summit and up into the head of Bowser Creek, turned up into the glacier, and went up until the clouds met the glacier. I turned back a little and kept working northward until I turned around again and started up the Frank Mackey Glacier. I couldn't get up it, so I went a little further north, started up another glacier, but didn't get up it either. I kept going around a couple more glaciers, and finally I asked Wendell where we were. He didn't know. I looked down at my compass, that beautiful Jap compass, and it was still heading north. It hadn't changed a bit since I left Ketchikan.

I crossed over a couple little ridges and there was a river that looked like it was flowing west or southwest. Well, one thing about it, I knew if we went down the river we would hit salt water somewhere in Alaska.

We started down the river, and the river got a little larger and a little larger, and pretty soon we came to a little cabin. Dawson looked out and said, "Oh, we're clear over on the Unuk

River! We're coming down the Unuk River now, and that's old Tommy McQuillan's cabin down there. You just turn to the left and go up this river, and we'll hit the Leduc Glacier." We swung around the corner, and sure enough there was the North Fork of Leduc Glacier.

We were going to land at about the 3000-foot level on the glacier so I took a pass over it as near as I could. The clouds were coming into the upper end of the glacier so I couldn't see anything. Wendell said, "When they land out there, they generally throw out a bunch of boughs so they have a little depth perception." Well, we didn't have any boughs, and it was the first time for me, so I set up for the area he pointed out making a nice stable approach. I got quite close to the snow, and all of a sudden everything was white. I got a little scared and poured on the power because I was going to have to try to go around, and I knew that I had to get altitude and turn. I wasn't sure just how I was going to do it because everything ahead of me was clouds. Just then, bump-bump-bump, we were on the ice. I shut the power off and came to a nice stop. That was my first glacier landing and a bit of a surprise. That taught me a real lesson that stayed with me the rest of my life. I learned that snow whiteouts were as bad as glassy water, and coupled with restricted vis-

This picture dates from the first trip with Wendell. You can see how poor the visibility was by looking at the hill in the background. A map showing the claims we worked appears on page 208.

ibility, they were worse. What I had just done was a no-no. The weather must be right or don't do it.

When I went to leave, it was getting along in the afternoon, and I tried to take off but couldn't go anywhere. The snow was so wet and soft, I couldn't get up enough speed to get airborne. So I taxied the airplane back to where we had unloaded the supplies. We hiked off to the side of the glacier and found a few old limbs to put underneath the plane so it wouldn't freeze in. We made camp as best we could and spent the night on the side of the glacier. Thankfully, we had brought snowshoes and enough camping gear in the first trip. Had we packed differently, we would have been very uncomfortable.

The next morning I realized we had burned up a lot of extra gas flying around the weather. I was a little worried about having enough gas to get back to Stewart so we snowshoed across the glacier and hiked across the nose of land that separates the north fork and the south fork of the Leduc Glacier. When we finally got over to the mining camp we found that we were the objects of a search. Nobody had been able to search yet, but they had us placed as overdue which, of course, was true—we were overdue. I was supposed to be right back out for the second

Kelly Adams and Don Ross did a lot of prospecting around Southeast. Here they're looking for copper in the Leduc Glacier area. The pair eventually discovered what became the Ross-Adams uranium mine.

Bob Young waits beside his aircraft during a stop at Wolfe's cabin on the Chickamin River. 42 Mike lays against the far bank, and Don Ross' cub in the distance.

trip because we had planned three trips to move all the stuff plus the two prospectors into the glacier. So the guys at the camp gave us coffee and food and were just super good to us. We told them we needed a little gas so they got a couple cans and gave me eight gallons of the aviation gas they had for their airplanes.

Much to our surprise, they had a Snowcat. It was quite a machine. We hopped in the Snowcat, and they drove around the mountain to our airplane. Again the snow was too soft to take off so the guy said, "Okay, I'll make you a trail that you can take off of." He made two or three strips that were about a half-mile long so I had a packed-down area to take off from. That takeoff went fine. I brought in a load of groceries on my second trip, and on my third trip brought in Paul and a final load of groceries. All the landings thereafter were more or less uneventful because after having done it once, it becomes easier (and there were no more weather problems).

Landing on the snow when the snow was a little hard was rough on the seaplane because the seaplane has rigid struts with no give. But when there is soft snow, it is quite a soft landing, really nice. Normally the soft snow doesn't bother you on the

Nine Lives of an Alaska Bush Pilot

The Granduc mine employees and their Snowcat pose for a shot while helping Wendell Dawson (right) and I get off the Leduc Glacier.

takeoff either as long as you aren't plowing snow over the top of the floats. On subsequent trips, everything worked out fine.

Depending on the weather, we would fly in over Summit Lake, or come up the Chickamin River. The Chickamin River route was longer, but less prone to weather problems, which the Leduc area had plenty of. All trips originated from Stewart, B.C. because of customs.

After those first few trips, I got involved in the prospecting myself, and Kelly got hold of a J-3 Cub on wheels, using Don Ross to fly it. I would help when I could, but mostly they landed that Cub on a little mud strip there on the beach close to Old Man Wolfe's cabin at the mouth of the Chickamin. There was not much room, but Don accomplished it very nicely.

Don and Kelly had found some good-looking ore, and a big American mining company was sniffing around, interested in the the project. That mud strip let them ferry supplies to Old Man Wolfe's place by seaplane, then ferry them up to the glacier using the Cub. Don started taking trips carrying supplies to the edge of the border between the Leduc Glacier, U.S. soil, and Canadian soil. The little dogleg strip up there was about 600 feet long. It had a little turn in the middle of it, and it came out through the willow trees to the riverbank. Wendell Dawson and

Paul Piper had cut it out with their jackknives so to speak. They didn't have much equipment to work with, but they made a usable strip for Don to land the Cub on.

This was really a rough strip, and on one of their trips, they nosed the airplane up, damaged the landing gear, and bent the propeller. With a lot of ingenuity, Kelly took some of the damaged pieces up to the Granduc camp and got some of the men at the camp to weld up the landing gear. They also managed to get the propeller straightened out enough to let Don fly the airplane out of there. What an exciting takeoff that must have been!

When Don got to town safely, I loaned Kelly the landing gear that came off of 42 Mike so he could put it on his little J-3 Cub instead of using the beat-up stuff. They mounted the airplane up on my landing gear and started making trips again.

Everything worked fine until the last of the season. Don had been taking mining company people in and out after looking at the mining claims. On the last trip out of the little dogleg strip with Paul, the afternoon wind picked up. It put him downwind, and he settled into the river bottom, wrecking the plane. The crash didn't scare Paul, but when Don told him to "Get out, it's gonna burn!" THAT scared him.

Pete Cessnun called me and said Don was overdue. I gathered a few things, and Pete and I made a flight up the Chickamin. We found the plane right away. Don and Paul looked all right so we made an air drop and flew back to town to figure a way to get them out. We got Don and Paul out shortly thereafter, but the mining company wanted some more work done. With the Cub out of commission, transportation was a problem.

We decided to put a crew in on a small lake near the Leduc, and I went back in, making food drops. They were not in a good spot. We did okay on the first drop, but the second one bounced off the river bank and into the river. Paul Piper and his partner made a great effort to catch it, but the river swept it away.

Kelly Adams was sure we had it made with the interest the mining company displayed. Kelly told Peggy "not to worry about one million dollars, but about how many million dollars" we would make off the claim. She is still waiting. It wasn't too long until our hopes of success went down the river like the food drop.

Prospectors are dreamers. Kelly's dream was to make enough money so he could drive a pink Caddie, smoke Cuban cigars, and fart through silk shorts. He spent a lot more time bent over banging on rocks than driving Caddies, but he did make a few profitable claims over the years.

Prospecting is a funny business. Depending on the needs of the moment, the mining companies will be very hot for different things. For a while it will be iron, then copper, then uranium, or purple fluoride, or whatever industry happens to need. I can remember when iron was the really hot thing, until someone found huge iron deposits in Australia. By year's end, all the interest in iron was gone.

Old Man Wolfe's Cabin

The Chickamin River became a pretty important stop to us. During the Leduc effort and for years thereafter, we would stop at Old Man Wolfe's cabin and spend time with him. If we had space, we'd occasionally take him to town. I always remember the first time I saw Old Man Wolfe in Ketchikan. He was always dressed up in a suit and a hat when he came to town. He had this funny-looking riverboat that he had built. It was probably 20 feet long and maybe six feet wide, built out of little thin strips of wood that he had nailed together. It had a little one-lung Universal for power and a little roof on it with four posts holding it up for a little shelter to keep the rain off. He had a little shed for the boat and kept it beached most of the time. At high tide he would put it in the water. Wolfe came to town once a year to buy his supplies and go back out to the Chickamin.

Old Man Wolfe was a character. He had been a cowboy and a prospector in his early days, and when he came to Alaska, that was it. He was home. He never married. He really liked to prospect, and he had made a little money prospecting in Arizona. He never found anything in Alaska, but he had his homestead at the mouth of the Chickamin. He actually had two homesteads—a home site of 6 acres and a homestead of 80 acres. I know this because I thought a lot of Old Man Wolfe so I helped him get the papers for the property.

Duke Island Iron Claims

At that time iron was a big thing. U.S. Steel was staking iron claims all over the country. Paul and I knew where there was some iron on Duke Island so we went down and staked it only to find out that U.S. Steel people were down there staking claims too. We staked a batch of claims in Hall Cove and thought we had something going there, but it never did pan out. The iron was low grade ultra-basic with a lot of titanium in it which is hard to separate out. U.S. Steel had claims staked all over. They went to the trouble of patenting some of them. To this date nothing has come of it. Recently I heard they had even sold off some of their claims for people to build cabins on.

Nucleometer and the Purple Claims

I was bitten by the uranium bug so this was the era when everywhere I went, I was flying with a nucleometer fastened to the airplane. That meant I was flying low into every little nook and cranny I could get into. It was a funny thing; the tighter the valley you got into and the further into it you got, the better the readings were. It was kind of a sucker thing for us, but we soon learned that when the mountains started to close in on

Although Al Wolfe was something of a hermit, his home on the Chickamin became an oasis and emergency shelter for many over the years. Wolfe himself was a former cowboy who retired into Alaska's bush. He came to town once or twice a year in the boat seen in the background.

you, what little uranium activity there was would be concentrated so you would get a higher reading, even though there wasn't a higher content of uranium.

As fate would have it, one day I had a trip down to McLean Arm. On the way back, I decided to fly the nucleometer past Bokan Mountain, but on the way there I hit some heavy tubulence and had to turn aside.

Don Ross put together a group of prospectors the next year looking strictly for uranium using a nucleometer. On their first serious expedition they flew over Bokan Mountain, and into a massive uranium deposit which the investors sold for close to $1,000,000. This eventually became the Ross-Adams mine.

When Don Ross and Kelly Adams located their deposit of uranium, I took Paul over to Kendrick Bay to look around. He found what we called the Purple Claims right alongside the uranium claims staked by Ross and Adams. They contained purple fluoride with some uranium—it was an interesting exposure. We staked the claims, but they never did amount to anything.

Power-off Landing

I was flying the nucleometer way back into the center of Etolin Island when all of a sudden smoke started drifting up through the cockpit. It smelled like electrical smoke, but I wasn't sure so I turned off all the electrical stuff. The smoke persisted so the next thing I thought best to do was to turn the engine clear off. I turned the engine off, pulled it up to where the propellers stopped, and we were on a nice silent glide. The smoke stopped, but we were quite a ways off of the water.

The amazing thing I found out was that with the propeller standing still, the airplane glided much further than it would with the propeller turning. The turning propeller acts like a brake. Just as the best braking of a car comes before the wheels slide, the same is true of a propeller. As long as it was turning, the propeller was resisting all it could. The minute it stopped, the plane would start sliding so to speak, and your glide would improve. I glided around and around, and I had plenty of room to get to the salt water. I ended up in Burnett Inlet and greased down a nice landing. I had a lot of confidence in power-off landings because I believed in practicing my emergencies and didn't give a second thought to turning the engine off to make a landing when I had a clear landing area.

Examining the engine, I found the generator belt had burned up, creating lots of smoke and a little bit of damage to the wiring. I was lucky to get out of that one as painlessly as I did.

Weary Landing

Another day flying the nucleometer we wanted to go up into the Hyder district so I started out early in the morning and flew and flew and flew. I think we flew about ten hours that day. When we started out it was a beautiful sunshiny day, and there was a brisk westerly wind. We took off out of the harbor in great shape. Coming back I guess I was getting tired. When I finally got home to land, it looked to me like the same old stiff westerly wind was blowing, and the nice sunshiny day was still there. In reality the wind had shifted a bit, but I didn't notice until it was too late.

I knew I was going to make a pretty close landing and turn into the hangar as I came off the step. I touched down, and obviously I was rummy because I was going downwind heading for the hangar much too fast to get stopped. I turned a little to the left and missed the hangar, but ahead of me was a dock with

Don Ross and Kelly Adams refueling their plane on the banks of the Chickamin.

pilings on it. I did everything I could think of to get it slowed down. I finally came off the step, and just as I was going to smash into the dock, I tromped on the rudder pedal and swung the wing around 90 degrees. The wing went between the pilings as the plane slid sideways toward the dock. I jumped out and managed to grab a piling, but as the backwash from my landing came in, it tipped the airplane a bit and smashed the wing tip on the dock. Kind of taught me a lesson.

Bronson Lake Gold

I took Paul to a small lake in the upper Bronson Creek area where he had seen a gossen (stained rusty area) he wanted to explore. First we flew over the spot and dropped some tools and supplies, and then I landed in the lake. Paul packed the rest of his gear and some dynamite to the prospecting area. He found some very interesting low-grade gold but because of its remoteness and the price of gold being $32 an ounce, we didn't spend a lot of time there. That was his only trip there, but looking back on it now, we sure missed the bonanza. Two different companies have done extensive gold mining there at Bronson Creek and nearby Johnny Mountain.

Red River Claims

I was prospecting with Red Williams and Mac McReynolds, looking over the Red Lake area when we located some copper staining and some molybdenum in the Red River area. We decided we had better go in for a closer look. Red and Mac wanted to explore a canyon located down the river quite a ways, and I got the bright idea to land in the lake and give them a rubber boat to take down to a big straight stretch in the river. It looked pretty shallow from the air so I said, "You guys go down there and measure out the straight stretch to see how long and how deep it is."

When I flew down the river, they had everything set up with stakes in the water where it was shallow. It gave me plenty of room. I could touch down in the shallow water, but I couldn't come off the step until I got into the deep water. I had to make a little S-turn up into some timber before I could finally stop. I did this several times and got their camp gear in. They worked the area for a few days until it came time to pick them up to get out of there.

After my previous trips I realized that the river was deep enough to handle a heavier load. I had been taking off empty, but with the heavier load I thought I could start my takeoff from back inside the timber, come around the left-hand turn, hit the straightaway, and go. So the first trip, I took just one passenger. I got back in the timber and started my takeoff. I got on the step, slacked off the power, and taxied around the corner. Then I poured on the power, took off, and got my passenger out of there successfully.

The next trip going back in, I thought, "I can improve on that. I can go out of the corner full-bore." Little did I know this would be a bad move. As I came out of the turn, the airplane skidded sideways, and I realized that I was going to slide sideways into the bank and tear the floats off from underneath the airplane. Just a good reaction, I think, from driving buses and cars on the ice so much, kept us from disaster. I tromped on the right rudder and drove straight into the bank. The airplane hit the bank, slid up on it, and sailed into the muskeg about 30 feet. It took us several hours to work the airplane back into the river. That was enough of that maneuver. Later on I realized that the proper way to make the turn was to put in opposite aileron and bury the float on the outside of the turn so it wouldn't slip. It's kind of unnerving to do it unless you're pretty familiar with your airplane.

We did quite a bit of work laying out claims on the Red River, and finally Tom Osborne from ASARCO (American Smelting and Refining Company) came up to look at the property. Right away he decided it was worth drilling. ASARCO set up a little camp above the river, and we made many trips moving drill equipment and guys to and from their work in a very steep canyon that we called Tom's Canyon. This went on for several months. The molybdenite and copper deposits extended all the way from the Red River through the mountain to Humpback Lake, but the ore was very low grade. After the results of their drilling, ASARCO decided to give the claims up. Later when the Carter Administration turned Misty Fjords into a national monument, we lost our claims as well as all helicopter access to the area.

A trip to support Walt Simpson's blasting efforts on the Stikine took me down the Bradfield River. The spectacular copper stains I saw brought Paul Piper and I back a few days later. (See map on page 208.)

Chapter 5,
The Bradfield Claims

I flew many trips delivering dynamite to Walter Simpson and Alex McFee who had the job of blasting snags out of the Stikine River for the Canadian government and keeping the river clear for the riverboat, *Judith Ann*. On one of my trips, I took a new pass on the way home. I went up the Iskut River to the Craig River, up the Craig through a high pass, and down the North Fork of the Bradfield River. Going down the Bradfield, I spotted a large green copper stain on the side of the mountain. I couldn't wait to tell my prospecting partner Paul Piper about it. When I took him up to see the stain, he said it looked pretty good, but how do we get to it?

The Bradfield is a fast river, but about twelve miles up the river I saw a straight stretch that I thought I could land in. Paul wanted to go alone, but I felt it would be much safer if he had a partner. Arnt Antonson, a young fellow I knew, would do just fine. The next day we loaded up 42 Mike and headed for the Bradfield River. I managed to get the plane down all right and tied it up to the beach. We had to keep the nose of the floats in to the beach or the current would take the plane away from us. For takeoff we had to turn the plane around, get the engine running, and then cut loose and go downstream.

Paul said he would like to have me pick them up in one week in the same place. Two days later I got a call from a Fish and Wildlife boat that was tied up in the mouth of the Bradfield saying they had two men who were waiting for me to pick them up. I could not understand what had gone wrong. I was not supposed to pick them up for a week. When I arrived at the Fish and Wildlife boat to pick up Paul and Arnt, they had a big story to tell.

After I left them on the riverbank, they discovered they had to cross the East Fork of the river before they could get to the green stain area. They constructed a log raft and tried to get across, but the river was too fast, and they ended up going down the main river very fast. Around the next corner the raft was headed for a sweeper (a log laying crosswise to the current) with the current going right under it. Arnt could not swim so Paul tied a rope around his waist and to the raft. Then he jumped in the river and headed for the bank to try to stop the raft. He could not hold the raft and was pulled back into the river current. When the raft got to the sweeper, Arnt jumped on the sweeper, and the raft went under it with Paul soon following the raft. Paul was pulled down and got hung up under the sweeper. All Arnt could see was Paul's hair which he got a hold of and managed to pull Paul's head above the water. Then with great effort, Paul made it to the top of the sweeper and on to the bank of the river.

They lost everything so their only choice was to go down the river and hope some boat might come into the estuary. There were lots of grizzly bear on the river so they made it down the river in jig time, and their luck held out. The Fish and Wildlife boat was coming into the estuary when they arrived.

In July Paul wanted to try once more to get to the copper claims. I agreed to let him go by himself. He said, "You know, we need to land and get beyond the big river." I landed with Paul sixteen miles up the Bradfield River. I was able to get past the North Fork of the Bradfield River, land in the fast part of the river, slow down a little, and turn out of the current into a small side stream. It was pretty tricky, but it was fun, and we got Paul past the big river where it was possible for him to reach the 32 claims he had staked. We named them the Ptarmigan Claims.

We didn't know how to go about selling or promoting our new find. Out of nowhere a man by the name of Beckworth came along and wanted to look at the claims. He put on a big front and had us pretty excited. He hired a Dean Johnson helicopter and took Paul Piper and my partner Duey Barber in to look at the claims. Things looked pretty good until he handed us a paper to sign that would have cheated us out of the claims. We never saw Mr. Beckworth again.

Takahashi

Del Smith had just gotten his helicopter pilot's license and his first job was for the Takahashi Company that was interested in drilling our Ptarmigan Claims. I had been landing the airplane sixteen miles upriver (when I look back on it now, I don't think I want to do it anymore) and taking supplies in. From there they had to be hiked in another three or four miles up the river and up the mountainside and clear up on top of the mountain to where the mineral deposit was.

Del's job was to move the core driller, his drill, and supplies as close to the mountaintop as he could. My job was to move people and fuel to a place close enough for Del to ferry the people to the mountain and back without having to be clear full of fuel. With minimum fuel weight, the helicopter would perform at its very best. Considering Del's low time in the helicopter, and the under-powered helicopter he had, this was very exciting work.

Del found a place that he could land short of the mining operation, and started ferrying supplies. George Roberts, an old-time prospector, was the driller. It was hard on George because he had to carry the stuff a lot farther than need be, but it was a big accomplishment for Del and I.

George completed the drilling job and wrote a nice little report on the claims that satisfied the Takahashi people and enabled us to make a lease agreement with them.

Having made a deal with us, Mr. Takahashi, a Japanese fellow from Seattle, started to explore the property. One of the first moves he made was to put a float near the Harding River. Arrangements were made to use Jack Anderson's cabin nearby. We anchored the float in front of his house so I could unload supplies without having to fight the big tides. Supplies were litered to the beach by skiff and flown in to the claims by helicopter.

Takahashi hired a survey company to do a magnetic survey of the claims. The survey company in turn hired Boeing's Airocopters to fly the survey. Calvin Mojek was the pilot and Bob Fisher the mechanic. (Later Bob Fisher would become our FAA inspector in Southeast Alaska.) The claim was primarily iron and copper ore, and it looked like there was a whole mountain of it. I took fuel to them and tried to keep track of them. We left an umbrella tent at one of the points of the river where I could land. We kept the food in a cache up in a tree so that the bear could not get it. We never ever left anything in the tent because that would invite the bear into the tent.

On one of my trips into the landing, I found the tent missing. On close inspection I found the tent torn all to pieces and scattered over 100 yards down the beach. What had happened? The Airocopter crew had left their lunch in the tent. The tent had a ridgepole in the center, and the bear obviously had gone in the tent. He knocked the ridgepole down, and the tent collapsed around him. He must have panicked and roared down the riverbank leaving pieces of tent along the way. It would have been a sight to see. The crew had broken the rule: No food in the tent.

River Landings

I believe that Russ Simpson and I are the only ones who ever landed a seaplane above eight miles on the North Bradfield

Here's Paul Piper and 42 Mike upriver on the Bradfield. See the current boiling out of the side stream in the background? You had to be extremely careful up there.

River. I estimate the river current is over 15 mph in that area. It is too fast to comfortably secure an airplane to the beach so we had to resort to turning into a little side river that had enough water and enough length to let us come off the step. To depart, we had to get as far back in the little side stream as we could and be on the step by the time we hit the main river. This worked. One day Russ Simpson got ready to depart but failed to get on the step before he hit the main river. The current immediately turned his airplane upstream instead of downstream. Now his only choice, using minimum power still on, was to drift backwards down the river, keeping his eye out the door and the window for trees and shallow spots. He finally drifted far enough down the river so he could make a takeoff upstream. After that Russ said to me, "You can take all the Bradfield trips. I don't want any more of them."

I remember one day I landed a geologist by the name of Cleve Ball on the North Bradfield when the tongue of the river was running two feet high. Cleve was quite impressed with the landing after he got safely out of the airplane.

River landings sometimes seem innocent, but with a fast current, even on the big rivers, you cannot turn around without going to the bank and manually turning the airplane around. I know of one pilot who tried to do this on the Stikine and rolled over. Once you get broadside you start heading straight for the bank, and the more power you add, the faster you get there. What's worse, the more power you add, the farther the upstream float buries itself in the water until you finally tip over. If you can't turn in the river with 1000 RPM, don't try it. Go to the bank and turn your airplane around.

Grizzly Bears

The mining claims in Bradfield Canal were getting a lot of attention, and Takahashi sent a geologist representing Standard Slag Company to do some work on the claims. Joe Soloy, whom I will talk more about in the next chapter, was flying helicopters in the area and was available to do some work for them.

I had landed the airplane about seven miles up the river. Joe and the geologist had gone up the river in the helicopter, and Danny and I had delivered some fuel for Joe and were waiting on the river. Danny wanted to go goat hunting so we climbed up the mountain looking for a goat. Danny soon shot his first goat, and we brought it back to the river where we had left the plane.

When Joe came back from the mining claims, it was late so we had to spend the night on the bank of the river. We had rolled out our sleeping bags on the ground and then tried to decide the best thing to do with the goat. Because of the number of bear around, we decided to hang it on a root wad, which was the butt of a tree that had washed down the river, and the roots of it stuck out like claws. We could tie the goat from one of the roots, and it would be suspended in the air high enough that a bear couldn't reach it. Down below on the bottom side of the root wad, the river had washed out a hole, which was full of water so it looked like a pretty safe way to hang the goat.

After we hung the goat up on the root wad, Danny said, "If a bear starts to get this goat, what are we going to do?" Well, about that time we looked up the river bar, and here came a big grizzly bear heading right for the goat. We fired a couple shots into the gravel around the bear, and he took off. Then Danny said, "We'd better tie something on the goat so if the bear comes down in the night and starts eating the goat, we can hear it and scare him off." We emptied a couple of tin cans, put some rocks in them, and tied them to the goat so it would rattle if the goat was disturbed.

We crawled into our sleeping bags and had no more than gotten to sleep when rattle-rattle-rattle, we woke up. It was a bear working on our goat. Joe got the flashlight, and Danny and I both got our rifles. Here we were standing up barefooted with only our underwear on. Joe shined the flashlight over our heads, and Danny and I knelt down side by side with our rifles. The bear had gotten on top of the log and was reaching around with his paw and pulling the goat to him. When the light hit him we could see the bear with a big white piece of the goat in his mouth. We both fired at the same time, and the bear disappeared. Now it was nowhere in sight. A crippled bear is a bad thing.

Very cautiously we approached the log with Joe behind us

shining his flashlight. Danny and I walked barefooted in the gravel on the riverbank, and we very, very cautiously approached the root wad with the goat hanging on it. No sign of the bear. Not a sound as we stood there. Then we heard a dripping sound in the pool underneath the root wad and saw blood running down into the pool. Joe shined the light up on top of the root wad, and here the bear had fallen into sort of a crevice between the roots. The bear was stone dead. On examination the next day, we found that both bullets had hit the bear. One had hit him in the neck and the other in the heart.

Mr. Stevens, the geologist with Standard Slag, was really impressed and wanted the bear hide for his den. We very carefully skinned it out so he had a good bear rug with a head mount and the claws left on it. It was quite a tedious job, but Mr.

Bill Huff (left) and Angus Lillie were among the "ground troops" on many of our mineral explorations. Both men had reputations as hard workers—Angus Lillie in particular. Lillie would work alone in the field for weeks. Here the pair are working on Banded Mountain.

Paul Piper asked me to help him move this bear out of camp one morning. Paul had shot it in self-defense that night FROM HIS HAMMOCK! Bears were a constant worry throughout our experience in the Bradfield area.

Stevens thought it was the best thing that ever happened to him—a grizzly bear for his den.

On another occasion I came into camp and Paul Piper said, "Would you give me a hand? This bear's too big, I can't move it by myself." I don't know how big the bear was, but it took the two of us to move it, and we managed to roll it into the river to get rid of it. Paul had shot that grizzly from his hammock, and it was lying dead right under him. Can you imagine having that experience in the middle of the night?

Midnight Bomber

While Takahashi was working on the Bradfield Canal iron deposit, he quite often brought Japanese people in to look at it. I guess they were potential customers for him. On one occasion he had a couple of Japanese geologists with him, and we spent the night on the boat *OseeJoe*, which provided the quarters on salt water at that time and a place to tie up the seaplane. On this occasion Carl Larsen, an electrician from Ketchikan, was the skipper of the boat. The Japanese fellows got to talking to Carl and found out that Carl was on a certain island in the South Pacific during WWII, and every night a Japanese bomber would drop bombs just to harass them. They called it the Midnight Bomber, and it turned out that one of these fellows was the pilot of that bomber.

One day they wanted to go trout fishing so I took them to a nice lake a couple of miles up the Eagle River. The lake wasn't too big, but I was able to make a circular landing. They got off on the riverbank, and immediately in front of them was a big pile of bear dung. That was it. Back in the airplane they got. They were scared to death of bear. That was the end of our fishing trip.

On one other occasion Takahashi wanted me to take a couple of the bosses from Fuji Iron and Steel trout fishing. They were very nice fellows, but they couldn't speak English. I took them into Leduc Lake which was one of my favorite lakes. It had been planted with rainbow, and every rainbow you caught was about 20 inches long and very lively. They caught enough fish to have a nice feed, and they were so pleased because they thought I'd taken them to my very special private lake. In Anchorage they were taken out to the rivers where they caught spawning fish which they knew weren't good. So catching these nice rainbow trout from this beautiful lake was a real special thing for them.

For a while Takahashi had us pretty excited about our claims. They figured it was a whole mountain of high-grade iron. They even brought in some engineers from Lockheed to survey the route for a monorail to bring the ore out to salt water. You can imagine our disappointment when they gave the claims back to us.

Utah Construction Mining Company

At that time Utah Construction Mining Company was working Mount Andrews iron and copper claims on Kasaan Peninsula, which were the same kind of mineral that we had on the Bradfield. They decided to lease our claims. After an examination of the claims, they decided to move a camp and a drill crew into the property. They loaded up a barge with everything they needed and had it towed to the Bradfield River. The barge was moved in at high tide to the upper part of the flats.

They were worried about the safety of the barge if the river flooded. They asked me what I thought about it. I told them I was the wrong guy for that question, but there was an old recluse (Ham Island Slim) who had been doing some hand logging on the river who might know the answer. Everyone was afraid of him. He lived back in one of the little sloughs nearby. I had seen his cabin from the air and thought I could find it. Two of us took a skiff and started paddling up this eerie slough. It was like the Florida Everglades with lots of unfriendly bugs flying around and vegetation hanging into the water. When we arrived at the cabin, there was smoke coming out of the chimney. I hollered hello several times with no answer. I stepped up on the porch and tapped on the door. I could see him in there with his back turned to me. I tapped several times more with no response. Finally I told him that we represented a Utah mining company, and we needed him to help us with mooring the barge. That did the trick. We explained our situation, and he came right out and showed us where to put the barge. From then on he was a lot of help and looked after us.

Food and Mail Drops

Before I started flying the helicopter, Bob Young flew all the loads up to the 2000-foot level on the Ptarmigan Claims. The camp called us one day and wanted us to pick up some food and drop it to them with the seaplane because the helicopter wasn't around. Joe Soloy wanted to go in with me to see how the camp was set up so that on his next helicopter trip in, he'd know more about the area. I took Joe and the food up the river. I made a pass over the camp, which was up about 2000 feet. We made a successful drop, but after I dropped the food, I had to go out over the valley. There were a lot of clouds in the valley, and we hit a severe draft of wind that took us right into the clouds briefly. I turned back and got out of the clouds, but it was quite a scare for both of us. I learned a lesson—you don't go in downwind over that ridge. Just a learning experience all the way around, but it was a narrow squeak.

I had the job of dropping the mail to the crew. It was the

cheapest way for them to get their mail. On one occasion I flew over camp, and nobody was close by. I had a good streamer tied on to the package, and I was going to drop it as close to the cook shack (tent) as I could. I made a good drop—I hit the cook shack. Evidently I caught someone napping when he was supposed to be working because he came running out of the tent like he was shot.

Lost Driller

The next year Utah hired Boiles Brothers Core Drilling Company to do some deep drilling. After the drillers and equipment were moved in, I got an emergency call. I was to pick up Frank Ness, the big boss of Boiles Brothers, and take him to Sumdum where one of his drillers, a college football star, had been crossing a glacial stream and apparently slipped and fell into the river gorge.

This was one of those days with a low ceiling and visibility varying from one to five miles. It took me over two hours to get there. I had to follow the shoreline most of the way, slowing down when the visibility was less and speeding up when it was greater. If visibility got too bad, you just landed and stayed on the step until it improved—providing the water wasn't too rough. Everybody flew that way and didn't think much about it. Very rarely did anyone have trouble because of that type of flying.

We all worked Ellis Air's radio frequency 4668 on the HF Radio. Most of the time we would be talking to an Ellis Grumman. On this trip I remember talking to Joe Diamond in a Grumman as I was following the shore in Fredrick Sound, and Joe was on the other shore. He said, "It's OK on this side. I've got a couple miles and one hundred feet." If somebody told you it was down on the water their way, you would try a different way.

I finally arrived at Sumdum Camp in Endicott Arm landing carefully to avoid a lot of icebergs that day. It was a very sad situation with no hope of finding the boy.

River Landing With A Helicopter

I had become quite confident in my ability to handle the

seaplane in the fast river, but a few years later when I was flying a helicopter, I was coming out of the lower camp area on a nice, bluebird day, and the thought ran through my mind, "If I had an engine failure what would I do?" Of course the only possible place to save the helicopter was the river, which I had landed on so many times. A little practice wouldn't hurt so I set up for an autorotation to a nice straight stretch in the river. I shut the power down to idle and autorotated to the river. I flared at the bottom, leveled, and pulled pitch—a beautiful autorotation to the water. On touching the water and settling in, the current grabbed me and was thrusting me into the bank. The blades were going to hit a tree, and I would be rolled over in the river. The adrenalin hit full force, and I racked in the power and pulled pitch to get control of the helicopter. I had come within a foot of wrecking the helicopter.

Utah Backs Out

Utah eventually gave the claims back to Paul and me. Paul thought there was enough copper in the boulders in that area to concentrate it and sell the product. Now it was up to us to do the assessment work. I furnished the transportation and Paul did the work. Paul always did twice as much work as was required of him. He built a nice little cabin on the lower claim. On the claims by the big green stain, Paul almost completed a building for a mill. He did it all with a chainsaw and nails. He cut every board. Finally Paul gave up, and I tried to hang on to the claim by doing assessment work.

Angus Lillie spent some time on the claims, and my son Dan put a new roof on the lower cabin. The bear were giving us a real bad time so we devised a wrap-around of barbed wire. That did it. We found the barbed wire had left its mark on several bear, but the cabin was still standing. We had some interest in gold on the claims, but I had failed to ask Paul about it, and only he knew the best spots for gold. Finally we gave up.

A few years later another company staked a bunch of claims for gold, but in a couple of years they gave up too. I still have a soft spot in my heart for those claims, and I stop there from time to time for some reason or other. Memories, I guess.

Chapter 6,
First Helicopters

On July 19, 1951 the first helicopter, a Bell 47 piloted by Sam Chevalier, arrived in Ketchikan as part of a U.S. Geological Survey mapping effort. He gave a few people rides and left town two days later. In June of 1955 two more helicopters arrived in Ketchikan, both were old Bell 47s with pontoons. John Scott was one of the pilots, and the owner of Continental Helicopters. Continental had a contract with the USGS to use the helicopters to do some surveying of mountaintop locations for mapping Southeast Alaska. All of the local airplane pilots, of course, were very excited to see the first helicopters, and they gathered on the dock to watch the helicopters take off.

First helicopter in Ketchikan, July 19, 1951. Sam Chevalier poses for a photo with Bell 47, N182B. The helicopter's arrival made the paper that day. (Photo by Del Richardson, courtesy of Terry Richardson.)

The Bells could land almost anywhere with those big bag pontoons. Better yet, they could actually hover in midair so long as they stayed close to the ground. What a feat! (Today's helicopters can hover at various altitudes, but it takes a lot of power to do it. It's called "hovering out of ground effect.")

It wasn't long before one of the helicopters had a misfortune. Flying on glassy water in a helicopter is very difficult because the helicopter is very unstable in all directions—vertical and horizontal. Before taking off, the glassy water is like a mirror. When the craft first lifts up, the rotor wash creates a big ripple on the water that is very easy to see. However, as the helicopter moves forward, you fly away from that ripple. As the helicopter speeds up, it starts to aquire "translational lift" from its forward speed, until at about 17 miles an hour the helicopter starts flying like an airplane, leaving the hover cushion completely. If there's glassy water in front, the pilot can't see the surface and can fly into the glassy water. The old helicopters were kind of underpowered, and you didn't dare pull them up too steep on takeoff, which made them more vulnerable to problems in a glassy-water takeoff.

John Scott had left his passengers off on a mountain near

Joe Soloy and a young girl aboard a Hiller 360 (called an A-model). Note the open cockpit and control stick coming from above.

A Dean Johnson, Inc. Hiller B-model on the Bradfield River. (Note enclosed cockpit, controls on the floor.) Paul Piper stands in front, Dean Johnson behind.

the head of Bradfield Canal and then flown down to salt water to wait. John and his mechanic were sitting on the water on this beautiful sunny day waiting for the call from the people on the mountain to come get them. When John got the call, he fired up the helicopter and proceeded to take off. As he left his hover cushion, the helicopter settled slightly and flew right back into the water and tipped over. It was a nice sunshiny day, and they both got out of the helicopter okay. The big old pontoons floated it very nicely upside down. They laid on the pontoons and actually got sunburned waiting for a rescue. Finally they were picked up and brought to town where they arranged for a boat to salvage the helicopter and take it to Ketchikan.

We got acquainted with John Scott while the helicopter was being rebuilt. He was excited and enjoyed Alaska. Everything was interesting to him. He especially liked the fact that I had a seaplane that I could use to fly him up to see his operation. We had been doing a lot of prospecting so I knew the country quite well.

John Scott finally got the helicopter rebuilt and was ready to take off north for the next phase of his job. I talked to John and his boss and got permission for John to carry our nucleometer on his flights. He flew the silly thing all over the state before John wrecked the helicopter near Fairbanks. We got our instrument back in the mail.

There was a flare in mining at the time, and U.S. Steel was

very interested in three or four low-grade iron deposits in Southeast Alaska. They hired Dean Johnson out of McMinnville, Oregon to move their people around so they could stake their claims and do some exploration starting with Duke Island.

Dean landed in Ketchikan with an 360-model Hiller helicopter that had no cabin, just a windshield—the rest of it was wide open. It had wooden blades, a 178-horsepower Franklin engine, and an overhead stick for control instead of the standard floor stick like most helicopters had. The 360-model was on skids and had racks on the skids to store gear. He landed in an open field right across from Northern Bus Company garage, which was my business at the time.

Dean and his mechanic tied the helicopter down for the night and put some canvas engine covers on it. The next morning everybody had to go watch the first takeoff. The early helicopter pilots seemed to think they had to show off to demonstrate the helicopter's real versatility, which was really totally unnecessary. It was like when the airplane pilots wore a helmet with a scarf streaming out behind as their MOD. Dean made a wild takeoff, and something flew off of the helicopter. It turned out to be one of the engine covers they had accidentally left on the rack of the helicopter. When Dean took off, the cover flew into the water and floated. He tried to dip the front skid of the helicopter underneath the canvas cover to lift it up and bring it back to land. He hooked onto it a couple of times but kept losing it. Finally the cover sank, and he couldn't recover it. They came back a little chagrined to see the little mistake they made in front of the public.

The next year Joe Soloy came to Ketchikan, flying for Dean Johnson, to continue with the mining exploration work. Joe and his mechanic, Al Hutane, made quite a good team. Joe was thrilled with Alaska, and I got quite well acquainted with him because every time the helicopter got into trouble, they'd call on me to airdrop something or to land in the closest lake or river and carry in their supplies. On one occasion I airdropped a battery with a parachute to them, and another time I carried in a set of tail rotors. It seemed like the helicopters were prone to accidents, but most things were easily fixed, and they were on their way before very long.

Joe wanted to see a little bit of Alaska so I said, "Let's take the helicopter and go see Old Man Wolfe on the Chickamin River." Joe's helicopter was limited to a two-hour fuel supply so we took a few extra cans of gas with us, and flew out to the Chickamin River. We landed at Al Wolfe's homestead, which was quite an impressive step back in time. No electricity, and Al himself, who was a cowboy from years gone by. Al had always wanted to go up on a certain mountain to see if there was mineral there, so Joe took Al and I up the river to the spot Al was interested in. Joe landed just a couple feet from the edge of a thousand-foot cliff so we had to be sure we were walking in the right direction when we got out of the helicopter.

After we finished our exploration, we all got back in the helicopter, and Joe lifted off. Now mind you, this is a helicopter with just a windshield, and you're sitting right next to where there is no door. You put your seat belt on and lean your head out, and all there is beneath you is a pair of skids.

One moment we were hovering peacefully, the next we were spinning around and dropping toward the rocks a thousand feet below! Wolfe and I hung on for dear life while Joe smoothly got up airspeed and flew away.

Turns out those early helicopters were horribly underpowered—you had to be very careful how much pitch you pulled, and when you pulled it, because the blades would slow down quickly if you overdid it. You could pull pitch aggressively for a tiny moment, but you had to be able to flatten the collective and rebuild that stored energy, or you ceased to be an aircraft. Due to the helicopter's lack of power, pilots loved to land on a cliff facing into the mountain because all they had to do was spin around and dive off the cliff. Once they got past 17 miles per hour airspeed, it was easy for them to get their flying speed up and fly away. It's kind of a wild maneuver for anybody to observe, but it's not difficult, and with the old underpowered helicopters, it made sense. Unfortunately for us, Joe didn't bother to tell us what he was doing. When Joe went to fly, he lifted off into hover, whipped the ship around, and dove straight off the cliff.

In later years that pedal turn takeoff was a maneuver I used often. It was one of the ways my instructors taught me to get off of a mountain. The trick was remembering to tell your passengers what you were about to do.

During this time I got my first introduction to the controls of a helicopter. Joe gave me my first dual instruction in a Hiller 360, or A-model. In return I checked him out in my seaplane, 42 Mike.

Joe was so impressed with the country that he was able to talk Dean Johnson into leaving the helicopter in Ketchikan for the winter. Now that the helicopter was spending the winter in Ketchikan, it needed an overhaul, and Joe needed a place to do it. We let him use one of the stalls in our Northern Bus garage so, of course, we spent a lot of time watching the overhaul. The Hiller at that time had a lot of finite-life parts, plus a lot of things that just needed to be inspected—including the blades.

Re-Tracking Wooden Blades

The old Hiller helicopters had wooden blades with a metal leading edge and a metal beam going down the center to hold them together. The aerodynamic part of the blade was made out of balsa wood covered with fabric and had a steel tip on it, which made a very light blade that performed well.

When the helicopter was parked outside overnight, the blades were secured by tying one blade down to the tail boom which left the other one sticking up in the air. In our rainy climate, moisture would accumulate in the lower blade and make it heavier. Joe and Al had to continually track the blades to keep them fairly even. Sometimes the old blades would really get out of whack, and the helicopter would shake terribly.

In those days they had a very crude system for re-tracking blades. Red chalk was applied to one blade, and yellow chalk to the other blade. They would then start the helicopter and very slowly raise a piece of belting hanging from an offset length of pipe until the tips of the turning blades struck the edge of the belt. The blades left two chalk marks—a high and a low. They could tell which blade, the red or the yellow, made the mark, and then they would adjust the tabs on the trailing edge of the blade so the two blades would fly together and not shake much.

Pitch-Change Links

When you adjusted the blade tracking, sometimes you would need to adjust the pitch-change links as well. The pitch-change links changed the total amount of pitch that you could pull by moving the collective up or down. Pulling the collective up pulls the main blades down, which adds more pitch and takes more power, but when the engine quits, you also have to be able to put the collective clear down, which actually puts the blades into a reverse pitch so the downward speed and weight of the helicopter will keep the blades turning at a flying speed. The blades on the Hiller were turning up around 360 RPM, but if you got them down below 280, they ceased to be a blade, and started shaking and stop-banging which is a violent thing that scares the pants off of you.

The collective was attached to the pitch-change mechanism. To adjust the range of pitch, the pitch-change link had rod ends which could turn in or out to get the proper length. One evening Joe and Al were in the process of adjusting the pitch-change link, and they had worked late into the night. The mechanic had gone ahead and put the bolts in at the right spot, then called it a night. You always put the link bolts with the head in the direction of rotation so that just the turning of the blades would tend to keep the bolt in.

Well, for some unknown reason the mechanic made the change in the change-link and put the bolts back in, but he failed to put the nuts on because they were going to do some more adjusting the following day.

In the middle of the night, Joe got an emergency call from a little mining camp over at Mt. Andrews. Someone was ill and needed to be taken to town. Joe was very gung-ho on rescue and really wanted to help people out so he made the night flight. I can't remember how much light there was, but there was enough light to fly. Flying at night with helicopters is no fun without aids or instruments, which none of the early helicopters had. All you had was air speed and a compass.

Joe made it over there, brought the guy back to town, and parked the helicopter. At daylight the next morning, he went to work and got ready to fly the helicopter again. He climbed up on the helicopter to do his pre-flight inspection, and all of a sudden his face went stark white. Where were the nuts on the pitch-change links? He had flown that night flight with no nuts on the bolts that hold the pitch-change links. If one bolt had vibrated off, he would have lost all control of that helicopter. Joe had failed to do his pre-flight inspection that night before he flew. That was one of our early experiences that really struck home.

New Students

When the overhaul was complete, in order to try to make a little money, Joe picked up a few little jobs and had Dean Johnson send up a couple of students. Del Smith was one of those students (Del now owns one of the largest helicopter and airplane companies in the world, Evergreen International, Inc.). Back then Del had just gotten out of the Army and wanted to learn to fly helicopters, so here he was with his Army leather jacket and Army cap in Ketchikan, ready to go. Joe did the training off of the little vacant lot across from our bus garage, which was right next to the water, and also right next to a favorite neighborhood fast-food restaurant called the "Toot 'N Tell."

You couldn't have asked for better visibility for Joe, and I'm sure the "Toot'N Tell" customers had a lot to talk about with one of the only helicopters in Alaska taking off just across the way.

Start of TEMSCO

Sadly, later that year Dean Johnson had a fatal accident in the Super Cub he used to spray crops in Oregon. Joe said, "They're going to pull out of Alaska. I have a job lined up and this would be the ideal time to start a helicopter company. All we've got to do is raise $40,000 to buy a helicopter. That's what it's going to cost to buy a brand-new C-model Hiller."

This wasn't completely out of the question. I had a lot of friends, and we decided to start the company with Joe as the operator. Since we didn't know Joe very well, we felt we should have somebody local work with him. My friend Bob Young came in and helped Joe with the management and learned to fly helicopters. We planned to start off with one helicopter, and as soon as we had two pilots, we'd buy another helicopter. After that

Earl Walker and I would get our licenses, and that would give us four local pilots. We could beat the world.

We started the company and did everything wrong that we possibly could have done. We gave Bob and Joe sixty percent of the company. Their investment was a Piper PA-12 seaplane. The investors (there were eight others besides Joe and Bob) all loaned money rather than investing it. We started out with a $40,000 debt right off the bat, and had horrible financial problems. Joe Soloy was president, I was vice-president, and Bob Young was secretary. At one of our first meetings, we came up with the acronym TEMSCO from the words: Timber, Exploration, Mining, Survey, Cargo Operations. We named the company TEMSCO Helicopters, Inc.

We sent Joe and Bob down to Palo Alto, California to pick up a brand-new 12C-model Hiller, 5326 Victor, and bring it to Ketchikan. Soon afterwards, TEMSCO started operating out of a shed at Peninsula Point north of Ketchikan.

White Alice
White Alice was TEMSCO's first job. White Alice was the nuclear early warning system being built by the government to

Joe Soloy (front) and Bob Young with our first Hiller 12C.

send VHF line-of-sight radio signals from mountaintop to mountaintop. The radios would transmit a direct signal that couldn't be intercepted. The line had many outposts and ran all the way up to St. Lawrence Island in northern Alaska and into Canada. Joe's initial job was to go out and test these lines-of-sight so sites could be selected for building the control stations in Southeast Alaska. Some of the stations were built on mountains such as the one on Duncan Canal where our job was. It was about 1800 feet high on the mountain, and it shot a signal up the line to Annette Island for a distance of 60 to 90 miles to the next White Alice station.

I was the vice-president so I spent all my spare time at TEMSCO even though I was not on a salary. I still had my bus company to run, but I did everything I could, such as getting a Canadian license and looking after the office and the radio whenever needed.

Support Work

Earl and I did ongoing support work for TEMSCO using our seaplanes to take people, parts, and fuel all over Alaska and Canada. I had already done a lot of stream survey work for the Fish and Game Department, and TEMSCO acquired all the survey work from the Canadian border to Petersburg, including Prince of Wales Island. We flew between fifty and one hundred feet above the treetops, and an average day of survey work was about five hours of flying.

When we weren't doing that, we did escort flying for helicopters—both for TEMSCO, and for others. The helicopters' engines really weren't very reliable, which made long trips over water risky business—particularly for helicopters that didn't have floats.

Earl and I soon decided we'd been flying commercially long enough without a license, and we'd better do something about it. So we went to Corvallis, Oregon and took our commercial airplane training from Nancy and Arlo Livingston. Both of them were excellent pilots. It took us about three weeks to finish our course, pass our tests, and get out of there. Now we could do all the work we'd been doing—legally.

Servicing communications equipment by delivering things like this com shell on High Mountain became a large part of TEMSCO's business.

More Helicopters

In the spring it was obvious we had a little more work so we were going to need another helicopter. We bought Arlo Livingston's Hiller 12B-model, and with it came the training of one pilot. We sent Bob Young to Corvallis, and Arlo and Nancy taught him to fly. Bob brought the 12B, 5311 Victor, from Oregon to Alaska and was ready to go to work with it.

One of the first jobs we had with the 12B was for the FAA. A Grumman Goose amphibian had been damaged while landing in Purple Lake during a training flight, and they needed to inspect it for damage and cause. Bob landed at Annette Island airfield to pick up the FAA men, and when he took off he made the typical beginner's mistake of pulling more pitch in the blades than he had power to pull. The helicopter settled, and the heels of the floats hit the ground first causing the blades to come down and chop the tail boom off. Fortunately none of the flying debris got near the people on the ground, but Bob's pride and the helicopter were smashed. A month later 5311V was flying again.

Through my contact with Mark Anthony, a geologist and college geology teacher from Fairbanks, TEMSCO got a contract for a helicopter. We didn't have the bigger helicopter Mark wanted so we contracted with Arlo Livingston who was excited at the thought of getting his brand-new Hiller 12E-model to work. That summer proved very successful, and we all fell in love with the E-model because it was a real performing helicopter.

During the summer Arlo had flown out of Juneau quite a bit. He liked the looks of the town so when he got back to Corvallis, he sold his business, and he and Nancy moved to Juneau to start a helicopter business. We were very friendly competitors, and Arlo always called on us to do extra work for him, and we called him to help us whenever we needed it.

The following year the White Alice project went into the construction phase, which meant a lot more work for TEMSCO. We had two helicopters, a B- and a C-model, and neither one of them really qualified for the job. We made do for a while, but later in the season when we finally got the White Alice job, we had to buy two Hiller 12E-models for ourselves at $60,000 apiece.

The White Alice job consisted of moving people and supplies up to the top of the mountain where they started building the road from salt water to the top of the mountain from both ends at once. It was a rush program during the Cold War period so it had to be built all in one year. The E-model was really putting in the hours and doing a great job, but at the end of the White Alice job, we didn't have much in the line of work.

We now had four helicopters, and with four helicopters the accident ratio increased considerably. It seemed like every time we turned around, the airplane had to take a set of blades out here or a tail rotor out there, or a battery or something was needed for a helicopter. By August of 1961 we'd had a really bad year at TEMSCO, but finally we got a break.

The Canadians called for one of our helicopters to help fight a big forest fire. We finished our work for them successfully in spite of an expensive little mishap. Bob goofed one day and nicked the blade of the helicopter on a tree. To get him back to work quickly, I tied a new blade onto the little Piper Pacer—the blade was almost as long as the airplane—and flew straight to Terrace, B.C. We got permission from Canadian customs to go directly in, deliver the blade, and return with the old blade. I landed in the river at Terrace, and on the banks of the Skeena River, we made the change of blades, tracked and balanced them. It was a very easy, quick way to get the helicopter back in service.

Revenue from fighting the fire helped a lot, but by the next year TEMSCO's business just sort of disappeared, and we were really in trouble—behind eight months on our payments for the two Hiller 12Es and behind $25,000 on our insurance payments. Things weren't working out so Joe Soloy announced he wanted to sell out and left to go fly for Granduc, a mining operation across the border in Canada. When Joe left the company, the first thing I had to do was personally guarantee Hiller the payments so we could continue business. That left Earl Walker, me, and only one helicopter pilot, Bob Young.

We desperately needed another helicopter pilot.

Helicopter Training

I talked it over with Peggy and told her I would really like to fly helicopters commercially. Since our son Dan was through with his schooling and his military obligation, he could help us run the bus company. Later Peggy said to Dan, "We can make a living running the bus company so let's let Dad go play with the helicopters." I often remind her of that statement.

Armed with the support of my family, I went out on a limb. I told Bob and Earl, "If we buy Joe out, I'll learn to fly the helicopter and work full time for TEMSCO."

That was the start of my helicopter flight training. At that time we didn't have any legal instructors, and I guess we didn't need one because Bob taught me how to hover and how to take off and land. The standard training procedure was to take off and hover about two feet above the ground—hover sideways, left and right, turn around, do a 360 with your tail in the wind and your tail downwind. We also practiced hovering around a point, a maneuver where we hovered around in a circle keeping the helicopter pointed directly toward a spot in the middle of the circle.

Our early mentor, Arlo Livingston, standing next to one of his crop dusters.

It took all the manipulation of the helicopter to control it. As we went into the downwind and upwind situations, all the controls changed so we had to be very careful. This was excellent training in keeping the throttle and pitch coordinated.

We didn't have anybody who could go beyond this point in our training so we had Arlo Livingston come down and give Bob and I some instruction in autorotations, which were required for me to solo. When he arrived he said, "Okay, let's the three of us get in this helicopter, and we'll go do an autorotation."

The wind was shifting around at the pullout at Peninsula Point that day so Arlo took off and flew around until he got into position to make an upwind approach to the basin. I was sitting on the right outside, Arlo was sitting in the center, and Bob on the left-hand side. We came over the pullout, and he chopped the power to do the first autorotation. To autorotate you chop the power to simulate an engine failure and push down the collective. You descend at a speed of about 1800 feet a minute with the collective clear down and roll the throttle to idle. This keeps the blades spinning at flying speed, and actually stores some energy in them by speeding them up a little. When you get close to the water you flare, that is pull your nose up to slow down. Then as you get closer to the water, you lower the nose. Just as you touch the water, you pull in pitch with the collective to give the helicopter a little lift, and the helicopter will gracefully slide onto the water doing about 15 miles an hour or less.

Arlo went through this procedure on the first autorotation, and as he pulled pitch at the bottom, the helicopter hit the water and the nose tucked. He was pulling pitch for all he was worth, but the nose dove, and the water came halfway up on the bubble. I thought for sure we were tipping over, but because he had pulled pitch at the right time, the helicopter bobbed back to the surface. Water ran off of the helicopter like water off of a duck's back, and all of our hearts were fluttering. Arlo revved the engine up and pulled the helicopter off of the water. He landed it on the pullout and said, "Something's wrong with this helicopter. I don't think I made a downwind landing." Well, there was a possibility that he had, but there was also something wrong with the helicopter.

When we installed the floats, apparently our mechanic didn't understand where to position the floats on the helicopter. As it turned out, the floats were one foot too far back which didn't give enough flotation in front of the helicopter to perform the autorotation. When this was corrected, Arlo gave me a good hour session on autorotations, and I got to where I could do a pretty good job with them.

Flying Solo

Two interesting things happened after I learned to fly solo and prior to getting my license. One was when we had a lost preacher. A Methodist preacher had gone up Deer Mountain to make a long-range hike across the mountains and was to end up in White River. A day later the airplane went to pick him up, and he wasn't there. A search started, and a couple of days later, they finally spotted the preacher in a river valley where there were a lot of salmon and a lot of black bear. He was waving a handkerchief, but he apparently couldn't walk so they came to TEMSCO and needed a helicopter to rescue him.

The helicopters were all out working, and I was the only one there. I had the B-model, but I didn't have a license so I couldn't do it. They said, "You've got to do it. The preacher's been out there three nights now, and we've got to get him." So I said, "Well, okay, I'll tell you what I'll do. You send Jack Cousins (he'd located the preacher) over to George Inlet, and he can locate the preacher for me by circling him. I'll come over with the helicopter and land wherever I can and pick the preacher up and take him to the beach in George Inlet where Jack can take him back to town. That way nobody but you two will know I did it because if I'm hauling people without a license, I'm liable to never get my license."

I took off, and Jack spotted the preacher for me. I found a little muskeg which looked pretty good—it was pretty narrow, but it was big enough to get into. I had a couple hundred feet for a takeoff area, which you kind of needed with the old B-model Hiller. I landed in the muskeg and shut off the helicopter. Then I hiked down the creek and got the preacher. I was surprised to see that he had been eating dead salmon. Actually when you get right down to it, parts of the salmon were still pretty good—the bear liked it, and the preacher said it wasn't too bad. It was sure better than nothing. The preacher's feet were so sore he couldn't walk so I assisted him by half carrying him back to the helicopter.

This was my first landing and takeoff in a confined area. I lifted up about a foot and made a running take off. I flew him down to the beach at White River in George Inlet, and Jack took the preacher to town in his little Luscombe seaplane. Well, the preacher wanted to tell the media and his congregation about the rescue, and he wanted to mention my name. I said, "No, you can't." He said, "In my sermon, I want to thank you for rescuing me." I said, "You can't mention my name, or I'll never get my license." It was a big disappointment to him that he couldn't thank me publicly for rescuing him. He honored my request begrudgingly; anyway, it didn't interfere with my getting my license for my helicopter rating.

Carl Manzonie Crash

Not long after rescuing the preacher, I went out looking for Carl Manzonie. Carl was one of the local pilots and a friend of mine who had been working for Pete Cessnun for about five years. He had about 5000 hours flight time, and he was really good.

Some men that were planning to go goat hunting asked Carl to fly them over to the mainland. They wanted to look the area over first, so Carl took the three of them in a 180 Cessna and headed inland. Apparently he tried to out-climb Deer Mountain in a show-off stunt and stalled the airplane just before he reached the top of the mountain. It crashed in a little lake at the base of the Deer Mountain Ridge.

We had airplanes and helicopters flying wherever we could to try to find them. (My logbook shows 15 hours of searching for him.) Several days later someone flying an Ellis Air Goose finally saw something that looked like an airplane in the water, and sure enough it was—all the people were killed.

Settling with Power

Terry Wills had gone up to the lake to help Bob Young bring the bodies out. In the process Terry lost his billfold so he came to TEMSCO and asked Bob if he wouldn't take him up to find his billfold. Bob said, "Ken's flying enough now. He can take you up there." So Terry was my actual second passenger. He was a good airplane pilot so he didn't mind riding along with me even though I didn't have my license yet. I took off and started climbing. The helicopter was underpowered and didn't climb very well. I figured I had to get up to 2000 feet to get into the lake, and I was planning to climb up to 2500 feet before I started into the valley where the lake was.

A helicopter with a bubble doesn't provide any real good way to orient yourself to level unless you can see the horizon, but I was too new to realize that. As we climbed, I put us into a little steeper climb than I should have and started losing airspeed without noticing it.

There's a condition that occurs with a helicopter called "settling with power." This condition occurs when you have power applied, in other words, you're pulling pitch, and you're going less than five miles an hour forward speed, and you're settling downwards more than 300 feet a minute. The blades cavitate like an outboard motor when it gets air, and they speed up, but they don't do anything. The more pitch you pull, the worse it gets.

The helicopter started to shake and shudder and was falling a lot faster than I wanted it to. I wanted to be climbing! My rotors were up to speed and I was pulling pitch, what was wrong?

No one had ever told me about this, but I had read something about "settling with power" in the Hiller manual, and it mentioned that when this occurred, you reduce the power and bottom the collective, going into autorotation. I rolled the power off and put the ship into autorotation, shoved the nose forward, got into flight, rolled the power back in, and started a more gentle climb. It worked, but Terry Wills' eyes were as big as saucers. He didn't have a clue what was going on, but he knew it wasn't right.

We landed on a little knoll right in the creek bottom in the center of the entrance into this steep-walled little mountain lake. Terry hiked around to where the airplane had crashed about a half-mile from where we landed the helicopter, but he couldn't find his wallet. So it was back home for us—with me a lot wiser.

Helicopter Rating

September 12, 1962 we finally got an FAA inspector, Richard S. Thwaits, to come down from Anchorage and give me a check ride for my license. He had less time in the helicopter than I did. He was to observe and tell me what to do, but he was not to touch the controls. I made an autorotation to the water from 180° and one straight in, no sweat. The inspector was elated at the fact that I had done a good job. He thought I was really something special.

Now I had my helicopter rating. I was flying 5326V, our original helicopter which was a Hiller C-model with a 210-horsepower Franklin engine. It was still quite underpowered and prone to fouling spark plugs and breaking starter bendixes so the standard equipment aboard ship were tools, spark plugs, and extra bendixes.

First Commercial Flights

One of my first commercial flights was into White River drainage area with the Army Engineers to examine some of the terrain for a possible road into White River. I went in and landed on a little knoll successfully, and when the engineer had done his work and came back, I fired up the helicopter and lifted off into a hover.

When you're flying a helicopter basically what happens is when you pull pitch, you blow enough air down to actually hover on a cushion of air. You can tip the helicopter any way you want to, and it'll move on the cushion of air. The closer you get to the ground, the less power it takes to hold a hover. This is called "ground effect." You don't appreciate ground effect as much when you're flying over a smooth surface, but when you go off of a knoll, your ground effect suddenly drops away, and it takes a little more power to fly than you anticipated.

This was my first takeoff on my own in a condition like that, and as I was leaving the knoll, I felt the ground cushion disappear. I pulled more pitch, and the power started to fade. I had pulled too much pitch. This was the basic thing that you learned flying helicopters, and it was instilled in me well enough that I did the right thing. You want to pull more pitch, but the right thing is to go down on the pitch and keep that RPM up. So I tipped the nose down, dropped the collective, and got up to flying speed. We flew off over the trees, and I breathed a huge sigh of relief.

This was just a simple introduction to underpowered helicopters and learning to use them. Flying these helicopters turned out to be good training for me because later on when we were flying heavy loads, this built-in technique was really helpful. It is kind of like driving a car. Once you learn to shift gears without looking where you're shifting them, you just do it automatically. That's what you have to do with a helicopter—you have to get to where all those reactions become automatic. Then you start to be a pilot.

Building Helicopter Time

At that time the Forest Service required 50 hours of pilot time in order to fly them. In order to accumulate enough hours,

I flew as many trips as possible. It didn't really matter what the trip was, just anything to build time. I took the helicopter on prospecting trips and fun trips of any kind. In fact we inaugurated what turned out to be an annual event—taking the kids out in the woods to gather Christmas trees and hauling them back with the helicopter. Every year we'd haul enough trees in for everybody in the company and our friends and their friends. The minute they saw the helicopter coming in with a load of Christmas trees, all the friends arrived at TEMSCO to pick up their trees. Sometimes we had to make an extra trip because all the trees were gone and none were left for us!

I made several trips to Annette Island where Pan American Airways came in with their DC-3s and their four-engine Stratacrusiers. Every time the weather was down, the Grummans that serviced Ketchikan couldn't get into Annette, but with the helicopter I could fly low and follow a beach line. As long as I didn't have to cross glassy water, I could get into Annette Island airfield and pick up a needed package or drop off a passenger when needed. Those trips weren't a money-making venture, but it let TEMSCO do some favors for people and helped me gain hours.

My most famous trip to Annette as far as I was concerned was when Pete Cessnun, who was quite a Republican at the time, called me up and said, "It's snowing hard, and I've got Ted Stevens stuck in town here. He's got to be in Washington, D.C. tomorrow to be sworn in as a Senator. We can't get him over to Annette, and the airplane's going to leave in 45 minutes so we're getting desperate." I flew Ted Stevens over to Annette Island so he could catch his plane and gave Frank and Peggy Larson a ride back to Ketchikan on the return trip.

To this day Ted Stevens is still the U.S. Senator for the State of Alaska, and now he's one of the head Republicans in Congress. I thought it was pretty important to get him over to Annette Island Airport on time.

One way or another I accumulated 50 hours on my logbook, and my first job for the Forest Service was over in Polk Inlet spraying a large volume of spruce trees that were infected with the spruce budworm. We worked with two helicopters and a big

PBY Flying Boat rigged with spray gear. It would spray the larger areas, and we would spray the smaller wooded valleys. We used DDT mixed with diesel oil to spray.

I started out with one of the Forest Service officers who wanted to get the lay of the land. It was a nice warm day, and we took both doors off so he could see better. As he was sorting through his aerial photos, he laid one on the floor. A gust of wind took it out the door, and immediately we heard a screeching noise in the back end of the helicopter. I made an autorotation down to the water and landed. I shut the engine off, and we looked around to see what had happened. The shredded photo had gone through the cooling fan. No damage was done, but it was just another lesson learned about keeping things in the proper order in the front seat—especially when the doors are off.

We proceeded with the spray job flying about 50 feet over the top of the trees. I never did hear whether the spray job was successful or not. Later on I know the spray was discontinued because they said it was killing the eagles off, but I never saw any evidence of that.

Terry Wills was visiting the camp in his Cessna 180. While

That's me having a lighthearted moment with the original TEMSCO hangar out at Peninsula Point.

we were waiting for weather, the PBY pilots got to know Terry and took a liking to him. They let him fly the PBY—quite a thrill for Terry!

The next year we continued to do any kind of job that came along. Tight on dollars we sold our Hiller 12C, N5326V, to Richard and Merrill Wein in Fairbanks. We'd already gotten rid of the B-model, so now we had just the two Hiller 12Es. They were first-class helicopters at that time so we could proceed with our work. Bob had a contract with Del Smith at Evergreen to spray crops down in the Oregon-Washington area. I took care of the local helicopter work, and Earl Walker flew the airplane.

By March of '63 I had accumulated about 164 hours and was flying our Hiller 12E with the 305 HP motor—it was a real strong helicopter, and I loved it. Later the Hiller was rated at 340 HP. You weren't supposed to use all the horsepower, but with dual carburetors on the 305 HP engine, the horsepower went up to 340. We were restricted, however, and were only supposed to pull 25½ inches of manifold pressure, but in reality we ignored that. The Hiller was a strong ship, and you'd pull everything it would pull. As long as you kept the RPM up in the 3200 range, it didn't abuse the engine, and the ship handled it very well.

The latter part of the 1963 season I got a job with the Livingstons on the Snettisham Power Project out of Juneau. They were just starting to do the survey work and needed another helicopter to satisfy the Army Engineers' requirements. We surveyed the power line all the way into Juneau, which was about 35 miles. It was an interesting job, and I was low on time so all those hours were very valuable to me.

A few months after I left, one of Livingston's 12Es was flying on the Snettisham project where they were doing some blasting. Just as the helicopter flew over the blast area, somebody shot the blast off and literally blew it out of the sky. Rumors immediately started circulating amid a lot of hard feelings. We never knew whether that shot was intentional.

Things slowed down that winter. We were lucky to get a trip a day, but it helped keep the wolf from the door. Fortunately in February the Army Engineers hired us to move their camp, drilling equipment, and fuel into Grace Lake on the back side of Revillagigedo Island. They were going to drill at the outlet of the lake to see what problems they might encounter if they were to build a power dam for Ketchikan. This turned out to be a pretty good job—it lasted several months in the dead of winter. I did all of the flying and really enjoyed the winter challenge. There were a couple of trips a week plus breakdown trips for parts. I moved most of the fuel for the helicopter up to the camp, but left four barrels on the beach planning to move them before the tides got too big. This fuel turned out to be a big help in getting the rescue going for the Granduc avalanche not long thereafter.

Railroad to nowhere. Thirty-five years later the twisted and broken railroad leading into the Granduc Mine disappears off the cliff. The avalanche blasted most of the buildings, a railcar, and much of the mine's equipment into a tangle of wreckage, now scattered across the valley below.

Twenty-six men lost their lives that day.

Chapter 7,
Avalanche at the Granduc

The 18th of February 1965 wasn't pretty. Blowing southeast and snowing at 35 to 45 knots, it was a nasty, gusty day—the kind of day you'd like to spend inside the house.

The last several days had been like that—just below freezing, wet, cold, and blowing to boot. Trying to service the Granduc copper mine had been an effort in frustration. The weather would look okay long enough to convince a person to load up and make the effort, but by the time we got close to the mine, the ceiling was so low you couldn't get over the ridge into Stewart, much less fly into the mine. The Granduc took supplies from Stewart, B.C., but during weather like this, supplies would accumulate in Stewart, waiting for a ride up over the hill. On the U.S. side, the Grace Lake Army Corps of Engineers drilling project was suffering from the same problem. Fuel intended for Grace Lake had to be laid down at sea level because low visibility obscured the pass leading into the lake.

It had been snowing hard the previous few weeks, but over the last couple of days warmer weather had started dumping heavy, wet stuff all over Southeast. Sixty-some inches of semi-wet snow had fallen in the last 24 hours, and people were getting concerned about their homes and businesses. If the weather kept up, or it started to rain, any building that didn't get swept off would get crushed under the weight of the snow.

Out at the Granduc, conditions were worse. Wet, heavy snow piled on top of dry powder creating an unstable cornice above the mine. As the miners started sweeping snow off their various buildings, something on the hill above them broke loose.

Floating silently down the hillside, the roar of the avalanche couldn't be heard over the wind and weather. According to one survivor who had been out sweeping snow off a roof, a gentle breeze suddenly blew across the compound, causing several to look up. At that instant, WHAP! The avalanche was on them. A wave of snow scoured through the mine complex, destroying most of the buildings, and burying a great many of the workers. The wave left the Granduc in shambles. The communications building in particular had been destroyed, leaving the remote camp cut off from the outside world—at the worst possible moment.

One of the survivors patched together a radio using a spare battery and a radio out of a Cat on the airstrip above the mine. With it, he put out the first distress call.

Apparently the weak HF radio signal barely hissed out of the speakers, but it was clear enough to understand. Relayed by the local radio communications center, the signal from Portal Camp made it to Webber Air, where immediately the pilots there began organizing a rescue.

Webber Air called us at TEMSCO to let us know there had been a problem out at the mine, and they might need some helicopter assistance. Soon Dick Borch hurried in, alerting me and Bob Young of the disaster, and asking to use the telephone.

Destruction at the mine site. Note the Canadian Sikorsky taking off in the background. (Photo courtesy of Howard Brand.)

Throughout the rescue, conditions weren't good. This little Canadian chopper was one of the first on the scene. (Photo courtesy of Howard Brand.)

Borch began alerting the Ketchikan Volunteer Rescue Squad while Bob Young and I began getting the helicopter and our personal gear ready to go.

When the phone rang again, I answered, and found myself on the line with AKL, the 1965-equivalent of today's marine operator. (AKL was boosting the signal and sending it directly to us over the telephone line.) The operator patched me directly to the survivors radioing from the damaged Cat bulldozer. "We need help; we've had an avalanche, 50 men are buried. We need help right now. Bring doctors, medical supplies, whatever you can. Our camp is wiped out." Sitting near the radio, I answered, ending with "I'll see if I can get permission to come into Canada." The miner replied, "Forget the permission, just come."

Bob and I talked the situation over, looking at the rapidly-degrading weather, snow, and failing light. Daylight in February is a scarce commodity, especially on a cloudy day. By now it was well after noon—we only had another hour or two to make the long flight to the glacier. Bob said, "I'll go if you don't want to." I responded, "No, I really want to go." Bob finished, saying: "I'll get the ship ready while you go home and change."

Quickly I called Doc Wilson, and began getting my part of

Nine Lives of an Alaska Bush Pilot   **147**

the makeshift rescue into gear. Webber Air was doing the same, calling people up and making preparations for a rescue effort. Quickly pulling the gear we needed to survive the night took time, and adding rescue items for the mine took longer. Daylight was fading, and if the weather socked in, the mine would have to wait as long as several days for any sort of relief. Those broken and injured by the tons of snow and shattered buildings couldn't wait that long.

We had our winter clothes on, I took along a tent and sleeping bags, and had a little heater that I'd planned to give the camp up there. We had medical supplies, our gear, everything loaded on. Fact is, we were going to take a nurse with us, but at the last minute it looked like we had too much gear in the helicopter so the nurse was not taken.

Leaving the TEMSCO pullout, I headed to the Webber Air dock to pick up Doc Wilson, and after coordinating with the other pilots there, we took off, trying to reach the mine before it became too dark and nasty to fly.

To get into the Granduc camp, helicopters and aircraft normally flew from Stewart, B.C. over a 5000-foot mountain range. Remember, this hadn't been possible for weeks due to weather, and that evening's snow wasn't helping at all. To reach the Granduc, rescuers had to start from Ketchikan, fly to the Chickamin River, then follow the river up to the Leduc River to its source at the Leduc Glacier. The Granduc mine complex perched on a little knob of land above the south fork of the Glacier, around 1500 feet above sea level. There is a slightly shorter route into the mine, coming in over Manzanita Lake, but with such low visibility, the circuitous low-level route up the rivers was the only option available.

On our way out, it was a rough ride, and I had to go the long way around. I went to the Grace Lake Army Engineers camp, where I landed and fueled up again.

In the preceding months we had helped lay out the Army Corps of Engineers test camp at Grace Lake. The crew had been working out in the weather for months, and would be ideal rescuers. Wilson told the people at Grace Lake that they might be needed for an assist in the rescue work, and the engineers immediately went into high gear.

Doc and I proceeded up the Chickamin, then up the Leduc River until we got to the south fork of the Leduc Glacier. It was snowing so bad I could hardly see. I tried to get up the glacier, but I couldn't find a spot to land. The foot of the glacier was supposed to hold an airstrip, but the snow was so bad I couldn't find a thing. We searched the area, but to no avail.

I finally set down in the snow very gingerly, and when I shut the helicopter off, we looked out and the blades were just ticking a snow bank on the other side. I stepped off the helicopter and I went into the snow so deep I couldn't get back up on the helicopter without help. The big floats supported the weight of the helicopter in this soft snow very well, sinking in only about a foot, but boy, when I went in I went clear to the bottom. Wilson helped pull me back up onto the floats, where we took stock of the situation. Donning snowshoes, we frantically stamped out a landing area, then planted a lantern we could leave as a beacon to come back to. By this time night was falling, and with 50 people or more buried in the snow above us, time was running out.

My hope was to try to get into the camp with the doctor and the aid I had. So I took off again from this location. I had taken the door off so I could see as best I could, and I got halfway up the glacier. I could put one pontoon down, but I couldn't find any place that I could put both pontoons down. It finally got so dark that I couldn't attempt to fly up any more so I went down to where I'd left the lantern and made another landing.

About that time we heard an avalanche starting from way up high in the mountains. I jumped back in the helicopter, fired it up, and we lifted off the ground. Surrounded by blowing snowflakes and inky blackness, I was instantly blind. White-out from all directions. If I didn't find a reference point, I would add myself and Dr. Wilson to the list of Granduc casualties.

I angled back in for a nearly-blind landing, knowing that the avalanche was still coming. There was nothing to do. . . I just guessed that I'd landed in a spot that wasn't in a valley coming off of the mountains. I set it back down, and we had nothing to do but shut the engine off. As the rotors wound down, the bass rumble of the avalanche built up, overwhelming the whine of the transmission.

We could still hear this avalanche coming down the mountain, and it was getting closer and closer, and finally with a great big swoosh, it came out on the snow about 200 feet from us.

Radioing Ketchikan, I gave the word that we were forced down by weather, and that we would be spending the night at the foot of the glacier—just a few miles from our destination. Ketchikan radioed back, saying that the Granduc had a Snowcat running, and they would send it down to pick up the doctor.

Although many people had been freed from the grip of the avalanche relatively unharmed, many were seriously hurt. The miners desperately needed Doctor Wilson.

Forced to settle in for the night, we tied the helicopter down, and pitched a tent under the tail boom. In a matter of half an hour, we pulled the tent together, relocated our bags, and laid down to try to rest.

Again a slope broke loose, and the rumble of the snow thundering down the hillside poured adrenaline into our veins. With nowhere to run, we clutched our sleeping bags and prayed.

This occurred several times during the night—neither one of us slept a minute. We were just in a position where it was up to the good Lord whether we were going to get hit with an avalanche or not.

Morning broke clear and cold with excellent visibility—but the Snowcat from the mine did not appear. (The Snowcat had rolled trying to reach us, and had to be abandoned.) Airborne rescuers from Ketchikan were inbound on the radio, but the morning's freeze stopped my helicopter in its tracks. Everything froze. All that wet snow froze. All over the helicopter, all over the blades, it was a horrible mess.

I worked feverishly to scrape ice from the tail rotor, shaft, and the ends of the blades using whatever pieces of metal I could find loose in our gear. It wasn't helping the paint job, but the helicopter was starting to look flyable. I thought I might be able to start it up and get it moving enough to shake some of the ice loose, but it was shaking too much.

Now I had to perform a feat—here we were out in the middle of the snow, and I had to get the ice off that blade so that I could fly. Casting around for tools, we found ourselves shy of most everything. We had come planning to help rescue people from the snow—not scrape ice off the rotor. The best we could come up with was the bottom of a steel oil can. Now if we could only reach the rotor blades, we might be able to fly.

Balancing precariously on the Hiller's long metal tail boom, I began to slide my way out onto the tail, reaching above my head to scrape with one hand and hold on with the other. At the base of the tail, the transition section offered reasonable traction, but as I moved out onto the boom, I had to balance on the pillar blocks that supported the one-inch driveline running across the top of the tail boom. The Hiller's driveline is a thin-walled aluminum tube. While strong and stiff in terms of acting like a drive shaft, a relatively small ding in the hollow shaft destroys its structural integrity. If I slipped and stepped down on the driveline, I risked catastrophic tail rotor failure when I tried to power up.

Well, in the process of doing it, I heard the motor of a helicopter, and here came a helicopter over the mountain, a Hiller. Instead of going straight into the camp, he came down to check on my situation, and we gave him the high sign that we were okay. Then a Bell helicopter came over. He came in the same way, coming from the Stewart side over the mountains and into the glacier. He also made a quick low pass by to see if we were okay. By that time I had the engine started, and it was still a little rough, but it was getting flyable now so we loaded everything into the helicopter, took off and flew into camp.

The devastation from the slide was almost total. The cookhouse, helipad (with Hiller helicopter), powerhouse, the small railroad out of the mine shaft, the recreation hall, three bunkhouses, everything had been swept off the mountain by a monstrous wave of snow. It seemed the entire mountainside above them had cut loose, carrying rocks, trees, dirt, and untold tons of snow right over the top of them. Thankfully one bunkhouse survived. The miners had frantically tried to dig their friends and co-workers out until it was too dark to see and had succeeded in finding many of them alive. Bonfires provided the only real warmth, and miners crowded around the fires to thaw out before going back to digging. Broken and bleeding, the injured avalanche survivors crowded into the bunkhouse. They all were suffering from hypothermia, plus a wide range of physical injuries.

When I landed up there, the helicopter pilot who lived at the glacier threw his arms around me and gave me a big hug. His helicopter had been destroyed in the avalanche, and they'd known that I'd been at the bottom of the glacier all night long trying to get to them. They knew the conditions we'd gone through to survive the night, and they said I was the happiest sight they'd seen.

Doc Wilson and I unloaded the survival gear we had for the miners, and the doctor immediately went up the hill to the mine's makeshift hospital area. Dozens of people needed serious medical attention immediately, and if they weren't moved off the mountain into town soon, many wouldn't make it.

Unfortunately, after a brief stretch of clear weather in the morning, the weather had quickly deteriorated. The Canadian pilots had been able to clear the ridge to fly into the mine, but now they couldn't go back. If they were to evacuate anybody, they had to go down the mountain, not up.

Now the other two Canadian pilots (one of them was a Frenchman) and I got together, and they said, "How are we going to do this?" I said, "Well, I've got good communication with Ketchikan. We can't trust the weather to make a full-blown evacuation of these people over the mountain to the Stewart side so the logical thing to do is set up a camp on the Chickamin River at Old Man Wolfe's cabin. I'll get the wheels in motion, and we'll get the rescue operation started.

They said, "We don't have enough gas to go down there and come back." I said, "I've got gas across the canal from Old Man Wolfe's cabin, and if I can squeeze my gas enough to get out there, I'll be able to bring over about four barrels of fuel.

Canadian S-58 offloading supplies for the rescue. Weather trapped the Canadians on the U.S. side of the ridge much of the time. One had an engine failure and had to make an emergency landing. (Photo courtesy of Howard Brand.)

I quickly took off, and began unreeling my HF-radio's trailing antenna. Using the trailing antenna, I could make contact with Ketchikan. I told them the rescue was starting and that the Canadians and I were going to bring the injured down to the Chickamin River. Ketchikan would need to send boats carrying aviation fuel, doctors, rescue workers—everything they could to the Chickamin River and Old Man Wolfe's cabin.

Hearing me over the HF radio, Arlo Livingston in Juneau came on the air asking, "Do you need more help?" I replied, "We need all the help we can get. We have 100 people to move out of the mine down to salt water where they've got quarters. We still have people buried, and we don't know whether any of them are alive, but it's very doubtful. We need all the help we can get because we've just got three helicopters that can hold two people at a time, and it's an hour round trip to the Chickamin cabin and back."

Livingston said he would send a couple of helicopters right away. So far the surviving mine workers had found more than a dozen of the 50 people that were missing, and in truth the rescue was going as well as could be expected under the circumstances. Still largely cut off from the outside world, the miners needed real help to find and rescue any remaining survivors and to evacuate their wounded. With three helicopters on station but low on gas, the entire effort hinged on getting that first load of fuel from the cache.

Thankfully I had just dropped a couple of barrels at sea level prior to the rescue, intending to bring them on in to Grace Lake the following day. They were close to the beach, and relatively close, but "close" was still a matter of several minutes flying time.

On the way down, I got to Wolfe's cabin, unloaded the passengers with minor injuries, and with the engine still running I took off immediately for the gas cache. My gas gauge was registering the point to where you don't fly. We always had a rule that we'd leave 50 pounds in, and I was down to 30 pounds, and I had about three miles to go. It was about the hardest three minutes of my life to get to that fuel cache, and boy, when I got there I landed so quick you couldn't believe it.

I pumped the tanks full of gas and rolled some barrels out of the snow, quickly rigging them for the flight back to the

Wolfe's cabin later during the rescue. Even at sea level, conditions weren't good. (Photo courtesy of Howard Brand.)

Chickamin. Meeting the Canadians there, I got the two Canadian ships fueled up and gone again, then pumped aboard enough fuel for one more trip.

In the meantime Ketchikan was putting together a full-blown rescue effort. The call was going out up and down the coast for air support, but if the weather closed in, it would take hours before really substantive help could arrive. U.S. Coast Guard cutter *Cape Romain* and Canadian patrol boat *Nanaimo* and later, Canadian fisheries patrol vessel *Laurier* were all underway to the Chickamin site, led by a handful of smaller boats from the Ketchikan Volunteer Rescue Squad. Even at the cutter's robust 20 knots, they would need most of a day to reach the camp at the mouth of the Chickamin, miles from the avalanche site. If anyone was going to provide real help to the mine, they had to do it by air, and do it now.

The two Canadians, and a large Coast Guard helicopter arrived back at the site within minutes of my return, creating something of an aerial traffic jam. The weather had deteriorated all morning to where it was barely flyable. Now with the confusion and poor visibility caused by blowing snow, the scene was becoming dangerous.

I had landed and was being loaded with a couple more people when the heavy rotors of the Coast Guard's HH52A started shaking the air. As the big bird started coming closer to the landing zone, the already heavy snow was blowing crazily. For the Coast Guard helicopter, my Hiller, the Canadian Hiller, and the Canadian Bell, visibility near the ground was becoming critical.

I lifted off to start back, but the snow was so thick I couldn't see anything so I set back down. In the meantime the Coast Guard made their landing and loaded a few more victims into their helicopter. Their bird was big enough to handle stretchers so the rescuers on the ground loaded them with some of the most seriously injured.

The big HH52A employed one pilot flying by instruments, and one pilot flying by his vision. Working together, they had a little better chance of being able to pick out a landmark and hover successfully. However, when they lifted off, they immediately lost their vision. Neither of the pilots was able to pick up sight of some land and get control of the helicopter. Flying on gut instinct they managed to point the helicopter away from the hill and get clear, but they never came back again.

By this time the weather was really grim up on the mountain, but the approaches were clear enough that Southeast Alaska's pilots turned out in force. The engineers at Grace Lake were cut off due to the terrible visibility, but at least the helicopters made it in. One entire working shift at the mine was underground at the time of the avalanche, and when they dug their way clear of the snow blocking their tunnel entrance, they became the front-line ground troops for the quickly-developing rescue effort.

By the time we got back to the river on about the third flight, helicopters were starting to come in. Arlo Livingston and Chuck Geisel had come in from Juneau. It had taken them about three hours to get down from Juneau, but they got there. Two bigger Canadian helicopters arrived, and before the day was over we had ten helicopters in the area, which was unbelievable.

No one among the fleet (with the possible exception of

One of the injured being flown out from Wolfe's cabin. (Photo courtesy of Howard Brand.)

Arlo) had any idea there were that many helicopters that close to the Granduc, but in typical Southeast Alaskan style, when serious trouble came up, everyone dropped what they were doing and came to help. The two Canadian Sikorsky's (an S-55 and an S-58) took over the heavy lifting of supplies and the evacuation of the most seriously injured, while the smaller helicopters focused on the walking wounded, fuel, and personnel transport into the mine.

With more helicopters flying and additional support on its way in from Ketchikan, a formal rescue started taking shape under the direction of the mining company. Thanks to the other pilots' rapid response, as of the third round-trip as much help was going up the mountain as were victims coming down. Of the 50 people buried in the avalanche, 20-some had been recovered alive so far, but there was real loss of life.

A special avalanche crew was brought in from Canada, and orders were given to not take anybody in unless they were authorized by the mining company. (The mining company later offered to pay for all the effort by the rescue teams.) Because of the severity of the situation, and the problems getting people into the site, the pilots had to make every trip count.

By the end of the first day, the first support boats had arrived, and river boat teams started working with wetsuit gear on to haul supplies closer to the mine. The big boats couldn't come anywhere close to the shallow mudflat that surrounded Old Man Wolfe's cabin, so small boats had to liter the gear onto the sandbars where the aircraft could pick it up. This was the busiest Old Man Wolfe's cabin ever had been.

Knowing that the big Sikorsky helicopters were coming, the sea arm of the rescue knew they would need a lot of extra aviation fuel. Thankfully the stream of boats coming out from Ketchikan were more than able to meet the demand. The *Cape Romain* arrived stocked with avgas, plus a doctor, and outboard motor fuel. In the end, the rescue had quite a surplus of avgas—barrels of fuel remained there for years afterward.

Governor Egan diverted the Alaska State ferry *Taku* to Stewart to act as a floating shelter for the injured, but because the weather was so severe, the passes between Stewart and the

Getting the survivors off the glacier was only half the battle. Stan Bishop (left) was part of the boat operation, unloading supplies to the beach, and transferring survivors to boats and aircraft at Wolfe's cabin. (Photo courtesy of Howard Brand.)

mine stayed cut off. Hundreds of beds, blankets, a commercial kitchen, and the ship's boats, all ended up in Stewart, wasted.

By now the news of the Granduc avalanche was making ripples on the national news wire, and reporters started showing up, trying to bum rides up onto the mountain. Several attempted to weasel their way in ahead of rescue workers, doctors, or loads of vitally needed equipment. Rather than try to help the rescuers, they were trying to make the rescuers help them at the expense of the injured on the mountain. If ever there was a low moment for the media in Southeast, this had to be one of them.

I had snapped pictures in the few minutes that we had blue sky up at the camp, and I had those pictures with me. They didn't show too much, but they did show some of the conditions, and these reporters were just giving us a terrible time. So I finally said, "Well, look, you guys, we can't take you in, but I've got a roll of film here," and I gave it to one of the reporters. Instantly other reporters swarmed around that reporter, like a pack of dogs thrown a single bone.

The story of the Granduc would blanket the news that night

up and down the West Coast, focusing attention both on Southeast, and the viability of helicopters for remote search and rescue operations like this one. With dozens of men lost, and many more badly injured, the Granduc would be recorded as one of the worst avalanche disasters in Alaska's modern history.

There were people from *Life* magazine that were just begging to get some information from us; it was a really hot item.

Howard Brand was the only other member of the rescue crew who had a camera. One of the *Life* representatives offered him $2,000 for his film, but he told them, "No, it belongs to the rescue squad."

The Granduc occupied the nation's attention for two days, until Malcolm X was assassinated. Then the reporters were all gone. Granduc was history.

When rescuing victims of an avalanche, time is critical. The compacted snow holds bodies fast—like so much icy cement—restricting the victim's ability to breathe, plus restricting the air volume available to him. If he wasn't crushed, the victim can often breathe for a while, drawing what little air remains in the snow around him. However, the heat of his breath melts the

Another picture of Stan Bishop and the boat crew, ferrying supplies from bigger boats anchored offshore. (Photo courtesy of Howard Brand.)

snow in front of the nose and mouth, forming an icy crust. As the victim continues to breathe, and more snow melts and refreezes, eventually the icy crust becomes a solid cap, blocking all air flow.

If the victim survives the initial crush of the snow, and the asphyxiating pressure, and can find an air pocket under a board or piece of debris, he finds himself locked inside tons of powdered ice, slowly freezing to death.

After half an hour, well over 50 percent of those buried are dead. After a day, 90 percent. Clarence Moore was discovered alive under the remains of the tool shed 24 hours after the avalanche, but now, three days had passed, and the bunkhouse that had been serving as a hospital was becoming a morgue.

According to Al Soucie, who had driven a tracked vehicle in from Stewart, whenever the bulldozer would come close to a body, the snow would look dark, almost black. When the rescuers saw dark snow, they would stop the Cat and dig with shovels, knowing a dead man was close.

I had landed the helicopter and was watching, and the Cat had just taken a pass to plow an area of snow, and these guys got all excited. Here was a pair of eyes blinking at them. The funereal mood disappeared, and rescuers leapt into action, overjoyed to find a survivor. His situation was critical, but discovering a survivor after 72 hours in the snow catapulted the entire rescue back into high gear.

Turns out that as the avalanche began to settle, the snow had rolled Finar Myllya up against a piece of plywood (ironically, part of the destroyed helipad). The plywood resisted the flow just enough to create a pocket of air, giving Myllya enough space to work his lungs, and a little extra air to breathe. A photo that would later appear in the October 1987 edition of the *New Alaskan* shows one of the Hillers landing on the exact spot where Myllya was buried. When recovered, Myllya said there was someone near him so the rescuers started digging frantically. They did eventually find Myllya's co-worker, well-separated from the shelter of the helipad and frozen solid.

He said time went by pretty fast, it was just sort of a daze.

Survivors waiting for a ride. Note the snow load on the little building in the background. (Photo courtesy of Howard Brand.)

He could hear nothing, but his biggest surprise was when they found him. Those were the first sounds he'd heard. He was immediately hustled on the big Canadian 107 Vertol that had come in, and Doc Wilson went in to Ketchikan Hospital with the guy.

Ketchikan General Hospital had used the last few days well, prepping their available treatments for hypothermia. The initial wave of survivors were starting to stabilize, freeing up some of their critical-care equipment when Myllya was flown directly to Ketchikan. Horribly frostbitten, Myllya's hands, lower arms, feet, and legs were all solid chunks of ice. The characteristic black color of frostbitten flesh covered his extremities, and if he didn't get serious help right away, gangrene infecting the dead flesh would quickly kill him.

Ketchikan General knew they needed to work a cold weather miracle of survival, and put the word out for a hyberbaric (compression) chamber like the ones used by divers. At the time, there were only two in North America, and the only one available was in Buffalo, New York. They filled the decompression chamber with nearly-pure oxygen, put Myllya in it, and as they raised the pressure inside, Myllya began to recover. Thanks to everyone's efforts, he survived the incident with the loss of just a few fingers and toes.

The two big Sikorskys were working back and forth on the rescue, moving huge amounts of cargo up and down the mountain. With dozens of other airships moving in and out of the area, the air was getting positively crowded.

During this heavy-lifting phase, one of the Sikorsky's broke squelch, calling out an engine failure—he was going down. If he couldn't get down out of the trees, the Sikorsky's blades hitting the heavy timber would likely make the entire ship explode. Frantically nursing their power into a sort of assisted autorotation, the pilots managed to get their bird down into a big meadow at the junction of the Leduc and the Chickamin Rivers. They'd lost a cylinder, which forced their emergency landing, but everything was okay. It was just a matter of getting a new cylinder installed, and they would be back on their way.

Recovering the rescue team from the glacier suffered from the same problems with weather. In order to help guide the pilots, buckets of oil were thrown onto the bonfires, providing a light, plus lots of smoke.

Eventually 19 bodies were loaded aboard a DC-3 for evacuation to Annette Island. More would come later, but this was most of the total. As the pilot built up speed for takeoff, his gear hit a puddle, spinning the aircraft out of control. No one was hurt, but the bodies had to be moved again, adding another indignity to an already difficult and grisly situation.

By the end of a week, the rescue and evacuation of the mine was winding down, letting everyone take stock of the situation. Granduc would later move their mining efforts to the other end of the site, hoping to avoid another such incident in the future.

At the same time, the miners began drilling a tunnel clear through the mountain to the Hyder side. When completed, they could remove the ore without crossing the U.S. border, and wouldn't have to go through customs. This also gave them an all-weather land route for bringing in supplies, and evacuating their injured in the future.

Later on I got to take a trip in through the mine, which was ten miles of tunnel from the Stewart side into the mine, and it was one of the most interesting experiences I ever had.

When the Granduc Mining Company came out with a letter to their stockholders, it stated that Granduc had taken care of everything during the rescue, providing the first helicopters to the scene, and generally overseeing all the rescue effort. This ruffled the feathers of a lot of people, but most wrote it off as a case of the head office not knowing the details.

But the people at the mining camp knew, and they appreciated what we did.

TREASURY DEPARTMENT
UNITED STATES COAST GUARD

ADDRESS REPLY TO:
COMMANDER
17TH COAST GUARD DISTRICT
P.O. BOX 2831
JUNEAU, ALASKA

o
• 5720
1 MAR 1965
Serial 394

Mr. Ken Eichner
TEMSCO Helicopters, Inc.
P. O. Box 57
Ketchikan, Alaska

Dear Mr. Eichner:

During the recent disaster at the Granduc Mine, your organization participated in the rescue operations which resulted in the successful evacuation of over 120 survivors.

The untiring efforts of all participating personnel were in keeping with the long standing tradition to render assistance to persons in distress or imminent peril.

May I express my most sincere appreciation to you and the personnel of your employ whose assistance contributed immeasurably to the success of the overall operation.

Sincerely,

GEORGE D. SYNON
Rear Admiral, U. S. Coast Guard
Commander, Seventeenth Coast Guard District

Sweeping vistas were just one of many benefits of doing work with the Geological Survey. For a rockhound like me, working Mt. Saint Elias with the geologists was a thrill.

Chapter 8,
TEMSCO's Early Work

By 1965 TEMSCO had more internal problems. Bob Young sold out and took our 180 seaplane 93 Queen with him. That left me as the only pilot. Earl said he would get his license so we sent him south to Pacific Aeromotive, Inc. in Burbank for helicopter training. His instructor was one of the original Whirly-Girls, Loretta Foy, who was an excellent pilot. She taught Earl to fly the little Hughes 269-A which they used for instruction. Earl acquired his helicopter license and experience in the little 269 and came back to Ketchikan ready to fly.

I got Earl all checked out in the 12E and sent him to Petersburg, where we had established a hangar. I had been running back and forth between Petersburg and Ketchikan working in both places. Earl did a great job up there and eliminated a lot of my wasted time.

Now we had to buckle down and try to work our way out of debt. I felt all alone—all decisions were on my shoulders. I was not experienced in hiring pilots, bidding jobs, or dealing with bankers. TEMSCO had a board of directors, but they were less experienced than I was so they rubber-stamped anything I wanted to do—right or wrong.

There was not much to running the company with just the two of us flying, and Elsie McGowan who agreed to be our secretary, office girl, and bookkeeper. Our biggest weakness was maintenance. We had two mechanics, Wendell Jones and Gary Daubersmith, who were good with airplanes but not experienced with helicopters.

We needed another helicopter so we went down to talk to Okanogan Helicopters about buying one of theirs. Turns out they wouldn't finance us and neither would our bank. Somehow Del

Smith of Evergreen Helicopters got wind of our need, so to help us out, he offered to buy a 12E and sell it to us direct. He would carry the financing so we could pay him instead of the bank. With Del's help, we had the aircraft we needed.

Odd Jobs

Earl and I were working hard to nail down any job we could, so we bid on some unusual things. We bid on a spray job up in Sitka and got it. We rigged the helicopter up for spraying, and I took my son Dan with me as a ground crew. We put on our wet suits and flew the helicopter on skid gear up to Sitka. If we had had an emergency en route, the helicopter would have sunk immediately so the wet suits were really a good safety precaution—if a bit silly-looking. We completed the spray job successfully and came back in the same manner.

When Jay Snodderly moved to his house on the beach off of Pond Reef Road, he asked me to move his piano for him. It was very difficult to get to the property, and of course the road didn't go down that far. It was my first piano move, and he said I did a good job and didn't charge him too much—that makes a happy customer. After that I moved several pianos.

Laying Wire

Ketchikan Public Utilities used our helicopters wherever they could. As long as we weren't in a populated area, using the helicopter was a lot faster and a lot less trouble than using their truck to pull line. We rigged up a carrier so we could carry a spool of wire under the helicopter easily. The KPU men would grab one end of the wire and hold it while I lifted it up and laid it over the power pole. Then I would hover right down the power poles and lay the wire out over the cross-arms so all they had to do was climb up and hook the wires onto the insulators and sag them properly.

To do this, we took the floats off and put the lighter skids on so the helicopter could lift more weight. We were lifting close to the maximum—about 900 pounds of wire on a reel plus the carrier. When we were out near Mud Bay on South Tongass Highway, the KPU men pulled out a little extra line and hooked the carrier on to the cargo hook. I lifted up to get the wire laid on the first cross-arm, and they gave me the high sign to go. I

KPU staff hook up a roll of wire to the Hiller in Mud Bay. That's me in the cockpit.

had just started to go forward when the line came up tight. Somebody had goofed in the wrapping of the line. There was a knot in the line that cinched up the reel. I was just barely able to stop the helicopter without being tipped over on my nose onto the highway. I backed up and set the reel down on the ground. The guys were very chagrined; they apologized all over the place. They got the line untangled, and I started out again, very gingerly, expecting it to come up tight again, but it worked that time. I laid miles of wire this way.

Setting Power Poles

Southeast Electric had the contract to put in power poles and string wire from the Beaver Falls power plant to town. They hired me to help do the job. After the right of way had been cleared, they dug holes in the ground and put in two 55-gallon barrels with the ends cut out to act as a sort of socket for the power poles. I flew barrels of gravel in to firm up the holes, then

Erecting power poles was a fun job for a helicopter pilot. It involved lots of unusual loads and precision flying.

started erecting the poles themselves.

The poles were staged at Saxman Terminal where I had a clear area to take off with them. Some were rigged with cross-arms, and some were not, depending upon the guessed weight. We found that on a rainy day the poles weighed much more, but most of the work was done in the winter in freezing weather. I had the door off of the helicopter and was dressed so heavily I could hardly move. Between fuelings I would tap my thermos bottle for a drink of hot coffee. It was fun work.

There was nothing between the Saxman staging area and the water so, on some occasions, I actually drug the pole in the water for a ways until I could get up enough speed to lift it. I would fly to the next hole and start an approach trying to bullseye the barrel hole without having to jockey around. There were two men at the hole who would help a little when they had to. As soon as the pole bottomed out, I would hold it erect until the men could tie off the three guy lines that were already on the pole.

One pole weighed nearly 1600 pounds. That was too heavy. It was located up behind the Coast Guard Base, but it was on the wrong side of the hot power lines. I was able to pick up one end at a time and move it. I finally got it in a position to try to erect it. When it was nearly up, it slid into the hole pulling me with it until it hit the bottom of the hole—about a six-foot drop. That was a thrill!

Wrecked Helicopter Recovery

I was sitting in the office on a blustery day with heavy snow squalls and nice weather in between when we got a radio call from Earl, saying, "I'm upside down on Johnson Creek on the Iskut River. Nobody's hurt, but I need help to get out of here." So I hopped in 52 Victor and took off for Johnson Creek. The shortest route to Earl was north to Bradfield Canal and up the river past our Bradfield claims to High Pass into the Craig River, down the Craig River to the Iskut to Johnson Creek. All went well till I got to High Pass where I got caught in a snowstorm. I landed near the top of the pass and waited an hour before the snow stopped. Then I cleared the snow off the helicopter and was on my way. When I arrived, sure enough, there was Earl's helicopter upside down and pretty well torn up. I took the two passengers back to Wrangell then went back to get Earl.

He explained to me what had happened. He got caught in a sudden snowstorm and needed to land. We had always told him to pick an object that you could see, like a little tree or something, and land just as close to it as possible so when the wind starts to blow the snow around, you still have the tree in sight, and you won't lose your bearings and crash. You'll be able to see that it's stationary, and you can make your landing on it. Well, Earl chose the cut bank of the river to get up close to, and when he got close to the cut bank, the rotor wash started blowing snow up the cut bank, recirculating it around until he couldn't see anything. Earl had actually set down—there were imprints of his floats where he had very lightly touched. All he had to do was put the collective down, and he'd have been there. But he'd lost all visibility, and out of the corner of his eye, he saw a little bit of sunshine. He turned toward the sunshine and started a rather fast takeoff not realizing how far he had tipped himself forward. In the process he dragged the left float in the snow. The straps on the front of the float broke, and the float rolled underneath, which caused the helicopter to flip upside down. All the

64 Victor upside down on Johnson Creek, on the Iskut. Earl got out okay, but the helicopter was a mess.

imprints of the float dragging and the original landing were all still plain on the snow, so I took pictures of them from the air so we could talk about it later.

Recovering the helicopter turned into quite a little fiasco. The blades were gone, and the tail boom was chopped. Any time the helicopter has an accident like that, it means a total overhaul of all the machinery. The bubble was broken, but the floats were still okay. Now it was a matter of getting it out of the Iskut River and to a repair shop.

We didn't know much about the helicopter business or the overhauling of helicopters, but I was bound and determined we were going to get the wrecked helicopter out before the ice broke up and took it down the river. I got Johnny Minnick, who was an airplane mechanic working for us at the time and Don Moore, whom we were breaking in as a helicopter pilot, to come with me to salvage 64 Victor. Well, not being helicopter mechanics, we really didn't know what to do. The helicopter was lying on its side. We knew we had to take the engine off because I couldn't lift the helicopter with the engine on it. We finally got the torn blades off the rotor system and most of the engine unhooked from the helicopter, but darkness was coming on so it was time to go in. We jumped in the helicopter, I hit the starter, and it just made a slight groan. It wouldn't do anything.

Johnny and Don just stood there in a daze and looked at me. I said, "Hey, fellows, we have to get those tents pitched, and get in them. We've got sleeping bags and everything we need, but we have to get those tents pitched before it gets dark. In a short while it's going to be so dark we won't even be able to find the tents." We managed to get two tents pitched. With the emergency gear from both helicopters, we had two mummy bags and a tarp for each of us.

To make the Hillers adaptable for our kind of operation where there was always a possibility of being stuck overnight, we had remodeled the back cushions of the seat so they would hold three mummy bags and three tarps. We kept snowshoes tied on the engine mounts, and in the baggage box mounted on the tail boom we kept a tent, ax, fire starters, first aid kit, funnel, and a Ford wrench to open barrels with. On the floats we had a fuel pump tied down. All this came in handy. Bad weather and mechanical problems were fairly common.

We got into our sleeping bags. It was 30 below that night with the wind blowing, which put the chill factor down lower yet. I think I was awake all night long just trying to keep warm. Come daylight, I jumped up and got the little one-burner gas stove that we carried with our emergency gear going. I put some ice in a little can and started melting some water. We also had a little tiny two-cycle engine with a little generator on it that I carried for this kind of a cold start. I held it over the heat for a little bit, and I got it started. With the generator, I was able to put what we called a dipstick heater, a 75-watt tube heater, in the engine oil tank, and to use a little heat lamp for heating the carburetor to get the helicopter engine warmed up before trying to start the engine.

I went over to the wrecked helicopter and got the undamaged battery out and put it in my helicopter. About that time an airplane came overhead looking for us. It was Chuck Traylor out of Wrangell. We tried to talk to him on the radio. I don't know if he ever got the message through or not, but he could see we were all okay. I tried to tell him our batteries were dead, and if we didn't show up in a few hours, we were in a lot of trouble.

After we had warmed the oil and the carburetor and exchanged batteries, I was ready to try a start. I rolled the throttle three times to prime the engine and then hit the starter button. It groaned a bit, and then bang—it started. That was a great relief. We flew into Wrangell, landed, and rejoiced.

A couple days later we went up the river and finished the job. It took about three trips to bring all the pieces out, but we successfully salvaged the helicopter and shipped it to Ketchikan. After talking to the insurance company, we sent the helicopter down to Okanogan Helicopters in Vancouver, B.C. for repair.

TEMSCO Mechanics

My two mechanics didn't see any future in TEMSCO Helicopters, and they departed so I hired Johnny Minnich, who had just gotten his A&P license and could sign off the work we had to do on the helicopters. With summer's work beginning, I

Bill Hornbaker (left) and Stan Maplesden coach me down for a landing on one of the dollies we used to roll helicopters in and out of the TEMSCO hangar.

knew I had to go hunting for a real helicopter mechanic. I had already had too many mechanical emergencies, and if I was going to make TEMSCO successful, I had to find some good men.

My greatest inspiration in the helicopter business was Del Smith, who was now operating eight Hillers, so I headed for Evergreen Helicopters in McMinnville, Oregon. Del Smith and Curley Barrick were a great help to me. They gave me a list of all the Hiller mechanic employees who had not moved to the East coast when Hiller sold his company to Fairchild Aircraft

Company. Curley had worked in the factory with most of them, and he strongly recommended Bill Hornbaker. I needed a really top-notch Hiller mechanic, and these names were some of the best men in the business. After a few phone calls I took off for San Francisco to meet with Bill. He was interested, but his wife Arlene had doubts. I suggested they come up to Ketchikan and see what they thought of our company. At that time we were working out of our little Quonset hut hangar. We had two helicopters and a third one being rebuilt in Canada.

They arrived in town on a nice sunny day so I took them out fishing for silver salmon. Arlene hooked on to a real good one. I think that made their decision—they accepted my offer and moved to Ketchikan with their two little boys (Roy and Russell) and their dog.

Engine Failure

Just as Bill Hornbaker got to town, Earl called me and said 52 Victor was acting up with an occasional miss. Hornbaker was ready to go to work so we flew to Petersburg. Bill checked the helicopter in every way and said it was okay. I took it out for an hour and did everything possible to prove it was okay. Earl was happy so we went home.

On a sunny afternoon the next weekend we got a call saying Earl was upside down on the Stikine River. Nobody was hurt. The engine had quit, and Earl had attempted a forced landing in the snow. With his autorotation capabilities he didn't think he could slide on the snow, so he tried to make a full-stop landing. In doing so the heels of the helicopter hit first which would bounce the blades down—chopping the tail boom and, of course, flipping the helicopter over. So there we were out of commission again.

With a total rebuild on his hands, Bill needed help so he contacted Glenn Elliott, another Hiller mechanic, and Glenn, Peggy and their two children (Larry and Terry) soon moved to Ketchikan. Now we had two of the best helicopter mechanics in the world working for us. What a blessing!

When the rebuild of 52V got under way, they found a gasket on the air cleaner had not been glued in properly during the

I can't say enough about the value of good mechanics, particularly men like Bill Hornbaker and Glenn Elliott. Because of our remote location we had to do all our own maintenance—including total rebuilds of our wrecked birds.

previous rebuild. It had slipped into the throat of the dual carburetors and finally, after riding for a long time between the two throats, it slipped into one throat and choked the engine out.

Shooting Wolves for Bounty

We were bound and determined to make TEMSCO work so we did every kind of job imaginable. We figured out a way to do any little job that came along. The government had a $50 bounty on wolves, and I got a permit from Fish and Game to hunt wolves with the helicopter. Our charter rate was $110 an hour so it would take two wolves and a fraction per hour to pay for the helicopter. Since I had trapped wolves quite a bit before, I had a good idea where we might find some.

One morning after a good snowstorm my son Danny and I took off on a wolf-hunting trip. We stopped at Twelve-Mile Arm where Johnny Stacker had a cabin, and asked if he wanted to go wolf hunting. Johnny was a trapper in the wintertime and a ship's carpenter for Wards Cove Cannery the rest of the time.

Working on mountainsides to support mining exploration often meant landing our Hillers on makeshift helipads like this one.

Well, Johnny was elated to go with us. A little way up the Harris River we spotted five wolves. We were able to get three of them right away. We chased another one up the river and got it. Then we headed on up to Klawock Lake, and right in the middle of the lake were a whole bunch of wolves—25 at least. We took a run at the wolves with the helicopter, and we picked out one wolf. Danny nailed it right off the bat, but the other wolves took off like crazy going all directions, and we only got one wolf out of the whole bunch.

Later we figured out what we did wrong. Anytime we tried to cut the wolves off from the trees, which were their protection, they'd do anything to get away from us. We found out the only way to do it was to make a nice easy approach right straight into the wolves. A few of them would retreat, but the leader and a couple others would generally sort of challenge us and stand out. We were able to be more successful thereafter.

Shortly after we got back into town, we had a call from Fish and Game. They said, "Hey, there are some people in the Fish and Game who are making a big noise about this hunting wolves with a helicopter. They said there's no way the pilot can shoot them—he's too busy flying the helicopter. So you've got unlicensed guys in the helicopter shooting wolves." We said, "Well, if that's the case, give us some more licenses." So we got permits for Ellsworth Jensen, Don Moore, William Putvin, Bill Pattison, Dr. James Mortensen, John Staker, W. A. Hawkins, Bill Hornbaker, Ernest DeBoer, and my son Dan. Soon after we got the permits, the Fish and Game really put a stop to it. No more hunting wolves with a helicopter. And they fired Loren Croxton for giving us a permit.

This was all instigated by internal politics in the Fish and Game. I believe it was a break for Loren in the long run because he was a good biologist, and he went to work for the federal Fish and Wildlife which was a preferred job over the one he had. He is retired now and lives in Petersburg.

Prior to this we always carried a rifle in a little rack just behind the back seat in the helicopter. My pet one was a little .30 caliber semiautomatic military carbine that had a little clip that held about 15 shells in it. Most of our flying was with government people so we would have someone from either the Fish and Game or the Forest Service with us. They always wanted to sit in the right hand seat so they could unzip the window and shoot if we saw a wolf. Nearly everybody in the Fish and Game and the Forest Service had been able to shoot a wolf out of the helicopter, and of course they had it skinned and mounted and hung on their walls.

On one occasion I was surveying streams with Carl Rozier, a Fish and Game biologist at the time. As we came around a corner, we spotted a great big buck deer knee-deep in the water and a wolf standing on the bank waiting for him to come out. The deer had a big piece of hide hanging down from his hind ham where the wolf had nipped him. I didn't have my rifle with me—all I had was my .357 Magnum revolver. I handed it to Carl. He zipped the window down and nailed the wolf in one shot, which was remarkable for a handgun shot from the air.

Wolf hunting was a lot of fun for us, and when we were flying alone with the helicopter, so often we'd see wolves, and then the real problem came, how do you shoot one by yourself? The only thing you can do is land as close as you can. Well, you can imagine landing close to a wolf running probably 25 miles an hour, and by the time you get out of the helicopter, get your gun ready, and have the helicopter secure enough so you can step off of it, the wolf is going to be a fair distance out. So many times I've tried it, and the wolf was out of sight by the time I got ready.

On one occasion on the Unuk River, there was one lone wolf out in the middle of the frozen river. The snow was deep enough that he couldn't run as fast as normal so I was able to land and shoot the wolf. It hangs on the wall in my son's house. It was a small wolf, but it was a beautiful one because it had its winter fur. All the grey wolves on the mainland have a little dash of orange right around their ears—a telltale sign of the mainland Alaskan wolves.

Fuel Caches

The Hiller had such a short range that most of the time when we got to our location we had barely enough fuel to get back without doing any work. In order to do our customers justice, we set up over 100 fuel caches all over the area. We had a map with marks on it and a logbook to keep track of the number of full barrels and empty barrels in every cache. These caches were lifesavers when we needed them. They also were a big benefit to our customers because we could do their work without having to send another helicopter out with fuel. Their work was uninterrupted.

Later with the longer range and the faster speed of the Hughes helicopters and with all the environmental rules, the Forest Service made us remove all of our caches from the boonies—at least all they could find. The caches are all cleaned up now, and pilots depend on more permanent caches consisting of good fuel tanks with diaper protection for spills, good filters, and power fuel pumps.

Canadian Forest Fires

We were always pleased when the Canadians called us for help fighting forest fires. That was big money for us, with all the

Doing forestry work and water drops on fires helped keep our Hiller 12Es busy. This one carries a fertilizer bucket.

hours we could possibly fly. We jumped at the chance when we were called to go into Meziadin Lake in British Columbia to fight forest fires. This was my first big forest fire, and it was interesting and exciting. It was new country, and the only navigational equipment we had was our compass. It was really a matter of following a crude map of the area and following river valleys and lakes. Somehow I was able to do it without getting lost. The more you flew up there the better knowledge you had of the country, and the easier it was to keep yourself oriented.

Helicopters were used to take crews out and drop them off in certain areas. In some places they built heliports, and other places we landed in little meadows that had been cleared off with a chainsaw. We delivered hoses, tools, and food supplies to keep the camps going, and we made sure the crew didn't get trapped in the forest fire.

On one occasion I was ordered to pick up a crew that was being overrun by a fire. The fire was not fast-moving so we had plenty of time to do it—but without the helicopter they would have been in real trouble.

Water Drops

On another occasion the Forest Service wanted me to go up the Unuk River to do some water drops. There had been a lightning strike up there, and they had a pretty good little fire going. We bought a Canadian patent for converting a 55-gallon barrel into a water bucket and had just rigged up a brand-new bucket. It was the only one we had in Ketchikan. The new bucket was hooked on the helicopter, and I took off to fight the fire.

One of the problems we found in doing water drops was that when you land in a river, the bucket immediately washes downstream. It's just like an anchor when it's in the water so you have to dip the bucket in the river and then move downstream with it so you stay right over the bucket. That way you can lift it up without getting yourself all cocked off to one side, which could create an accident very easily.

When I arrived at the fire, I dipped the bucket in the river. As I made my first lift, I lost the bucket. One of the cables on the bucket hadn't been tightened, and the whole thing fell into the river. Much to my dismay, I dropped no water on the fire that day.

Later on we used our water buckets in all the forest fires we fought. Dropping water was a lot of fun because it was a precision thing. You tried to hit the fire in the hot spot, and you didn't dare go too slow or the wind from the helicopter would fan the fire. You had to do it just right—drop the water and not create a draft. It was really precise flying. The fact is most of the cargo work we did was precision work, and we got better at it all the time.

Kasaan Fire

One summer day the Coast Guard had one of their 90-footers out, and they were trying out their guns, shooting against a rock cliff over at Kasaan. They didn't realize that the explosives were pretty hot, and they accidentally started a small forest fire on top of the cliff. They called in their Coast Guard helicopter, and the Forest Service called TEMSCO in. We established a working zone for fighting the forest fire and started moving in the camp, equipment, and supplies. We had a couple of helicopters there hauling loads in, and the Coast Guard was trying to haul loads with their hoist, but they weren't doing very well. We'd make three trips to their one, and finally we asked them if they couldn't just let us haul it in since we could do it a lot faster. They accepted our offer and went on their way.

The next morning it was foggy on the hill, and we still had a lot of work to do. We figured we could work our way in through the fog, and we started loading up.

Going in with the helicopter with a gross load, you can hover along underneath the fog and do pretty well as long as you can see 50 or 100 feet ahead of you. You can creep along as long as you keep your eyes open so you don't find a tree where you don't expect it.

Of course we were always trying to do too much for our customers, and we were always hauling more than we should have. If we could get off the ground with it, we'd go. Well, in this case I came up the hill underneath the fog with this over-gross load. There was nothing but brush and scrub trees, maybe 10 to 15 feet high, and no open areas till we got pretty well up to the top of the hill. I slowed down to try to handle the fog, but the fog got a little thicker, and I had to slow down a little more. I went out of translational lift, out of flight back into hover, and I didn't have enough power to hold the hover. I dropped the collective, regained my RPM, and shoved the nose forward. Barely missing the bushes, I was able to squeeze away with it. Now I had no choice—I had to go a little faster than I wanted to into the fog until I got into the camp where there was room enough to land. This really taught me a rude lesson: You don't overload under those conditions.

Silvis Lake Rescue

One snowy day during spring avalanche time, we had an emergency call to the Silvis Lake area. Ketchikan Public Utilities built a power system there consisting of a power house at both the upper lake and the lower lake which controlled the flow of water down to the power plant at salt water. There was a road around the south side of the lower Silvis Lake that had been used for the construction of the dam and the power plant.

A crew of three had gone in to work on the power site, and

Nine Lives of an Alaska Bush Pilot

they took a little dog with them. Generally we flew them in to the site, but this time they decided to go around the edge of the lake on snowshoes. On the way back they crossed a slide area, and an avalanche struck. Two of the guys managed to get out of it, but Billy Spears and the dog were caught in the avalanche and were pushed down into the lake. They never did find the dog, but Billy's feet were sticking out so they dashed down to rescue him. Later Billy told of the experience of being covered up with snow and realizing he was getting close to the lake. He could see the water so he pushed his hands down trying to push himself back. Instead he pushed a hole to the water. The water started coming up around him, and it was going to drown him. In the meantime the guys got to him and hauled him out by his feet.

Billy was pretty banged up, cold, and wet. If they couldn't get him warmed up, he would go into shock and die—either of shock or hypothermia. It was a desperate situation, and they called for an emergency evacuation. The Coast Guard had left with their helicopter from Annette, but they couldn't find the place so KPU called me. I dashed up there with 52 Victor. I knew the area well because I'd done a lot of work there. It was snowing like heck, but with the window zipped down I was able to fly at 20 to 25 miles an hour at treetop level, and I was able to get in to the lake and right to Billy Spears. When we loaded him into the helicopter, he was in a state of shock but able to talk. We flew Billy right straight to the hospital.

This was a real close call—about as close as you could come. Can you visualize somebody being trapped in the snow and then having water creeping up around him, knowing that it was going to drown him in a few minutes? What a horrible experience. Billy is still active in KPU, and he is one of the nicer guys I know.

Quick Rescue

October 2, 1964, the *Ketchikan Daily News* published a little article that said "Two young Ketchikan Pulp Company boom men lost in the mountains while hunting yesterday were rescued by helicopter today. Fred Rufus, 21, and Jimmy Benson, 20. They were rescued at George Inlet in the White River country before noon today by Kenny Eichner and his trusty helicopter." It went on to say, "Eichner, sensing where the missing hunters were, went almost directly to them. He was gone less than an hour from the hangar."

Moving Boats

The Forest Service and Fish and Game were always moving boats around, and we found that if the boat wasn't too heavy, we could hook a line onto the center of the bow stem and lift the boat up in the air. When we started moving forward, it would go through the air just like it would in the water, only it would be a little more nose high. We landed the boat while we were still flying 20 to 30 miles ahead by touching the bottom of the boat on the water and then punching it off. It would go scooting along the water and stop. Then we would use our hover cushion to blow it into the beach so the crew could pick it up. It was a pretty good way to move boats around.

First Rides

Lots of people got their first airplane ride with me, and now lots of people were getting their first helicopter ride. In those days I liked to hover up to the top of a tall spruce tree and touch it with the HF antenna on the front of the helicopter. To this day there are still lots of people I take out for their first helicopter ride. It's kind of nice to have somebody come up and say, "Yeah, you gave me my first airplane ride," I guess that's rewarding in a subtle way.

Public Relations

In those early days helicopter pilots tended to show off a little, and I guess I was no exception. Passengers sometimes asked, "What happens if your engine quits?" I would say, "I'll show you," and just chop the engine off and go into an autorotation—sometimes to the water, sometimes to a river, whatever it might be. Later on we didn't allow things like that to happen because there's always a chance of an accident, and that's not a very wise thing to be doing.

One time we were sitting at about 2000 feet on the top of a ridge in the middle of a valley, and a storm was coming up the valley. I was faced into it, and visibility was getting close to zero up forward, but backwards it was okay. I rounded up the crew I was working with, got them in the helicopter, and fired it up. I lifted it off, flew off backwards, made a pedal turn, and chopped the power into autorotation. The visibility was going down, and I had to get to the bottom of the valley.

I hadn't told my passengers what I was going to do, and it scared them half to death. They weren't too happy with me. I learned something important—don't scare your passengers. If you've got to do some hairy maneuver like that, you had better forewarn your passengers.

Barren Island Light

In December of 1965, a Coast Guard lieutenant named Ralph Yetka came out to TEMSCO and asked us if it was possible to haul some batteries out to Barren Island, which is a little rock about 30 miles south of Ketchikan. The light on the island was out, and the Coast Guard had been down there, but the water was so rough they couldn't get on the rock. It was taking them more time and costing them more money to have that big ship stand by. Ralph was very pleased that we could do this so he and his helper brought the batteries out, and we loaded them on the baggage racks of the old Hiller.

We flew down and landed on Barren Island. Ralph and the seaman thought they would have to climb up the 15- or 20-foot tower with the batteries, but I said, "Just get one guy up there, and set the battery on the cargo rack float. I'll hover up there, and he can just set it right off." I hovered alongside the tower, and they were able to pick the batteries off the cargo rack and install them. In nothing flat they were all done with their job and back home at a minimum cost to them. After that we got quite a little bit of Coast Guard work.

This was Ralph's first helicopter flight, and it got him interested in aviation. Later on I'll tell more about Ralph, who turned out to be one of our best pilots and worked very faithfully for us until tragedy struck.

Long Distance Parts Delivery

The cable-laying ship *Long Line* called in to its office in Ketchikan requesting some parts while repairing the underwater telephone cables between Seattle and Alaska. It seems the Russians had been dragging in the area, and they had hooked onto the lines and broken them. In fact when the crew got the cable up, they could see that the Russians had cut a chunk of the line off so they could take it back home to show their engineers what kind of underwater cables we had perfected in the United States.

The *Long Line* was about 25 miles offshore of Cape Chacon, which was within the range of my Hiller, so I said, "Sure, I can take the parts out." I took a little extra fuel with me just in case, and I flew out there and located the *Long Line*. They had a nice heliport so I was able to land easily. They loved to have company so they took me aboard and showed me all around the ship. The cook had a great big lemon meringue pie that I got a taste of too. Those trips were always fun for me.

Canoe Rescue

Another day in the spring some local kids, the Antonsen girls, had spent the night across the bay on the beach of Gravina Island. They hadn't tied up their canoe, and when the tide came in, the canoe got loose. When I flew by with the helicopter, they were jumping up and down waving their arms. I could see what their problem was so I went in to Peninsula Point, unloaded my load, and went back out to see if I could rescue the canoe for them.

Just about the time I got there, a 30-foot pleasure boat with three people on it had grabbed the canoe and was taking off with it. I hovered the helicopter right in front of the boat and pointed at the canoe. They took off going as fast as they could go. I caught up to them again and hovered and kept pointing at the canoe. They just went inside and shut the window so I hovered right in front of them where they'd almost have to run over me and kept pointing at the canoe. I think they were trying to abscond with the canoe, but they finally got the message and let it loose. Then I went over and picked up one of the girls on the beach and took her over to where she could get a skiff and go rescue her canoe. It kind of ticked me off to see those guys trying to run off with her canoe.

Changing 300-Foot Tower Light

One day Southeast Electric's Bill Lattin called me and said, "We've got to change the light on the KTKN tower. It's a 300-foot tower, and we need to remove the light from the top of it. The light weighs about 100 pounds so it's not that easy to handle. We wondered if you could lift it off with a helicopter." I

All this for a light bulb. Taking the light OFF wasn't a problem, but putting it back ON, now that was tricky.

responded, "Sure, I think I can do that." He said, "We'll send Rocky Baird to climb up the tower and get the light loosened up. He will take the sling up, and you can drop a line down, hook on to it, and lift it off."

I had old 64 Victor that time, and when I got there Rocky was already up on the tower. I flew up alongside the tower until I reached the top of it. I stayed in fairly close proximity where it was easy to judge my position and got above the tower. I had about a 25-foot line hanging underneath the helicopter with a hook on it. It was swinging all over the place, but I finally managed to stabilize it enough, and looking over the side I was able to see Rocky well enough to give him the line. He hooked it on to the light and gave me the high sign to go. I lifted the light off and took it down to a safe landing area.

Then they said, "We want you to put it back up there tomorrow," and I said, "Boy, I don't know about that. I don't know whether I can do it or not. Let me know when you're ready." So the next day they gave me a call. It was ready, and I thought real hard. I knew there was no way I could tie the light on a line, hover over the top, and give it to Rocky. It would have been physically impossible for me to do it with the Hiller and not the best place for Rocky to be on top of the tower with the helicopter hovering over him. Then I got a bright idea. I was flying from the left side of the helicopter, and I could put a counterbalance on the right side of the helicopter so the helicopter would be in balance and put the light on my side so I could almost touch it. Then I could hover up to the top of the tower, lean against the tower, and let Rocky pick the light off. Rocky would be in a little a cage at the top of the tower. I figured this way I would have good control, and my only concern would be holding the helicopter against the tower. We decided to try it.

I hovered up and leaned against the top of the tower with the helicopter. Rocky reached over, grabbed the light, and set it down in his little cage. He gave me the high sign to go, and I took off. Well, much to Rocky's surprise, and I didn't know it until later, I'd been leaning against the tower hard enough that I'd bent it over quite a bit. The minute I left, the tower swayed back and forth with Rocky hanging on for dear life hoping the tower wouldn't go down. The tower stayed up, and he got the

Bob Baade with a bag of trout ready to be released.

light up all right. Rocky had the ride of his life.

Just to show you that fate works in funny ways, a year later in a little windstorm, that tower fell down right across buildings and everything else. Nobody was hurt, but it destroyed the tower, and I often wondered if I had any part in damaging it. Everybody thought it was just crystallization of the bolts, and one of those freak things that just happens.

Planting Fish

I always enjoyed flying Bob Baade around planting rainbow trout and grayling. You felt like you had accomplished something when four years later you checked the lake and found it loaded with big fish. Bob enthusiastically helped with all aspects of the program—even on his day off.

The Fish and Game people wanted to try a planting of mature sockeye salmon. The salmon were caught in Hugh Smith Lake and were to be transported to Bakewell Lake in the Quadra-Smeaton Bay area. They rigged up a tank to haul the fish in that was near my maximum load. They filled it full of water and dumped about 50 sockeye in the tank with something in the water to drug them a little. When I arrived at Bakewell Lake, I set the tank down in the stream at the head of the lake. Lyle Simpson was there to spill the tank of fish into the river. Much to our dismay half of the fish appeared dead. I parked the helicopter and dashed into the river to help Lyle resuscitate the salmon by grabbing them by the tail and wiggling them into the current forcing water through their gills. We ended up with very few dead fish. We managed to plant several hundred spawning salmon. A fish ladder had been built at salt water to try to introduce salmon to a new spawning grounds where only trout existed.

Palma Bay

In the fall of 1966 Wallace McGregor, a geologist for Cypress Minerals, wanted to go up to Palma Bay on the edge of the Gulf of Alaska, just past Cape Spencer to do two weeks of prospecting. I was always tickled to get jobs like this, even though it was really a bad time of the year. In the latter part of September, it rained steady up there, just poured. It was a fairly long trip, and it was a good way to break in a new pilot. Don Moore had just gotten his helicopter rating and needed to build time so I let him fly the helicopter up, and I flew the airplane. We met on the big lake at Palma Bay. Don flew the airplane back, and I stayed and did the job.

It was kind of a miserable job. Wally's funds weren't too good so I had to sleep in my little one-man tent. It was pouring down rain, and the tent would sweat—it seemed like I was wet all the time. The job went on pretty well though. We did a lot of recon on Mt. Saint Elias as high as we could work the helicopter trying to find mineral stains.

We found part of an old glacier camp on the Brady Glacier. Some nice nickel deposits were located there, but it's now in a park monument so it will never be mined.

There were a lot of bear in the area, and one of the geologists had a big German shepherd he always took with him in the helicopter. On one occasion we were coming into Palma Bay from down the coast a ways, and the dog was sitting up in the bubble when he saw a couple of big bear. I thought, "I'll just show these guys a good close look at the bear." We went down to harass this bear a little bit, and when we got close the dog went wild. He jumped forward, and the helicopter started to shake and vibrate. I didn't know what was the matter so I immediately got away

Palma Bay's spectacularly rugged coast.

from the bear so the dog would calm down. As the dog mellowed out, so did the helicopter so I didn't think too much of it.

The trip was soon over, and Lloyd Roundtree had flown fuel in to us with his Beaver. I wanted to get home in one day so I slung a barrel of gas under me and flew as long as I could on a tank of gas. Then I landed in the muskeg and pumped my tank full again. I didn't quite use all of the gas so I hauled the barrel to the second stop. Every once in a while the helicopter would get those shakes. I'd get up and look at the rotor system, and I couldn't figure it out. When I got back to town, I said, "Earl, I wish you'd go fly that helicopter a little bit and see if you think there's something wrong with it. Every once in a while it gets to shaking pretty bad." Earl and the mechanics looked it all over, and Earl went out and flew it. He didn't have any trouble with it shaking, but he said, "Let's try it again." He took it out again, and this time he said, "Yeah, there is something wrong." So one of the mechanics got up on the rotor system and discovered that the lock nut on one of the drag struts had never been tightened up. Over the course of quite a few hours, the drag strut had shaken loose and was moving back and forth. It was right on the edge of being a failure, and it could very easily have caused a catastrophic accident.

I think in learning to fly the helicopter the hardest thing was to determine when something was wrong and what it was. There were so many little hidden tricks and secrets as to what to look for and what might be going wrong that it was a learning curve all the time. Now the systems are managed so well that after you get a good hundred-hour or a good annual, you don't have anything to worry about. It's a pretty rare day that something extra crops up. But in the learning days things weren't that efficient, and there were lots of little problems that popped up like that, and some little problems turned out to be big ones.

Rescuing the Bittersweet

Interesting things happened in the helicopter business. One day we got a rush call from the Coast Guard base that the tender *Bittersweet* had run on the rocks out at Smugglers Cove and needed some extra pumps immediately. I flew out to the Coast Guard base, picked up the pumps, and dropped them off to the *Bittersweet* so she could hold her own against the incoming water and get back to the base for repairs.

Port Malmesbury Rescue

In 1965 Dick Borch was the president of the Ketchikan Volunteer Rescue Squad, and I was the vice-president. Dick called me and said the Coast Guard had a rescue going on at Port Malmesbury out on Kuiu Island. Two rescue squad men had gone with the Coast Guard helicopter and had gotten into some kind of predicament. It was a long flight for us in the Hiller, but Dick and I decided to load up the helicopter and head for Port Malmesbury and see what we could do.

A couple of fellows off a fishing boat had gone up the mountain, and one of them had fallen over a cliff and been killed. The Coast Guard had taken an Albatross amphibian and HH62 helicopter with Doug Giles and Don Moore from the rescue squad and was attempting to let them off on the mountain. The Coast Guard pilot was so nervous about trying to land on the mountain that he made the guys jump out of the helicopter from four or five feet, and in doing so Don turned his ankle and was pretty crippled up. The Coast Guard had left them there, and now they were stuck on the mountain with no overnight equipment.

Don and Doug had been able to bring the body part way down the mountain and were stuck on a ledge right next to a cliff and a big waterfall. There was not enough room to land on the ledge. The Coast Guard Albatross was on the water down below so I let Dick off nearby. I took a net on a sling and hovered near the ledge. Don and Doug were able to load the body in, and I brought it back down to the Albatross.

Now I had to attempt to rescue Don and Doug who were trapped on the ledge. They didn't have time to hike up the mountain before dark. I was able to get in very close to the cliff and put one float on the ledge—the waterfall was so close that bits of water were hitting the rotor blades, and the blades were throwing water everywhere. Doug Giles was the first one to try to get aboard. He got on the float and grabbed the door handle of the helicopter. I had both my hands full balancing with one float sitting on the ledge. I kept jerking my head and motioning that he had to slide the handle. I can feel that crazy feeling yet, trying to make my body motions tell him what to do. All of a sudden the door popped open, and he was able to crawl in. I took him down to the beach. Before going back up to get Don Moore, I took the right hand door off. With both men safely off the ledge, we poured in the last of our fuel and made the trip home in the dark. It made for a long day and kind of a frantic rescue.

Soloy Conversions

In the early 1970s Joe Soloy bought the design plans from Hiller for converting Hiller piston engines into turbine engines and started making conversions in his shop in Chehalis, Oregon.

Bill Hornbaker and I traveled to a helicopter auction in Nevada about that time. We successfully bid on five Hillers. We had four of them transported to Ketchikan and left one in Chehalis for Joe to convert to a turbine engine helicopter. The Soloy conversion worked well for us, and we soon had all eight of our Hillers converted. We flew them side-by-side with the Hughes until we standardized on the Hughes in 1981.

A Soloy conversion perched on a mountaintop in the Brooks Range. (Photo by Stan Maplesden.)

Close Call

One day I was working with the Forest Service up at Harriet Hunt Lake. They were doing some ground work in preparation for building a road up to the lake. Ben, the engineer, was there doing some blasting. The time was set up for me to pick the crew up. I came sailing into the muskeg, and Ben had just lit the fuse on the dynamite. He made one gallant effort to run out, exposing himself to the dynamite blast, and stop me from coming in with the helicopter. I got the message real quick and backed up doing a torque turn and flew away. Ben was able to get back into his protected area before the blast went off. I'd had enough experience with blasting that I was very alert on this occasion, and it saved the day.

Salazar's Close Call

Humble Oil had a camp over in the Saltchuck area—we called it Scout Camp. Lee Burroughs was drilling some holes for them out there, and the drill was on a steep little bank—not really room enough to land the helicopter. Mike Salazar had just moved the drill in, and on his last trip he tried to get closer to the drill. The drillers had already put their water pipe in, and it

Prospecting was a constant feature of our business. Here Terry Wills and Bill Huff load a TEMSCO Hiller 12E with supplies for claim operations up in Walker Cove.

stuck up a little higher than normal. Mike's blades clipped the top of the hose, and it damaged the blades and made the helicopter shake so badly all he could do was set it down. He ended up perched on the edge of the cliff, with the helicopter ready to go over the cliff backwards if he shut down. Mike kept the power on, and was sitting there with the helicopter shaking terribly, hanging on for dear life. The driller, a quick thinker, saw what was happening and got a rope on the front of the floats. He tied the rope to his drill rig, put a come-along on it, and secured the helicopter so Mike could shut the power off. It was a very close call, and a very brave thing for the driller to do. At a later date we came in, jacked the helicopter up level, put new blades on it, and flew it out of there.

Pond Reef Rescues

Wendell Jones was a mechanic for me for awhile before he went to work with the state troopers. On a cold, windy day the state troopers got a call saying that a canoe had tipped over in the Tongass Narrows out by Pond Reef, and there were people in the water. Some of the troopers dashed out to Pond Reef by car. When they got there, they couldn't help anybody because the victims were way out beyond their swimming distance.

Fortunately Wendell stopped at TEMSCO on his way out to Pond Reef. I had just landed the helicopter, and the engine was still running. He jumped up on the helicopter and told me, "Hey, a canoe tipped over out by Pond Reef, and there are some guys in the water." I said, "Get in. We'll go get 'em." So Wendell hopped in, and we got out there and located the guys in the water. They were pretty hypothermic.

I was able to land in the water, but it was rough. I was able to hold power on so that I wasn't sinking too deep, and didn't lose control of the helicopter. Wendell got out on the float, grabbed one guy by the collar, and got him onto the float of the helicopter. I was able to push the door open, and Wendell got him into the helicopter. He reached down and got the second guy and pulled him up on the float. I was able to lift the helicopter off with Wendell on the float hanging on to this second person. We only had a short distance of a half-mile to go to the beach so I just hovered over and landed. The troopers were there, and they picked the two guys up and dashed them into a home close by. The homeowners had been alerted to the emergency and had a tub full of warm water to put the guys in. They warmed the guys up and saved their bacon.

Positioning a drill.

The ironic thing about this whole incident is that two weeks later Wendell Jones was part of a state troopers' raid on a marijuana house. The troopers stormed in with their guns and nailed these guys to the wall. Wendell put a gun into one guy's back and the guy put his hands up. When they got the handcuffs on him and turned him around, low and behold it was one of the guys that Wendell had just saved. Things like that happened.

A few days later I arrived back at the pullout after a flight, and the helicopter was still running when the office girl called me on the radio and told me there were some scuba divers in trouble at Pond Reef. Without shutting off the engine, I dashed out to Pond Reef. The Pond Reef rock was still exposed when I got there, and two divers were hanging onto it. I hovered close to them, and they smiled and waved so I assumed there was nothing wrong with them and returned to the pullout. The office girl called me again and said someone had called and said the divers were still hollering for help so I dashed back out there and landed in the water beside them. One of them climbed onto the big bag float of the helicopter. I hovered him to the shore and returned for the second one. It turned out to be Pat Charles and Dolores Churchill who were just learning to scuba dive and had run out of air. They didn't realize they could drop their weights and swim to shore in their wetsuits.

Rescue At Duncan Pass

In late 1967, Earl Walker was flying out of Petersburg, and he was called to bring in some Fish and Game people who had been injured in an airplane accident. Evidently, the airplane pilot got caught just out of Petersburg in a heavy snowstorm in Duncan Pass. He ended up crashing, and the airplane burned. All the passengers got out of it, but Ken Durley, whom we all knew, had internal injuries that needed immediate attention.

Earl took off after dark in a snowstorm, worked his way in, located the burning airplane, picked the survivors up, and brought them back one at a time to town. I think Earl made three trips. Ken Durley got immediate surgery for his internal injuries, and it saved his life. We were real proud of Earl for that.

Alaska Air Carriers Association

We formed the Alaska Air Carriers Association in 1966. Arlo

Livingston and Kenny Loken were the first two presidents. Other people who attended those first meetings were Ed Todd, Pete Cessnun, Lloyd Roundtree, and Latin Bennett. We were trying to get all the air carriers in Alaska, primarily all the helicopter and airplane charter operators, to work together on various issues. We started the organization and tried to make it go statewide, but we couldn't get any participation out of the people in Anchorage

In 1968 I was the president and Pete Johnson was the secretary. Pete and I decided the only way to make the Air Carriers Association work was to take it to Anchorage. We put the package together and got enough help from Anchorage operators to have the meeting in Anchorage.

The second year we met in Anchorage, we got a lot more support. I was able to pass off the presidency to another member. I believe it was Richard Wein. Other members who showed up in Anchorage were Jim Pippen, Harold Esmelka, Orin Seybert, Dick Gallagher, Marge Baker, Dave Boughmister, Rex Bishop,

Earl Walker shown hovering in 5364 Victor, a helicopter similar to the one he used for the rescue at Duncan Pass.

Tommy Craig, Steve Smith and more. Soon the organization had grown enough that we hired Jim Dodson as an Executive Secretary. Jim did an excellent job, and he worked for little wages because he loved what he was doing. His dad had been one of the pioneer aviators in Alaska so he was really interested in the aviation business.

Our goal, which we did accomplish, was to represent our segment of the industry to the public and to get the respect of government agencies, especially the FAA. We tried to get some breaks from the insurance companies, but that was a failure. We also got the Alaska Aviation Safety Foundation off and running, and it is still going strong today. We held our board of directors meetings in different operator's towns which was great for getting acquainted with the members and seeing their problems. I was president in '68, '69 and '77, and chairman of the board in '78. When Orin Seybert of Peninsula Airways became president of the Air Carriers, he and the board of directors made a special trip to Ketchikan to present me with a jade plaque thanking me for my years of service. That gesture meant a lot to me.

Logbook Note

Just to give you an idea what our business was like in the 1970s, looking at one page of my logbook there are about ten items. It starts out: Unable to get into Ketchikan due to bad weather—RON (remain over night) at Johnny Stacker's cabin. Move men and gear to Nitchen Cove. Fish and Game Ken Durley Stream Survey. Pole setting North Point Higgins. North Tongass TV, six men and tools to mountain. KPU one man to the upper lake to check the line. Tongass TV Don Cunnings to the mountain. Wes Davidson, Jack Tibbles to inspect the Alaska Loggers repeater at Ratz Harbor Mountain. That's the way it goes, day after day. It was a busy time, and it was a fun business.

Chapter 9,
Mountaintop Repeaters

In the early days we used high-frequency (HF) radios for radio communications. The radios were very noisy, and you couldn't tune the squelch out. It's probably the reason I'm so deaf now. In the late sixties Jack Tibbles, the head electronics man at Service Electric, started experimenting with VHF direct line-of-sight communications using mountaintop repeaters. Today they're pretty well perfected, but in the early days there were all kinds of problems. Each company built their own repeaters. They weren't too dependable, but they worked most of the time. When they failed we had to wait for good weather to get up on the mountain with the helicopter to fix them. But the first step was to put a big radio tower up on top of a mountain, and until Tibbles came along, this really hadn't been done before. With great effort we hauled a radio tower up to Blue Mountain, 3400 feet high. The tower was a triangular affair about 100 feet high. We built a good foundation in the rock, drilled holes, and mounted inch-and-a-half steel bars to form the base of the tower. The tower itself was pipe construction, with lattice work you could climb up. Tibbles put a whip antenna up on top of it, and created a repeater that was working really good—until winter came along.

We found in Southeast Alaska, with over 180 inches average rainfall per year, the wintertime freezing rain at about 3500 feet was a real problem. On the back edge of Blue Lake Ridge, where this tower was mounted, the rain would hit the tower, and the ice would build all up. Finally the ice built up so much on one side of the tower that it just bent over. Those inch-and-a-half steel bars bent right over at 90 degrees. This was a real lesson for our mountaintop experience. We'd been working on White Alice repeaters early on, but these VHF units were a new tech-

Control Lake mountaintop repeater, caked with ice. Note the size of the tower relative to the men. Left to right we have Dick Madden (back to camera) Allan Linn, Barny Huddleston and Svend Larsen, all of Thorne Bay

nology. Eventually, servicing mountaintop repeaters became a natural extension of our business.

High Mountain

One by one repeaters cropped up all over the country. The Alaska Loggers put a big plastic cone about 20 feet high with the antenna inside up on Ratz Mountain, and a local community organization built a repeater on High Mountain for TV reception. High Mountain was an ideal spot for us to have a radio repeater. It was 2500 feet high and located right straight across from our TEMSCO office and hangars. We put our repeater there, and had it working smoothly.

One cold winter day I took George Ferrall up to make a final inspection of the TV repeater on High Mountain. The sun had just gone down so the temperature dropped an extra ten degrees. I was climbing up the mountain with full power, and when I started to level off, I couldn't budge the throttle—it was frozen at full throttle. I was in a predicament, still climbing, and there was nothing I could do about it. I called our base on the radio and told them my predicament, but I got no help. Nobody knew what to do.

Out of the blue, Arlo Livingston called me on the radio. He said they had had some problems with the throttle freezing too. He suggested I turn to one magneto only. I tried that, but it didn't work. He said, "All you can do then is shut the engine off." I prepared my passenger to assist me by turning the other magneto off so I could respond faster on entering autorotation. I was now 4000 feet high and climbing. George turned the power off, and I shoved the collective down and started to autorotate, but the blades started slowing down instead of holding their RPM. They started to stop-bang (stop-banging means the blades are not tracking which may cause damage to the mast and loss of the rotor system). Instinctively I shoved the nose forward while I still had a little control, got into a steep dive, and the RPMs started coming back. I started to level off again, and the blades started to slow again. I shoved the nose down again to keep up the necessary speed to hold the RPM. To make a landing on the water, I had only one choice and that was to hold my speed up until I was just inches off the water, then land like an airplane. I went for it and greased on a great landing.

After George and I settled down, I felt the throttle, and it was no longer frozen. Heat from the engine and the lower altitude had thawed the frozen throttle cable. I started the helicopter and flew back to the pullout. The mechanics now had to solve the frozen-throttle problem, but more importantly they had to adjust the autorotation RPM of the blades so the helicopter could hold RPM with a minimum weight configuration.

Gary Boles did most of the work on the facilities for the High Mountain repeater so quite often I would leave him up there and pick him up at the last minute. On one occasion, I hovered up the mountain due to low visibility, arrived at the heliport, and loaded Gary and his helper. I had picked up a little ice on the blades, and I warned Gary as I took off that it was going to vibrate for a minute. As I dove off the mountain, I bounced the collective which flexed the blades and shed the ice. I was able to fly off the back side of the mountain which had a little better visibility.

On another trip to High Mountain, moisture was hanging in the air as I waited for Gary and his helper to arrive at the heliport. As I sat there running the engine, I was picking up ice and didn't realize it. When we got loaded up and ready to fly, I had so much ice on the blades that I could only get 2500 RPMs with full throttle. With Gary's help we scraped the ice off of the blades. When I started the engine again and rolled the throttle up, I still only got 2500 RPM. The ice had accumulated in that short time. It looked like we were stuck on the mountain for the night. We scraped the ice off again, and as we were waiting there just after sunset, the moisture condition on the mountain disappeared. I fired up the helicopter again and was able to get the necessary 3200 RPMs. We flew down the mountain in the twilight.

Ratz Mountain Misfortune

These mountain repeaters caused a misfortune for us on Ratz Mountain. We sent one of our pilots, Martin Jetton, up on the mountain with Harlan Ohlson who was a radio tech for Service Electric. Harlan was working on the Alaska Loggers' repeater. It was a wintertime condition with two or three feet of snow on top of the mountain. You could walk in the snow, but it was very slow going. Before the work was finished, the weather closed in on them. They called to tell me their situation and I said, "Okay, I'll come up there and keep a check on the outside and let you know if I think you can get out." By the time I got up there, the top of the mountain was covered with fog. I circled around talking to Martin who was waiting in the helicopter. In about 15 minutes the weather started down, and there was no way he could get off the mountain. He was stuck for the night, and the weather was going bad fast—lots of high wind and snow.

The next day we got a radio call, and they said, "We survived the night, but the helicopter did not." The winds were over 100 miles an hour and had blown the helicopter off the mountain. Now they were stranded up there. It was still blowing pretty strong, and they couldn't see much. They were afraid for their lives, and I said, "I'll head up your way and see what I can do."

I flew up the ridge from the west side of Ratz Mountain as

"We survived, but the helicopter did not." Martin Jetton and Harlan Ohlson survived a blizzard on top of Ratz Mountain by spending the night inside the black radio cone at left. 84 Victor was almost a total loss.

far as I could go and got to within about 1000 feet of them. I called on the radio and told them the weather was not improving, but if they could get down to me, I could still get off of the mountain. They said they had suffered enough and wanted to give it a try.

Once they left the shelter, they were committed. They had to find me, or they were in a fatal position. I warned them to keep on the highest point of the ridge at all times as they descended, and they would find me. They took off and slugged down the mountain. Finally about 100 yards from me, two figures emerged wallowing waist deep in the snow. They were two happy boys. They said they had survived just by the grace of God. The previous night, when the wind came up, they had taken refuge inside the plastic cone that housed the Alaska Loggers' repeater. If the plastic sides of the cone—which were buckling in and out—had broken, they'd have been dead in minutes. The chill factor had been more than 100 degrees below zero.

We soon salvaged the helicopter. It hadn't blown clear off the mountain, but it blew upside down. The damage was almost as much as a flying accident. Because the blades were tied down, only one of them was damaged, but the rest of the helicopter was a mess.

Jack Tibbles at Service Electric finally got the radio repeaters working pretty well, and the word started getting around that we had reliable mountaintop repeaters. We tried to talk the FAA into putting repeaters up, but they said it was ridiculous to hire a helicopter to put them up. Every time they had to maintain a radio repeater, they'd have to get the helicopter to go up, and they just didn't have those kinds of funds. They pooh-poohed our idea, but a few years later they had to do it because the repeaters proved to be the best communications you could have.

Now there are quite a few mountaintop repeaters in Southeast Alaska, and communication is fairly good. In some ways it's not as good as the old HF radios that would reach out over 500 miles at times, but it's more dependable to have the VHF repeater.

Kassan Mountain Job

The pulp mill at Thorne Bay was going to put a repeater up on Kasaan Mountain so they could pick up a Canadian TV station and shoot it into their camp. An electronic device like a radio repeater needs a waterproof shelter, and the simplest way to build a waterproof shelter on the mountain was to take a 10,000-gallon fiberglass water tank and turn it upside down. The people who built the water tanks conveniently built a door in each one. On this occasion, Martin Jetton was working Thorne Bay with one of our helicopters, and Martin had moved all the men and equipment up to Kasaan Mountain. They got the base ready and were ready to put the tank in. Martin was flying a Hiller, and he couldn't lift the shelter up.

They asked Bob Day, who had just gotten a new Hughes 500 C-model, to lift the shelter in place. His helicopter had the C20 engine in it while ours had a C18, which was a little less powerful. Bob thought he could lift it, but he wasn't very experienced

Barney Huddleston beside a frozen mountaintop repeater. It's amazing how much ice will accumulate on them.

Nine Lives of an Alaska Bush Pilot

in cargo work. He lifted the load and got up just about high enough to put it onto the platform area when he started to lose control. He immediately descended back down and called us on the radio. If I would come over, he said I could use his helicopter. He knew that the helicopter would lift it, but he didn't feel he was capable of doing the job. So I went over and lifted up the load with his helicopter. It was a touchy load because it was right at gross, but I was able to bullseye it right in. The ground crew was pretty happy because I plunked it in with seemingly no effort at all. I'll have to admit I was lucky to be able to fly it in and hit it dead center on the platform. But once in a while you get lucky.

Fawn Mountain Heliport

Fawn Mountain was another mountaintop spot where we worked on repeaters. It was on the south end of town and was only about 1500 feet high. KATV, the local TV station, had rigged up a system where they could pick up the TV signal from Canadian stations in Prince Rupert. They wanted to lay insulated wire from the mountaintop down to the roadside and hook it into the telephone system to give the local people more dependable TV. My job was moving those guys in and out.

Fawn Mountain was one place where we finally got things "figured out." Wally Christianson was the chief engineer of the job, and he was very respectful of the helicopter. His crew built a shelter to house the equipment, a small tower, and a heliport. I had finally convinced people that when they started working on mountaintops, the proper thing to do was to build a heliport. The helicopter can't land just anywhere without eventually getting somebody in trouble. If we have a specific point to go to, it will be safer for the people operating around there. They'll all know where the heliport is, and they'll keep loose stuff away from it so it doesn't blow around and hurt somebody. The helicopter can land safely and be tied down if necessary. It makes a controlled operation. Christiansen went so far as to cut a narrow swath through the trees giving us a path to come into the heliport, and fly out the other side. Because of the path and the proper helipad, Fawn Mountain really worked out well.

Propane Tank Lesson

Mountaintop work provided a lot of good business for us including a service contract for a television repeater located in Seal Cove. The repeater was located at about the 1000-foot level and reflected a television signal from Ketchikan to Metlakatla. Propane gas generators powered the repeater, and we replaced the propane tanks regularly.

The rule is—you don't haul passengers with your cargo load. Whenever we did haul someone, we had to stretch a point and say the passenger was a necessary part of the crew. On this trip to the repeater, Earl Walker had Wally Christiansen on board, and he was carrying one of the propane bottles weighing roughly 750 pounds. This put him at a pretty heavy gross weight. Earl wasn't familiar with the area, and when he set the bottle down, he pickled it (which means punched it off).

It landed on the corner of a rock ledge about four feet high. As the propane tank tipped over, a sharp rock punctured it. A fog of propane sprayed out of the tank. The only thing that saved them was that Earl pulled up in a hover, and the downwash from the blades held the fumes down. If the fumes had gotten up into his engine, it would have ignited and blown him right out of the sky. There was a lesson learned—from then on we hauled propane bottles with tender loving care. Later, the installation of mountain repeaters for VHF radio and remote telephones all over the country meant regular trips for us hauling propane to them.

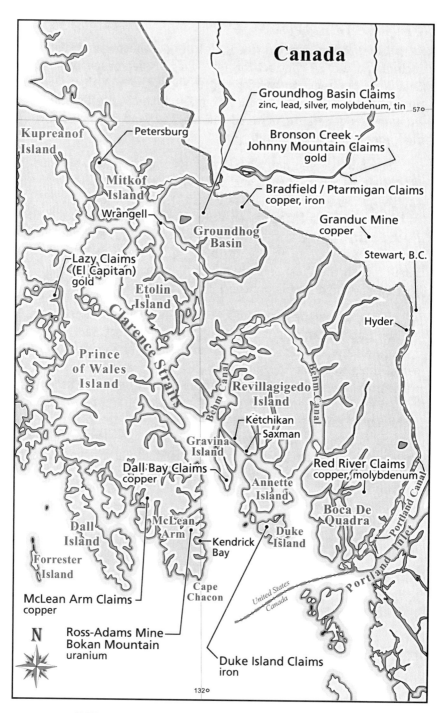

MINERAL DEPOSITS OF INTEREST

Chapter 10,
The Wolper Era

James Wolper and Wally Martin were a chapter in themselves. Jim was a big fellow, not too good in the woods. When I knew them, his partner Wally was in his 20s and in good shape. Jim said he was not a geologist, but the more you got to know him, you realized he was a very smart, shrewd man. As a self-educated geologist, he knew the right words to intrigue the mining geologists into recommending his properties to those who would lease his claims.

When Wolper found a good prospect, he would set up camp and move his crew in. Wolper, a bachelor from Abbotsford, B.C., would take in some of the boys from the detention home and bring them up to work in his camp, trying to improve the boys' lives. These boys were his crew in the summer.

My introduction to Jim came when he had a Phelps Dodge geologist looking at his claims on Gravina Island. Phelps Dodge hired me and the helicopter to take the geologist and Wolper out to look at the claims. When we arrived at the nearest landing spot, I shut down, got out of the helicopter, and hiked to the discovery pit with them. Wolper was pretty apprehensive about me looking at his claims, figuring that I might be jumping his claims in the future. Knowing I had done a bit of prospecting, he figured that was bad news, but he soon found out I was a real help to him. I would break rocks and find things he was looking for that would help him in his work, and I had no designs on his claims whatsoever. I knew where so many of the old discovery pits and trenches were that I was a big help to Jim. I could take him directly to a lot of the places he was hunting for. He soon was leaning on me to get samples in areas that he couldn't walk to, and we became quite good friends within a working relationship.

Jiminy Cricket

At that time TEMSCO had the Hillers and a Hughes 269B, N4341F, also known as Jiminy Cricket. The cost of chartering the Hughes was less than the Hiller by about 50 percent so Wolper liked to use the little Hughes. He was a big man weighing over 200 pounds, and when I loaded him, his prospecting gear, his partner, and enough gas to go do the job, we were squeaking out at over gross every time. The 269 was a fun little helicopter to fly, but you really had to be on your toes when you were going out in those overloaded conditions.

Jim Wolper holding court on a hillside.

The 269 had a fuel tank on the left side, and on the right side we had a box built in instead of an extra fuel tank. The box would hold one or two fuel cans which held approximately 10 gallons each. In place of one of the cans, we would generally put emergency gear. When we arrived at the area we wanted to work in, we took the extra can out and all the extra stuff we had so the helicopter would be more maneuverable, and we could operate in a safer manner.

Working with those kinds of loads, you always had to really fly that helicopter. You would come in to land on a very low approach and get right down to the ground while you were still moving ahead. You were moving at a very low speed but still in flight, and when you'd come out of your flight into hover, you were on the ground. The same with takeoff—you'd have to lift up, and if your RPM started to fade, you'd have to slow down, stop and touch down again. Sometimes you were in places where you couldn't land, but you could put one skid down and recover your RPM. This would give you a little inertia shot to get to a better spot where you might have a clean takeoff area—the preferred was downhill or over a cliff. It really kept you on your toes. I never had any problem with it. However poor Jim Wolper did have a problem.

One time I was incapacitated and let Mike Salazar take Jim Wolper and his partner out in the helicopter. Jim said, "We're going out to Dall Bay." Mike thought he was going out to Dall Island, which was a pretty long trip, so he put in full fuel and everything else, and went on this short flight out to Dall Bay. When they landed, Jim and his partner went out and did their prospecting. Mike got bored so he went looking for Jim and Wally, but he couldn't find them and got lost in the process. He finally found his way back to his helicopter, and by then he was all sweated up. Jim and his partner also came back and got in the helicopter.

They were in an area I'd been working in all the time, but I'd taken full advantage by getting clear back into the corner to take off and making sure everything was right before I left. Well, Mike was a little embarrassed from being away from his helicopter and being lost, and when he loaded the passengers in the helicopter, the bubble immediately fogged up because all the guys were sweaty and had rain clothes on. He didn't utilize all his area when he started his takeoff. Since he was overloaded, he couldn't clear the first tree so he tried to stop. The blades hit the tree, and the helicopter crashed. Wolper and his partner got out very easily, but Mike's foot was stuck underneath the rudder pedal. With their help Mike was able to get out, and we survived with just a wrecked helicopter.

Testing Ground

I used Jim as a testing ground for my new pilots. Jim was very critical, and if I sent a pilot out with him and Jim was happy, I knew I had a good man. You had to be able to get along with Jim to prove you could handle the public.

On one occasion Wolper wanted to go up on the mountain above the camp on Gravina to save himself a big climb. Wolper wasn't in shape to be climbing a 2500-foot mountain. Our pilot Don Moore put him up on the mountain, left him, and turned around and came home.

Later on Jim called for the helicopter, and I went out to Grant Creek Camp. He immediately started reading the riot act to me. He said, "Your pilot came out here and took us up on the mountain, and then he left us and didn't even come back after us. We had to walk off the mountain." They were really unhappy about that.

It turned out that Don Moore was starting to have some mental problems that finally got the best of him. He had to be put in a home where he eventually passed away.

McLean Arm To Glacier Bay

Jim created a lot of work for us. He had some molybdenum claims up in Glacier Bay that he hung on to just to antagonize the Park Service. (I think he hoped to sell the claims to them in the long run.) The Park Service was getting really rough on letting people so much as enter Glacier Bay—especially in a helicopter—but Jim had filed claims there years before, so he could just call them up and say what he was going to do.

He delighted in blasting and making a lot of noise in the park just because he had the authority to do that. We would make the long trip up to Glacier Bay from Ketchikan and perform his assessment work by doing a lot of blasting and making a lot of noise, to Jim's great satisfaction.

Jim also had claims on Gravina, out on Prince of Wales, on Hump Island, and quite a few other spots. He optioned his properties off several times which gave him money to operate on.

We made a number of trips out to McLean Arm on Prince of Wales Island where Jim had his biggest find. It finally ended up not being much, but there was definitely mineral there. McLean Arm is out where it gets the bad weather. Unlike most of Southeast, which is relatively sheltered, the mouth of McLean Arm is exposed to the open ocean. While McLean looks protected when you look at the map, it's a terrible place for weather. I have seen big ten-foot waves come hit the mouth and run clear to the back of McLean Arm. We had to be very careful when we flew in that area.

On one occasion we were out at McLean Arm, and we decided we were going to go to town. A storm was coming up, and it was getting dark, but Jim had a desperate reason for wanting to get to town so I said, "Okay, we'll give her a go." As we took off, it was getting dark, and it was really rough. I got up fairly high to clear the mountains, and looked down at the water. That water looked so ugly I didn't want to be over it any more than I absolutely had to, so instead of flying over the water which would have been smoother, I stayed over the land. In doing so we really had a rough ride—it was like riding a bucking bronco. Thankfully it wasn't very long before we were turning the corner at Guard Island and heading into Tongass Narrows, homebound.

Accidental Fire

Jim had a crew of four or five men at McLean Arm. I'd take two at a time and run them up into the muskeg. Two very interesting things happened on these trips. One day I left them off in the muskeg, and they said, "Come back and pick us up at four o'clock." This was a real hot day in the summer. I came back and looked and looked, but I couldn't find them. I looked around, and I finally had to go back and get more gas.

I continued to fly around looking for them, and finally I saw some smoke about a mile away—totally in the opposite direction from where they had planned to go. I flew over to investigate the smoke and found the crew trying to put out a fire. I don't know what they were doing out there. They had lit a little fire to attract my attention, and by the time I got there, they had a forest fire going. Consequently, we spent the late evening putting the fire out for fear the Forest Service would find out about it. It wasn't hurting anything. It burned a lot of muskeg and a few pine trees.

Dumb Stunt

We were back in the same area a few days later with a mining crew. They were going to blast some rock where they'd found some mineral. They wanted to set off some dynamite to try to expose enough of it to see what they really had. They said, "We'll be through by two o'clock easy so you can come pick us up then."

I came back at two o'clock and sat in the helicopter, and no noise, nothing, no word from them. They said they'd be through blasting by that time easily. I waited until three o'clock and still hadn't heard any sound from the guys so I hollered—no answer. Finally I decided I would go in and see what I could find. I started back in to the woods. I was walking on a little log when all of a sudden the blast goes off.

A rock came sailing through the trees and hit me on my left shoulder knocking me off of the log onto the ground. How the rock got through all those trees, I'll never know. I laid there for a little bit thinking what a dumb guy I was. I knew they were blasting, but I didn't know exactly where they were. I didn't dare tell them how dumb I was. So I finally sat up and worked my shoulder. It was so sore I could hardly lift my arm. I got back out to the helicopter and sat in it trying my arm to see if I could lift the collective and still fly the helicopter without telling them what happened. Actually once the motor is turning over and the blades are turning, the collective becomes lighter to lift; but when they're not turning, the collective is very heavy to lift. I figured that by the time I started up, I'd be able to lift the collective up enough to fly. The guys came out of the woods, and I flew two trips back to camp. I was the first one in bed that night. Never did tell them what happened. I always was ashamed of myself for pulling such a dumb stunt.

Beaver Rescue

Jim was always trying to go as cheap as he could so he had the helicopter contracted for a month out at McLean Arm. This time I wasn't flying it. We had Hal French flying it. Hal was a good pilot. We rigged up the sling gear on it, and Hal could move a 50-gallon barrel and take it wherever Jim wanted it so they were doing just fine. Jim sent Hal to town one day.

One of the fears all of us pilots have when crosssing streches of water is this: If the engine should quit, whether you are in an airplane or a helicopter, your chances of surviving were slim. To my knowledge there have only been a couple of airplanes that have had to land in the straits. On this particular day, Pete Cessnun had a summertime pilot flying for him who was coming in with a Beaver from Thorne Bay. He had a six-year-old girl with him as his only passenger, and he ran out of gas right off of Niblack Point in Clarence Strait. The Beaver is a good airplane, and he was able to get it down in the rough water all right, but the plane was dead in the water, and they weren't going to survive too long if it was blown onto the rocky beach.

Hal had just come in with the little 41 Fox and got the message that Pete needed somebody to get some gas out to this airplane before it drifted on the rocks. So Hal rigged up a five-gallon can of gas on a rope, hooked it onto his cargo hook, and flew out to the Beaver. The pilot stood up on the float and was able to catch the can as Hal punched the rope loose. He poured the gas in and was able to start the engine and taxi into a little cove where the airplane was grounded for the night. Hal picked up the pilot and the little girl in the helicopter and brought them to town.

Pete Cessnun sent Al Zink out to sit in the airplane and make sure that nothing happened to it. He took a little extra oil out too because the Beaver used a lot of oil. A few days later on an extreme high tide, I took Pete and some extra gasoline out to the Beaver. He warmed the engine up and took off out of this little tiny cove just before he hit the rough water. He saved his airplane and was pretty happy that everything worked out so well.

Barber/Pilot

Jim Wolper had some claims on Gravina, and Amoco Minerals was looking at one of them. They needed some work done over there, and we were breaking in a new pilot who had been a barber at the airport barber shop in Seattle. He'd learned to fly, and his greatest ambition was to fly for TEMSCO. A friend of his was working for us, and told him about a potential job. TEMSCO had him come up, and we checked him out. He wasn't really too bad a pilot—he was finally able to accomplish the things I wanted him to do, and we were getting kind of comfortable with him.

We sent him out to move Wolper's camp and move a bunch of drill steel—just a good day's work out there. He did everything very well. When he got ready to leave, he loaded up all the gear he had: gas pumps, nets, and slings. Then he went over and filled the helicopter completely full of gas. He was in a confined area where he had to clear some 100-foot trees. At the last minute the cook for the camp decided that he would go to town too so he came out and asked the pilot if he could go with him. The pilot said, "Sure, that would be fine."

What he did was a sad mistake. He tried to take off the wrong way in the muskeg, and instead of using all the muskeg, he took off against the trees and tried to climb out over them. He was absolutely grossed out, and the helicopter didn't have the power to do it. He was climbing as hard as he could climb, and the helicopter started to falter. He attempted to back right down the same trail he'd come up, and with the RPM fading, he didn't make it. He crunched my helicopter, my 52 Victor. I'd flown it 5000 hours without a scratch.

We got the message on the radio that he'd had a hard landing. I said, "Can you see any obvious damage?" He responded, "Well, not much." So I said, "We'll come over and check it for you, and maybe we can fly it home." When we arrived, here was this poor sad thing—52 Victor was totally wrecked. It was a real blow. Needless to say the barber went back to barbering, and we went back to rebuilding helicopters.

U.S. Borax

Jim leased his claims to U.S. Borax, and they started to work on them. The Borax people were very anxious when they called in on the radio, "Get the helicopter over here right away. We've got to move our drill into the drill site." The drill site was all prepared, and they were raring to go.

We had just hired some new pilots, including Stan Maplesden, who was one of the nicest young fellows we'd ever come across. He was what you'd call the All-American Boy, I guess. He'd just come back from Viet Nam, and we had hired him as a helicopter pilot and had checked him out a bit. We thought this was a great time to give him some experience. I told him, "Just fly over to McLean Arm, and I'll go over in the airplane and meet you there. I'll do the moving in the camp. Don't you do anything when you get there. It's very important, Stan, that you don't do a thing."

I took off in the airplane, and Stan had already left in the helicopter and arrived at his destination. The crew said, "Oh, we've got to start moving right away. We can't be waiting. We want you to haul this first load in there. Just move your helicopter right up here, and we'll hook you on to the load." Well, Stan couldn't say no, and the loading area was a little tight. Stan was not that familiar with the 12E, and the first thing he did was catch the tips of the rotor blades in a tree. Didn't wreck the helicopter, but it cost us a pair of $5,000 blades.

Much as Stan thought he was going to be fired over that, we figured this was a learning game, and those were the things that cost us money but also taught us lessons. He found out the hard way. Stan's dad was always impressed by the fact that Stan had caused TEMSCO a total of $10,000 worth of damage, and we hadn't fired him over it.

Drifting Helicopter

I was flying Jim out at McLean Arm in a torrential downpour one day, and he wanted to go into Copper Lake. We flew out of McLean Arm and around the corner into Stone Rock Bay and up the river to Copper Lake. Copper Lake is pretty well loaded with trees, not much room and not many places to land. We had the big pontoons on the helicopter, and there was a little delta coming out from a creek which had about two inches of water in it. The helicopter could land in that two inches of water and sit very nicely, very solidly on the bottom.

We landed the helicopter and proceeded to go in the woods. I went with them to do the prospecting, and about three hours later we came back to the spot where we'd left the helicopter—and no helicopter. It had rained so much that where there had been two inches of water, now we had a foot of water right where I had landed. We followed the flood downstream and found the helicopter floating out in the middle of the lake. This was a fall day when the temperature was down in the 40s, and sopping wet. What do you do? Do you dare go swim after it? If you don't, you're going to spend the night in the woods, and it's going to be mighty uncomfortable. If you swim after it, you've got to make it or you're going to drown. You've got to make a hard decision.

I finally made the decision to swim for it, but I took every advantage I could. I got myself in a position that was the very shortest distance to the helicopter, stripped off my clothes, and swam to the helicopter. I climbed aboard, started it up, and moved it back over to where I could find my clothes again. We reloaded the helicopter and got back to camp. Needless to say that was the end of the prospecting for the day.

I spent a lot of enjoyable days with Jim Wolper working those outside shores. Of course oftentimes they'd be doing something that didn't interest me so I'd go beach combing in all the rough little corners. Every time I came home from a trip out at McLean Arm, I'd bring back a bunch of glass balls. Finding those things was fun for me, and we decorated our house with them.

Working with Wolper out on those outside ocean beaches was a real challenge. In order to cover the places he wanted to go, oftentimes we would drop one guy off, and he'd cut down a tree or something and make room for us to land. We improvised a lot of heliports out of driftwood. It was a challenge at every step, but it was fun. I enjoyed that very much.

Jim was here for about four or five years, and then his health gave out. When he died, Wally his partner wasn't interested in coming back up here so that ended the Jim Wolper era.

Chapter 11,
Groundhog Basin

Groundhog Basin grew out of Bill Huff's work with Mark Anthony, a geology professor at the University of Alaska. One summer, Mark Anthony worked for Moneta Porcupine Mines, Inc. on a systematic search for minerals in Southeast Alaska. He and Bill Huff examined the Groundhog Basin area and found mineral, but Moneta did not care to pursue it (see map on page 208). Bill got permission from the company to prospect the area and use what he had learned while working with Mark.

We had just formed a partnership for prospecting: Bill Huff, Bud Hawkins, Angus Lillie and myself. I had just acquired my helicopter license, and Bill was anxious to get a claim staked on a galena vein (lead, silver) before spring. Prospectors always think someone knows what they know and is going to beat them to the claim. Spring was not here yet, but Bill wanted to get that claim post on the discovery vein even though it was covered with ten feet of snow. It was a nice, bluebird day, but the ridge Bill wanted to land on was solid white and at an elevation of 4500 feet. I was a very green helicopter pilot, but I had some seaplane experience landing on ice and snow so I had great respect for what I was about to do.

There was very little wind, and the snow was bright—the best of conditions. After circling several times I made a fairly flat approach to the ridge. Everything looked good, and I slowed down. Then, as I pulled pitch to stop and touch down, a big cloud of snow blew up. My heart was in my mouth when I felt the big bag floats touch solid snow, and I eased off on the throttle. We were there. Bill and I put on our snowshoes, which were always tied on the outside of the Hiller 12E, plowed around a while and placed a discovery post in the best spot we could find. Now Bill could relax until spring arrived.

Bunker Hill

Bill soon got Bunker Hill Mining Company from Kellogg, Idaho interested in the claims. The next spring Bunker Hill had TEMSCO move their camp into the lower area of Porterfield Creek. They hired Bill Huff to run the camp and Dave McCrillis to be the engineer with the geological team when they were staking claims. Chris Copstead, one of our local pioneers, was the cook.

Their camp was at the 750-foot level, and to pitch their tent, they had to dig down through six or eight feet of snow. The top of the tent didn't come up above the snow level. They dug the hole out completely so they were on solid ground, and I always wondered if they got run out of there with water when the snow started to melt. When I landed on the snow in front of their tent, the crew would come up out of their hole in the snow to see who had arrived and if they had mail. At best the work was slow until the snow left.

Bunker Hill worked the claims a couple years and then gave them back to us. While they were there they hired a geologist, Juan Munoz, to do some core drill work. The best thing they did was to build a cabin at 750-foot elevation that would be a base camp for a long time.

Prospecting Partnership

Bill was the most active member in our group. Angus Lillie was a troller so as soon as fishing slowed down, he would anchor his boat, the *Martha Amanda*, in a safe place and go wherever we wanted him to prospect. Hawkins and I had businesses to run so we worked weekends and took care of the needs of the guys in the field. I dropped in quite often whenever I was flying in the area.

Bill Huff got permission from Vona and Gary Boles to take their son Garr in the field with him. Garr was a great help to him. Bill reciprocated by furthering Garr's education. In fact by the time Garr was through with the prospecting, he had acquired his blasting license which he pursued as a trade for years, and he was one of the best around.

Bill was a rock climber with no fear, but he knew what he was doing. I think at times he took mining company geologists

Tom Pitman, Bill Huff, myself, and a Bureau of Mines employee compare notes at the Groundhog claims.

into areas that were so scary they would not recommend a second look. He also scared me once. Bill asked me to help him get a rock sample from a galena vein above Groundhog Basin's outlet. We left base camp, flew up the gorge to the Basin, and landed near the outlet. Bill pointed to the east ridge which was about 1000 feet high. We hiked up a ways till we came to a steep snowfield. It might have been a small glacier covered with snow. We put on our crampons and climbed up the snowfield. Near the top we turned left into a steep rock cliff. We arrived at a little rock nose that had a small level spot on it. Bill had me hang over the cliff with an open sack to catch the pretty silver chunks of galena as he chipped them off.

When the job was done, we climbed down to the snowfield and put on our crampons again. Just as we started out I noticed a very nice looking rock—a slab of rylite with manganese staining that looked like trees all over it. I thought it would make a great keystone for a fireplace. The slab weighed about 30 pounds. I grabbed it and started to follow Bill down that steep snowfield. There was a dropoff onto a pile of boulders at the bottom of the snowfield. The bright snow bothered my eyes, and my rock was heavy. Every step had to be planted well—one slip and there would be no stopping. Bill disappeared when I was only half way down. I was sweating and getting tired but never gave a thought to throwing the rock away. When I arrived back at the helicopter, Bill said, "What took you so long?" I still have the rock.

Tom Pitman from the Bureau of Mines came to visit Bill at base camp and wanted Bill to show him around. Bill wanted to go up to a ridge on the northwest side of Porterfield Creek so I flew them up to a spot at about 4000 feet. Bill and Tom got out of the helicopter, put on their packs, and disappeared over the cliff. I like to tag along on these trips and break a few rocks myself so I got out my rock pick and pack and headed to the spot where they had disappeared. I got to the edge and could see no way they could get down. I spent the next few hours waiting for them. The next day they wanted to go back to the same place. This time I was ready to discover their trail. When I landed I stalled a bit before I let them off and got ready to go with them. They went down this very steep narrow ridge. There was no way I was going to follow them.

Moving Bill's Camp

A little northeast of this area, Bill wanted to make a camp to prospect a nice little galena vein and some larger bands of zinc, lead, and silver. There was no place to land, but I could get one float on a shelf with enough clearance from the rock cliff for the helicopter's blades. Bill got out and unloaded his gear off the rack on top of the pontoon, and I left him there for a time.

On the next trip in Bill got on the radio and said he had a heliport built and wanted me to take a look at it. He had built a retaining wall and filled in an area big enough for the floats. When I landed, the tail was out over space, and the front of the floats were within a foot of a 3- to 4-foot rock bank. It was okay, but it sure looked like something in the Swiss Alps. The heliport was very hard to locate, but knowing its altitude I could find it.

Bill had made some other improvements as well. Old prospectors delighted in having a unique outhouse. Bill was no exception. He put two poles out over a 1000-foot cliff, weighted the poles down with rocks, and built a little one-holer out in space. When you stepped in the outhouse and looked down the hole, you could see straight down 1000 feet. Fortunately, I never needed to use it!

Avalanches

Bill Huff had experience during World War II in the kamikaze raid of the Japanese on Attu Island in the Aleutians, in the South Seas as a scout, and in Germany with the mountain rescue team. He had seen avalanches before.

After the Granduc experience I was more aware of the dangers of the avalanche, and yet there were still a lot of dangers I didn't know about. In our mining claims where Bill Huff was working at Porterfield and Virginia Lake and Groundhog Basin, there had been a big avalanche that came out of Porterfield Creek and almost got to our cabin at Groundhog Basin. This was really a spectacular thing.

We had always heard about the wind in front of an avalanche, but we had never, of course, witnessed one. One of the survivors at Granduc said there wasn't any wind in front of that big avalanche. So there was a question to be raised: What is this big wind in front of the avalanche they're talking about? Well, I saw the avalanche start up at the head of Groundhog Basin. It started out as a fairly little trickle, but it kept gathering snow as it went down, and it finally got to where it was a great big bunch of snow coming down. When it got to the bottom of the cliff and hit the ground, it was like a big blanket coming down flat on the ground and compressing the air underneath it with tons of snow. It hit the ground so hard it squirted snow out in a big circular motion 2000 feet in the air as quick as you could blink your eye. I realized then that the areas where big trees had been sheared off from avalanches had come from an avalanche going over a cliff. It hit the ground and compressed the air to velocities probably in the neighborhood of 200 miles an hour or better. It would just shear the trees off clean at that point.

This was the lesson I learned: When I saw an avalanche starting, I would get away from that immediate area so I wouldn't be caught in that updraft. If I'd been in the area where the avalanche hit and squirted snow up in the air, it would have totally destroyed the helicopter in flight.

Autorotations

On another occasion Bill had Mr. Tulley, a geologist from Cypress Mines, and a helper with him. It was on a weekend and Bud Hawkins was along. I had taken them up to the upper Porterfield area, and after the day's work was about done, the weather went bad. Wind gusts were very strong, and the clouds were rolling up the valley. We didn't have much time. We decided that Bill and Tully's helper would skirt the glacier and hike to the upper camp. Tully, Hawkins, and I would head for town.

I warmed the helicopter up, and we took off. I had to descend a couple thousand feet, but it looked like the clouds were cutting off my escape route. I wasn't getting down fast enough so I went into full autorotation, but a wind gust hit me and held me up. I was desperately trying to get under the clouds, and the weight on the helicopter in full autorotation was causing the blades to overspeed and to vibrate pretty heavily. Finally the gust eased off, and down I went. As I started to get close to the ground, I could see under the clouds. I pulled pitch and brought the blades under control. The minute this happened Tully gave a great shout of joy and started pounding me on the back. Well, I was just as relieved as he was.

Camp at 4500 Feet Elevation

At this time we were operating only one helicopter out of Ketchikan and one out of Petersburg—our total fleet. I was always squeezing in extra little jobs or doing a freebie for our mining explorations. This invariably put me into bad weather on the mountain or on a night trip home.

From our base camp at 750 feet, we went up the steep gorge to Groundhog Basin, which was a flat basin a little bigger than a football field surrounded by steep cliffs and a couple of glaciers at 2000 feet. Bill had a camp at 4500 feet right above the base camp. On this occasion I had squeezed the time to take Bill his groceries, but the weather was not cooperating with me. I managed to get to Bill's camp but told him to unload me quick so I could beat the weather. As I sat there while Bill unloaded me, I held flight idle and collective full down—all hands on the controls for fear the gusts might deflect the blades into the tail boom or lift me into the air in some manner. Bill gave me the high sign when he had everything and I could go.

The only way out was through Groundhog Basin. I lifted off being very careful not to let the wind take me backwards into the clouds. Once down in the basin, it looked like Groundhog Creek gorge might be plugged so I went into a hover and moved up to the outlet of the creek to find out if I could see down into the valley. The wind made my mind up for me. As I moved up close to the outlet, the wind sucked me right into the gorge, and I had to go into autorotation to keep my visibility. It was like riding a sled down a very steep hill, but it was whitewater underneath me until I got to the bottom. Once down to the bottom of the gorge, I had a few hundred feet of visibility, and I recovered from the autorotation and headed for a rough ride home.

Glacier Landing with Seaplane

Bill and his dog were in the upper camp, and Bill wanted a cobra drill very badly. Helicopter 52 Victor was getting maintenance at the time so I told Bill to mark a good spot on Nelson Glacier, and I would bring the drill to him with 42 Mike. The next morning was a bluebird day, and I took off in the floatplane and headed for Nelson Glacier. I took a pass over the glacier and saw that Bill had marked it off pretty well. Generally the wind blows down the glacier so your landing will be uphill and your takeoff probably downwind and downhill. I lined up for the landing and went on in. The landing was very rough. I had not realized that the new snow was gone, and all that was left on the glacier was old undulating eroded snow. Bill and his dog were happy to see me. We unloaded the drill and caught up with the news. Then I took off down the glacier, and the downwind takeoff was worse yet because it took longer to get in the air. It was very hard on the airplane. I won't do that again.

Humble Oil Claim Staking

In November of '68, Humble Oil acquired the Groundhog Basin claims, and they wanted 300 claims staked right away. It was midwinter with heavy snow everywhere, and it was my job to do the flying. We moved into the cabin at Groundhog Basin and spent a month staking 300 claims. It was a fun month. We had five guys in addition to me—Carl Jackson, Bud Hawkins,

Harold Keith the cook, Bill Huff and Dale Johnson the engineers. We all helped in the claim-staking job.

A lot of the work was done on the glacier, and we encountered some problems. We'd put a stake in one day, and the next day it was covered up with snow. We had to use tree limbs to locate the stakes when we came back to work the next day. We also had a problem with crevasses. Sometimes I would leave a man off to put posts in and have to go back and pick him up because he was stuck between crevasses.

We found working in the dry snow in the steep country was easier than if there had been no snow. We had some heavy winds to work around, and it was a real experience to fly in the wintertime with snow, winds, ice, freezing conditions, and whiteouts. After this job I wrote down how I thought you should handle those conditions.

I found out that we had to use a landing light. If you landed and were blowing snow, the landing light would give you enough light to see the snow that was still stationary. That told you the helicopter wasn't moving backwards, and you could land safely. Another rule for me was: If you have no horizon, don't go.

We learned all the tricks to keeping the helicopter overnight and getting it started, warmed up, and ready to go the next morning. We kept covers on the blades, engine, and tail rotors. We had no mechanic in the field so it rested on the pilot to do a good preflight check, grease all the fittings, check the oil, and drain the sumps. It was no problem—just a little longer day's work.

In staking the claims in Groundhog Basin, there were two sides to the terrain. One cabin was on what we called Porterfield Creek, and on the other side of the mountains where we were staking claims was the Marsha Peak area and Glacier Basin. Glacier Basin was a big flat area where actually we could have built a landing strip for DC-3s. We set up an emergency camp on the Glacier Basin side in case we got stuck and couldn't get over the hill. This worked out very well. Thank goodness we never had to use it. We thought a couple times we would have to, but at the last minute we got a little break in the weather and were

Bill Huff works with a load during the Humble Oil claims effort.

able to get out of there.

I worked with the crews on the ground cutting brush and dragging the lines—doing whatever had to be done. We had a great pile of 4x4s for post markers with all the metal tags nailed on them. It was quite a bookkeeping job to keep everything going and to keep it right. We used four staging areas so we could stay close to the working areas.

We had 300 claims to stake each measuring 600 feet by 1500 feet. We got the bright idea that if we had a 1500-foot rope we could stretch it out, and it would be the exact measurement for the length of the claim. I got up in the air with this 1500-foot line dangling on the ground. To judge when that line is going to touch the ground from 1500 feet was next to impossible, but you could tell it was on the ground when you saw it curling up. We had somebody on the ground hang on to one end, and I would start a descent forward and drop the line at the far end. With very little effort we had a perfect measurement for the length of each claim. Later we found it was just as easy to drag the rope

The Humble Oil job turned into an arctic adventure for all of us. Adapting our gear and acclimating to prolonged winter exposure took thought. Here's Bill Huff again, staking out one of those many claims.

with the helicopter and do the rough layout that way.

I made a few trips into Wrangell for groceries and other supplies. Carl Jackson was very good with a chainsaw and during all his spare time he cut planks for walks or any other improvements for our comfort. Once we had everything taken care of for the evening and ate our dinner, we played some very heated poker games. No money changed hands—just lots of matches.

Bill Hornbaker came up to camp to do some helicopter maintenance, and he was impressed with the beautiful rugged country but was worried about the helicopter working in the wintertime in such country. It took a month to complete the staking. The Humble Oil people were pleased with the job, and all of us were pleased to have completed the job.

High-Altitude Photography

In the spring Humble Oil sent Mel Erskine to head the exploration of the property. Mel was a very enthusiastic geologist, and he thought the property had great potential. One of the first things he wanted was to take some photographs so they'd have more to work with. It was perfect, clear-blue weather, and he said, "We've got a professional photographer here, and we want to take pictures. Do you think you can get up to 10,000 feet and hold it for several runs across the area?" I'd never been up 10,000 feet especially from sea level, and some of the areas they were photographing would be less than 10,000 feet below us, but I had no hesitation to fly up that far in the old Hiller—I'd just never done it before. I took off, and later on I found out some of the problems you get into when you get up that high with the Hiller.

There was no real way that you could line up what was level with the horizon because there's just a big bubble in front of you. We found out that at the factory when they were doing high altitude tests, some of the pilots couldn't do it—they got vertigo. To solve this, they covered the lower half of the bubble with paper so the pilot couldn't see down. It gave him a sense of security and also gave him a horizon he could line up on and keep level.

These guys wanted to go to 10,000 feet, and then they wanted to fly level across a good-sized area and snap some pictures. I got up to 10,000 feet, and at that altitude, your air speed shows 20 miles an hour less—two miles less per thousand feet up—so it was very difficult to tell just what was going on. My altimeter was fairly accurate, and I tried my best to hold it right on 10,000 feet. We flew across the area, and I thought I was very unstable, but the photographer was happy with the results, and the pictures were beautiful. One more experience in the helicopter business.

Big Move-In

After the summer exploration Mel picked out three drilling targets. The number one target was at the 5000-foot level in a breccia zone, and if that showed good mineral, they would move out on Nelson Glacier and drill two holes. When Humble Oil moved in, they put another geologist in charge, which I was very disappointed about.

On April 27, 1970 we had the big move-in of Humble Oil

onto Nelson Glacier. They parked the barge in Madden Bay, and we started hauling loads to the camp area. At times we had five Hillers working on the job, Martin Jetton, Don Moore, Mike Salazar, Larry Kemp, and I. We moved 200 tons up on the glacier, and some of the loads were pretty hefty. The loads included an arctic camp and all the drill equipment, and another the drill for the big drilling job. This went on for several days. Most of the time the weather was fairly good, but there were times when it was marginal at the top.

On one occasion we'd all been going in to the 5000-foot area. Don Moore came in a little high, and he got in the clouds and got lost. We didn't know what happened to him, and about 20 minutes later he showed up looking pale. He'd gotten disoriented in the clouds, but he'd been lucky. He came out of it and found his way back to the camp. He said he was all through hauling stuff up to Groundhog Basin and home he went.

Whiteout Conditions

The camp was at around 4500 feet, and the proximity of the glacier often created fog so we had to be very careful. One day I came into the camp from the lower side, and it had snowed heavily that night. The whiteout condition was really tough so when I landed I had a talk with the guys. I said, "Hey, fellows, when you're expecting a helicopter to come in, get outside with your snowshoes and at least make a mark on the snow because the whiteout condition is absolutely impossible."

The next day when I went up to camp, there were some snowshoe tracks out of the cabin, up to the cliff, and right over the cliff. A closer examination showed that from about 500 feet down the snowshoe tracks started again, but they had to go way around to get back to the arctic camp because it was so steep. Eric Muench had gone out to mark the landing area for us as I'd told him. In whiteout conditions he had stepped right over the edge and gone down the cliff. There was such heavy snow cushioned up at the bottom, it didn't hurt him a bit, but it was a long hike back up to the camp.

Improvising

Working one day in Groundhog Basin, I was required to set some people down in Porterfield Creek, which is just above the lower base camp. I'd been flying all day and was just getting ready to go into base camp to get fuel. I dropped my passengers off, and while I was sitting there letting them get out of the helicopter, the engine stopped. We always carried a little measuring stick to measure the fuel in the gas tank, and when I'd landed I was tail low and on a sloping hill. The pickup point for the fuel on the Hiller is up in the forward part of the tank so consequently when I landed tail low, the fuel pickup couldn't pick the fuel up and the engine stopped. I turned on the boost pump, and it was obvious that there was nothing there. I checked with my dipstick. It showed several gallons of fuel.

It was getting to be the time of day when you didn't want to be stuck on the mountain, and I figured by the time I hiked back to camp and got back up, it'd be dark. I could see what was the matter so I let the air out of the front floats until I got the helicopter sitting level. Then I fired up the helicopter and immediately flew down to the base camp and landed with no hesitation and not tail low. Then I pumped the floats up, fueled up, and was back to normal.

Number Two Drill Target

As soon as the camp was completed, the driller was anxious to get to work so they started to dig snow to try to get down to rock. After three days they still had not reached rock. The driller talked the geologist into going to the num-

Carl Jackson during work on the Humble Oil claims.

ber two target and started drilling through the ice. The driller foreman had worked at Granduc and liked to drill through the ice so they drilled three holes through 600 feet of ice and 2800 feet of rock. All of the holes showed very little mineral. It is a sad thing, but sometimes big companies lose control of their objective. Humble Oil gave the claims back, and we had the big job of moving everything off of the mountain.

El Paso Natural Gas

When El Paso Natural Gas Company leased the Groundhog Basin claims, they bought the arctic camp from Humble Oil, and we moved it back up to the 5000-foot area. El Paso didn't keep a helicopter on full time so there were many short trips to move a drill, deliver break-down parts, and make grocery runs. Occasionally one of their geologists would keep a helicopter all day.

They did a lot of work including an airborne survey showing a potential mineral deposit under a portion of Nelson Glacier. They drilled a lot of short holes and found mineral but did not drill a pattern to prove size. After two years they gave up the lease and offered us the arctic camp. We made the mistake of saying, "Go ahead and leave it." It had lots of leaks, and after a few years winds over 100 mph took it apart and scattered it all over the mountain and Nelson Glacier. Bill Huff kept a small shack a short distance from the arctic camp with room for two men. It survived the elements.

Bill's Tunnel

Bill Huff wanted to explore a silver zone at the top of the back of Groundhog Basin. It was so steep all his work had to be done with ropes, and he wasn't making much progress. We talked it over, and Bill thought that if he drove a tunnel into the cliff a ways and then turned left, he could intercept the zone. We bought a compressor and drill, and I moved it up to a little ledge that Bill could work from and also set up a camp. Bill started in on the tunnel and whenever he needed something, he would get hold of Stan Maplesden in Wrangell, and Stan would help him out sometime before the day was over.

It was a beautiful day when Stan got a call from Bill for something. Stan went right up to Bill's camp. While he was there

Bill needed some fuel moved so Stan obliged. When he came in with the fuel, Stan thought he could set it real close for Bill. Well, he got a little too close to the snow bank just above the ledge, and the helicopter did a violent flip in towards the cliff. No one was hurt, but how lucky he was. If it had flipped outward, it would have fallen over a thousand feet into Groundhog Basin.

I got the call from Bill and flew right up there. Stan had been flying our first Soloy turbine-converted Hiller 12E. He felt terrible, but as long as no one was hurt, we could live with it. Much to Stan's surprise, I flew him to Ketchikan and put him in another helicopter and sent him back to Wrangell—a much wiser pilot. With the kind of flying we had to do, I felt he had better fly right away before he lost his nerve.

AMAX Mining

AMAX Mining Company liked the looks of Groundhog Basin. They saw a potential of molybdenum mineral. Bill Huff had found some moly, and in the 1930s a company had spent a lot of time on a moly prospect there. AMAX leased the property and moved into base camp. After a couple years' exploration, AMAX brought in a big drill and started drilling deep holes near the outlet of Groundhog Basin.

Dale Johnson, Bill Huff, and Bud Hawkins working with a Hiller at Groundhog Basin.

Stan Maplesden

TEMSCO had bought a hangar on the airport at Wrangell and moved Stan Maplesden and his family to Wrangell. Stan was creating lots of business in Wrangell and was making all kinds of improvements. With AMAX so close Stan had good communications with Ken Fink, the head geologist on the job. Every day there was a trip or two over to the camp.

It seemed like every time things were going smoothly, and I took a partial day off to do some of the things I love to do, something happened. On this particular day, September 9, 1978, I wanted to go out to see Angus Lillie at our Lazy Claim, which was a little gold claim in El Capitan Pass. Bud Hawkins and I took the Cessna N168 out to see Angus. We tied the plane up to Angus' troller, which was anchored up in the little harbor close by, and started discussing our plans for the day.

About that time a helicopter buzzed us overhead so I got in the airplane and got on the radio. Brad Donovan said, "Stan's had an accident in Wrangell. You've got to go over there." That's all he would tell me. Now our plans were shattered. Bud and I got in the airplane and took off for Wrangell. The Cessna 185 was amphibious so we could land on the runway. Just a short distance from the runway, I saw the wrecked helicopter. Finding out that everybody had been killed was a horrible blow, and looking at the helicopter to try to figure out what happened was an awful task.

Stan was my favorite boy—he was just such a wonderful personality, just a nice country boy. He would rap on the door every morning when he was in Ketchikan, and we'd do our running or go up to the school and do our swimming or our exercise. Whatever it was, he was always full of fun. He loved to hunt and fish and do whatever came along. He was a good timber faller, good with a chainsaw, and just a hard-working kid.

We tried to find out what had happened. Stan had been over to check the Crystal Mountain repeater, and the helicopter acted funny so he came back to Wrangell and checked it. He could find nothing wrong. Soon he got a call from Groundhog Basin to pick up Ken Fink and the AMAX cook and bring them to town. Stan had his daughter Stacey wait at the hangar in

Wrangell for him. He took off for Groundhog Basin and picked up the geologist and cook and headed back to the Wrangell Airport. Something was going wrong with his helicopter, and he was heading straight for the hangar. Just short of crossing the runway, the blade failed. The helicopter crashed on the beach just short of the runway. Stacey said, "My dad does not fly that way." She knew something terrible had happened.

We took the wreck into Chuck Traylor's hangar for the FAA, NTSB, Allison, Hiller, and Joe Soloy to examine what was left and find an answer to the accident. At first it seemed impossible to find a solution, but Joe Soloy seemed to have a better handle on the problem than all the other experts. Joe was looking at the mangled blades. One of the blade tips seemed normal for a wrecked blade, but the other looked like the end had been blown out. After more disassembly they found the anode bar or adjustable weight was missing from one of the blades. This would account for the catastrophic failure.

On examination of the rod that held the weight, they found the threads were not full threads. The factory had been cutting the threads and decided to roll the threads because rolled threads are stronger than cut threads. To roll threads they had to under cut the rod by 20-thousandths of an inch because rolling extrudes the threads. Somewhere in the process the rods were cut instead of rolled leaving the threads 20-thousandths undersized. Engineers said the threads would fail within 5000 hours, and they failed in 4500 hours. The FAA then grounded all Hillers

Arctic camp at Groundhog Basin.

in the world until they were checked for the proper threads. We found eight other rods in our fleet that were bad.

We had the funeral in Wrangell, and we took all the helicopters we had in Ketchikan to Wrangell and made a pass over the cemetery in a tribute to Stan. This was a low point in my helicopter management, and I didn't know whether I wanted to go on or not. In talking to some of my respected customers, they said, "You can't quit. It wouldn't be fair to us. Somebody else would have to learn all over what you already know. We trust your ability to operate the helicopter company. We have great faith in you so please don't quit." Little by little it soaked in. Time heals all wounds. I stuck it out.

Amax worked the claims for another year, and when they gave up the claims, they gave us a lot of good data that had been collected over a four-year period.

Urangesellschaft

Urangesellschaft, a German mining company we had done a lot of work for, wanted to explore our Groundhog property. We were short of helicopters, and it looked like we were going to have to lease one. Our pilot Ray Hertager said his brother had a Bell 47 G2 that would perform well enough to do the job. I told Ray that it had to be on floats, and they had to have an experienced mountain pilot, which they assured me they had. The helicopter finally arrived in Ketchikan, and before I could add it to our fleet and work it, I had to be checked out in it as chief pilot. The pilot that came with the Bell showed me how to start the helicopter, and I flew it around for a little while. Soon we got the FAA down from Anchorage to check me out as chief pilot so we could operate the Bell. The check ride consisted of taking off, flying to High Mountain across the channel from our base, landing on the heliport on the mountain, and returning to the base.

Urangesellschaft hired Bill Huff and his partner Garr Boles to help them prospect the property. I sent the Bell and pilot up to base camp and thought I had things under control. Two days later I got a call from base camp that the Bell had chopped its tail off up in one of the upper basins, and we needed to pick the pilot and geologist up right away. I was in the process of checking a new Vietnam pilot, Jerry Edwards. Al Jones had just delivered a brand new Hughes 500 so I decided to take Jerry on a little training trip and also take Ray along to find out what his pilot had done to the Bell. It was a 45-minute flight to the accident site. The pilot did not have much to say, but two things became obvious. The pilot had made a downwind landing, and he was not used to pontoons on the helicopter.

It was just 2500 feet vertically to base camp so this would be a simple trip, and Jerry was capable of taking it. I told Jerry to take the pilot and geologist back to base camp and come right back to pick up Ray and me. Don't do anything else. This was around 6 p.m. After 15 minutes I started to get nervous. Where was Jerry and where was our new helicopter? Nine o'clock rolled around, and I told Ray we had better get off this mountain, or we would be spending the night there. I had never hiked off this mountain, but I knew which side had timber and which side had cliffs so we took off for the timber. We traveled as fast as possible, and just before we got to the bottom of the hill, we heard a Hiller 12E go overhead heading for base camp. It was dark by the time we got out of the timber, and we still had a ways to go. By 11 p.m. we arrived at base camp amid lots of excitement. Jerry told me that when he arrived at base camp, the Urangesellschaft boss insisted that he pick up Bill Huff, Garr Boles, and their geologist before picking up Ray and me.

The pickup point was up Groundhog Creek at the Rock, which was a square boulder big enough to land on in the middle of a very rough area. It was above the brush and the only level place in the area. Jerry landed on the Rock and picked up his passengers. I had been working with Jerry with cargo loads and stressing that with heavy loads, keeping the helicopter absolutely straight takes a lot of power to hold against the torque, and if he let it torque just a little, it would be easier. Jerry said as he lifted off he was thinking of what I had told him, but it exceeded the limits and his military training took over. He cut the power off and attempted a hovering autorotation to the uneven ground. The new helicopter was wrecked, but his passengers had only a few bruises. They all hiked back to base camp. After a radio call from base camp, Kelly Shunke had arrived from Ketchikan. I decided to fly the Hiller with Ray and Kelly back to

Ketchikan. It was a beautiful clear night. The next day Kelly went back to camp and took care of Urangesellschaft. The newspaper printed a note from the Coast Guard saying three TEMSCO helicopters had crashed at Groundhog Basin.

The investigation into the accident showed the tail rotor driveline had failed. It was the same thing that happened to me in my accident at Francis Cove which I'll talk about later. The Insurance Company paid off, but we lost our deductible. A little later Tommy Craig from Alaska Helicopters in Anchorage called me and said Hughes had a new tail rotor driveline in their parts catalogue. The factory never admitted that when they changed their tail rotor blades from light fiberglass blades to heavier metal blades, they needed a heavier tail rotor driveline. We immediately ordered drivelines for all our Hughes 500s.

Moving Bill's Camp

Bill was still enthused with the Groundhog claims so he and Garr worked on them. I serviced them whenever they needed something, and I was free. Bill also began making more frequent trips to town.

One day Bill called in for a move when I was very busy, but I was going to be free in the evening and in his area. I told him to go ahead and strike his tent. By the time I got up to the arctic camp area, a southeaster had come up, but I still had visibility. Bill wanted to move right across the top of Groundhog Basin to the edge of Nelson Glacier. To save time I always brought three nets for a move. We loaded up the nets, and I made two flights over to the new location. Then I took Bill and Garr over. I went back over to get the last load and hooked it up myself by landing close to the load and putting a longer rope from the load to the cargo hook. When I flew over to the new site, the gusts were really bad, and I was in trouble before I could get the load on the ground. Instinctively I punched the load off and got control of the helicopter. Now it was snowing on top of it all. Bill and Garr were vigorously waving me out of there. I hated to leave, but it was no place for that helicopter to be. I left and was happy to get out of the snow at a lower elevation. Later they told me I broke a few of their boxes, and all they could do was crawl under their unpitched tent and get into their sleeping bags. They were stuck for several days.

Groundhog basin claimed 34 Victor, a Hughes 500C, flown by Jerry Edwards.

Bill soon wanted to go to town again, and this time he wanted to move the camp out too. I said, "Bill any time you want to go back, just let me know." Bill said, "I can't. I'm just not strong enough." This was the first I knew Bill was in bad trouble. So off to the hospital in Seattle Bill went. Garr went with him and stayed close to Bill until the last.

Santa Claus

As Bill lay dying of cancer on Christmas Eve, my daughter Suzy and I decided to pay tribute to him by decorating a helicopter with Christmas lights and flying over his house playing Christmas music. To make the Hiller look like Santa's sleigh, we extended the length of the floats with 2x4s and strung Christmas lights along the floats and up the sides of the bubble. We borrowed speakers and a tape player from the local music shop to play our recording of Christmas bells. Honda generators powered the lights and the speakers. It was a clear night with a full moon that Christmas Eve, and Bill was surprised and delighted with our serenade.

After our trip north of town for Bill, we decided to fly over the city and to the south as far as we could see. We followed a car until it turned off the road. Then we turned back and returned to Peninsula Point. By that time, one of the generators had run out of gas, and only one side of our sleigh was lighted.

Many people saw Santa that night, and we got some good comments from them.

The next year we extended the trip to include Metlakatla. One little gal said she saw Santa Claus, and Rudolph winked at her. It made a lot of children happy so it was worth doing. We made the Santa trip every year after that, weather permitting. My last trip was in the A-Star which was a very quiet helicopter so it was even more effective. Dolled up with Christmas lights, it made a spectacular sleigh for Santa. Using night goggles made the trip safer too.

Ralph Yetka was a great help with the Christmas flight. He had a lot of ingenuity and was a willing helper throughout.

Before he died, Bill completed all the paperwork on the claims and made suggestions about what to do. Bill left me a note saying how glad he was to have made my acquaintance, and that the things we did together had been the highlight of his life.

Angus Lillie

Now Angus Lillie spent most of his time when not trolling for salmon working out of base camp. Many times he hiked up to arctic camp and prospected out of Bill's little cabin. He always left me a note saying when and where he was going. I flew a big dish for a TV into base camp, and Ralph Yetka showed him how to aim it. He was pretty comfortable and in a place he loved where he was able to see wild game such as moose, black and brown bear, goats, ptarmigan, martin, beaver, marmots, and wolverine.

Every time I got a chance, I would drop in on Angus and take him out to some spot he had trouble getting to, and we would break rocks looking for mineral. I had a bright idea to help Angus out. I would buy a three-wheeler and take it up to him. Much to Angus' surprise the three-wheeler arrived at arctic camp. All Angus knew about equipment was running boats and outboards. I explained the operation of the three-wheeler to Angus not thinking anything about his judgment as to where to go or not go. Next trip up to arctic camp Angus heard me coming and was standing by the three-wheeler with a rope sling attached to it. I asked Angus, "Doesn't it work?" Angus explained that he had been out on the ice with it and skidded part way into a crevasse. The more power he used, the closer he got. Somehow he got out of the mess, and that was all of a three-wheeler he wanted. Get it out of here.

Gary Boles was quite impressed with Angus one day when I took him up to check on Angus. We landed at base camp and found a note saying Angus headed up the south ridge to arctic camp a couple hours ago. We took off and landed in the outlet of Groundhog and shut the engine off. In a little bit we heard a shot, and after a while a figure appeared out of the mist coming down a very steep part of the mountain with a big pack on his back. Angus was 78 years old at the time.

On another occasion I was in the area, and I thought I would go up Aaron Creek and into Nelson Glacier thinking Angus might be at arctic camp. I found him out on the glacier too far from camp to make it back before dark. He was very thankful for that ride.

Angus' boat, the *Martha Amanda*, was as old as Angus, and it sank at the dock. This ended Angus' prospecting. He passed away on April 24, 2002.

Visit to Groundhog Basin

In September of 1999 my son Danny and I were up at Groundhog Basin with our Hughes 500D, 29 November, cleaning up some of the debris that was left by the winds that tore the arctic camp apart. All of a sudden the fog started rolling in so we had to get out of there. We had a sling load all hooked up, and I was able to get off the top of the mountain at the 4500-foot level and down into Groundhog Basin proper which is about 2000 feet above sea level.

Beyond that wasn't good, and I wasn't going to hover down the creek with a sling load so we landed the sling load and left it at Groundhog Basin. Danny said, "I don't think we can get out of here." I said, "We'll take a look." So I moved over to the edge of the creek and looked down. I could see all the way to the bottom. At the bottom of the creek, the visibility opened up. I moved over and started to autorotate on down. Danny was really

Cabin located near the lake claims. Winters were very hard on our buildings up at Groundhog Basin.

pleased when we broke out down below. It was a simple thing to do, but it reminded me of the first time I had to do it in 52 Victor.

In the summer of 2001 the Forest Service and Bureau of Land Management required us to remove any hazardous fuel, including empty fuel barrels, from our claims in the Groundhog Basin.

I still retain five claims scattered around the Groundhog Basin area. The glacier has delivered some nice looking "float"— mineralized rock not in place. I keep my eye on Nelson Glacier hoping it will recede to the point where it intersects a potential mineralized area. Between floats and aerial surveys I still think there may be something to develop in Groundhog Basin. Now my son Dan, grandsons Eric and Ken, and I are the only ones interested, but who knows what will happen!

Chapter 12,
Cargo Lessons

Occasionally a pilot would arrive at his destination only to find out he didn't have his cargo load underneath him. Somewhere in route he'd lost it. Probably the most embarrassing cargo drop that I know about happened to Bill LaMotta, whose brother Wes LaMotta started Columbia Helicopters—one of the biggest helicopter companies in the United States. Bill was the younger brother and was a salesman for Hughes. On this occasion he was taking a Hughes 500 on a demonstration flight to Anchorage. Along the way he did some demo flights for his customers. A situation came up where a fellow had drowned, and they needed his body brought to town. Bill volunteered to do it and get a little publicity for the Hughes. The cargo net containing the body was hooked on to the helicopter, and Bill started toward Anchorage. When he arrived in Anchorage, there wasn't anything underneath the helicopter. I don't know whether they ever found the body or not, but it created a problem for Bill.

Sling Loads

We also got into trouble repeatedly when we had a sling load that wasn't too heavy, and the ground crew hung an extra line on with something hanging below the net. Most of the time the pilots weren't aware there was something below the net, and the extra load would hit the ground prematurely sometimes damaging the cargo we were hauling. I remember one time I was loading cargo aboard a boat, and the crew hung a little generator below the net load. It was almost inevitable—I dipped the little generator in the ocean before I got it aboard the boat. Those things happened.

Once Steve Dillman was hauling an engine for a drill rig. It was too heavy, and his power started to fade. He didn't quite make it to the beach and set it in the water. When it hit bottom he regained his RPM and lifted it up on the beach. The mechanics had to take the engine all apart and put it back together again so it slowed things down a bit.

That was one of the problems of dealing with an underpowered helicopter or an overload. Later with the turbine helicopter, you had torque to spare. Instead of flying by brute strength and the seat of our pants, we started using our heads and our judgment and controlling the lift in a more accurate and safe manner.

Cargo Hooks

Airways and waterways were about the only way you could transport things in Southeast Alaska so the coming of the helicopter was a great thing, especially when it was equipped with a cargo hook. With a cargo hook you could hook on barrels of fuel, slings of lumber and net loads of materials and supplies. You could move all kinds of things into a remote area where there wasn't any other access. Exploration became one of our main jobs, and along with construction of logging camps, made for a lot of helicopter work.

The cargo hook is attached right in the center of gravity, right below the engine on a helicopter so when you lift a load, you're lifting dead center. The hook is designed with a finger that latches up. When you press an electric button, it releases the finger, and the finger opens and drops the load. Besides the electrical hookup, cargo hooks had a mechanical hookup: a little lever somebody underneath the helicopter could use to release the hook. Also, if the electrical system failed, the pilot could release the load by pulling an internal cable that ran from the cockpit down to the cargo hook.

These mechanical releases caused some trouble. If the manual release was not hooked up properly, it would automatically trigger the load release when the cable was stretched too tight or the load started swinging. This caused some embarrassing moments for me.

On special occasions like the 4th of July, I flew the American flag with the Alaska flag underneath it on a long line under the helicopter. We put a weight at the bottom of the line, and if you flew at just the right speed, the flag would stand out very nicely. It was always quite a sight for people to see. For the opening of tour ship season one year, the Ketchikan Chamber of Commerce asked me to fly the flags. So with the cruise ship at the dock and with national TV coverage, I did my flight with the flags. As I turned in front of the ship, the flag swung sideways and the emergency release dumped the flags in the bay. Some people thought the dropping of the flags was part of the ceremony, but most knew better.

Later Bill Hornbaker designed a manual release for the Hillers that was on the floor just outside the pedal for your right foot. It was basically a bent wire coming out of the floor at right angles, and when you kicked the wire, it would stretch the internal cable for the manual release. This worked okay. Later on we went to a manual lever that we could grip with our right hand and release the cargo manually.

One of the things we learned the hard way was that cargo hooks had certain poundage limits on them, and if the limits were exceeded, the hook would not release. We had previously thought if you had too heavy a load, you could just dump it.

Jerry Taylor was flying for South Coast Forest Products helping them clear all the trees and debris off the side of a hill. Jerry was facilitating the job by hooking onto some of the debris with a long line and putting it into the lake for them. He was using a cargo hook with a remote control on the bottom. One day he hooked onto something he couldn't lift, and the load shifted. The debris slipped off the cliff leaving him hanging with a load that was twice as heavy as he could possibly haul. Even though he was pulling full power, the helicopter was jerked downward into the lake. It all happened so fast, he was under the water before he knew it. They lost the helicopter, but Jerry got out of it. After that he decided he would prefer to be an airplane pilot instead a helicopter pilot, which was too bad because Jerry was an excellent pilot.

Cargo Work

I found out that the cargo work with the helicopters was more or less a delicate situation. We were always running up against loads that were a little over what you should lift, but you felt obligated to the customer to keep him happy. We did everything on a real short line because the closer to the ground we were, the more lift the helicopter had.

On the short hookup you either set the load down blindly or had a signalman out in front. Without a signalman you picked your landing area, and if the helicopter was overloaded, you would come in at the bare minimum flying speed—about 17 or 18 miles an hour—and at the bottom you flared, tipping the helicopter back which blows air forward and stops forward motion. Just about the time you needed the power, the load would touch the ground, and the helicopter could easily hover, and you could punch the load off. If the load wasn't too tender, you could actually flare just as it touched and punch the load off. We preferred not to be that rough with things, but it worked with certain loads, certain areas, or certain conditions. In muskegs you could get by putting a barrel of fuel in there like that pretty nicely.

Later on we found you could lift just about as much with a long line because you had the flexibility of moving forward a little before you lifted your load off. The minute you started lifting your load, it would automatically swing forward, which would allow you to move into forward flight quicker. You could actually get away with the same load on a long line as you could on the short line.

One advantage to flying a short line was that you were flying with your head up so it gave you a horizon or a ground level to keep your helicopter level, and you could move around easier. Later on when we started doing the long line work, the door had to come off so you could have your head out and look down. Well, that was great for seeing the work, but it was more difficult to fly because you didn't have a horizon, and you had to be able to maneuver the helicopter at a subconscious level. It was a little tricky to start with, but you soon got to where you could do a lot of things on a long line.

First Long Line Job

In July of '64, the Coast Guard had an emergency call out at McLean Arm. Ken Madsen was having some kind of trouble on his boat, and the Coast Guard Albatross flew out there and dis-

Aerial workhorse of the Groundhog Basin claims, a TEMSCO Hiller 12E shown on the site.

covered that it didn't amount to anything. On his return the Albatross pilot decided to make an instrument approach to Annette Island airfield. He was about 1800 feet high, and he was going to fly on an easterly course, intersect the Annette Island beam, and turn and land at their base on Annette.

About six or seven miles to the north of Annette is Dall Ridge on Gravina Island. The Albatross, which is a big heavy amphibious airplane, had a crew of four or five people on it. The pilot was flying on instruments, but he was really not on an instrument flight plan—he had made an impromptu decision to do this. The ceiling was down fairly low, and before he intersected the beam, he intersected the mountain, and the plane crashed and burned.

The wreck was discovered in the very tall spruce trees the next day, and everybody on board had been killed. This was one of my first really long line jobs. The crew had hiked in and recovered the bodies which now needed to be removed. I used a 250-foot rope on the helicopter. Dangling it between the trees, I got it down to where they could load the bodies up and move them out. I had never done any of this kind of long line work before, but I got the bodies down to the Coast Guard at a lower level where I could land, load the helicopter properly, and take them all into town.

Cargo Loading Lessons

There were many tricks to flying the various loads. We learned one of the first lessons from Joe Soloy when he was moving a bull gear to Margarita Cove for Wes Davidson. They used a piece of cable with an eye on each end to hold the bull gear, which was pretty heavy—500 or 600 pounds. They put one eye in the cargo hook, and Joe was able to lift it off all right. He headed out across the bay, and the load started to spin like a top. He went approximately a mile, and all of a sudden we saw a big splash, and Joe came back much chagrined. He'd lost this critical breakdown part for the Davidson camp. When the load started to spin with just the single cable eye, it unwound the splice in the cable and dropped the load.

I can only remember once when I punched a load off because it was out of control. I was hauling loads of lumber for a trail up at Harriet Hunt Lake, and it was a day when we were getting 60 mph gusts. I shouldn't have been working, but we were always hungry, and we were trying to make a go of the company. I knew that if I put it off, somebody else would do the job for me, and I didn't want that.

One load started swinging, and I had a rule in my own

One of our turbine Hillers flying a pair of floats out to a disabled DeHavilland Beaver.

book—if the load swung out far enough to where I could see it out of the corner of my eye, it was time to punch it off. So when I saw the load come up, I instinctively punched it off and then went back and said, "That's enough for today."

Whenever we lost a load, of course the critical thing was to look at what happened: Was it a cargo hook failure, was it a pilot error, or was it a failure of the people who hooked it up? Later on we had to set up the rule that from the cargo hook up was our responsibility; from the cargo hook down was the customer's responsibility. The customer had to have the proper sling and the proper gear on the load to handle it. We could give him all the advice in the world on how to rig it, but if it wasn't done properly, it wouldn't work.

I remember one time I was working with a Canadian crew that was doing a boundary survey. They were cutting the right-of-way for the boundary between Alaska and Canada. We went up the Unuk River to the Canadian border to set up their camp, and we also took them up on the mountain to start their cutting. They were really a hardy crew.

I was hovering in on a real short hookup, when the loader missed the master ring and hooked into some of the fabric in the net load. When I picked up the load, it only had one of eight legs of the net. The one point wasn't strong enough to hold the load, and I no more than got airborne than it plunked into the bay and sank. Much to their sorrow, it had a survey instrument in it that they were really unhappy about losing, but it was their ground crew who made the mistake in hooking up the load.

Close Call

One time we had an exploration drilling job over on Prince of Wales near Pin Peaks. We'd moved the camp in and moved the drill around a couple of times, and this particular time they wanted to move the drill about a half mile. I talked to the drillers, and they said, "You know, if you could move these timbers that we've cut down for a tripod, you're going to save us a day's work." I said, "Well, let's take one of them and see if I can lift it." Each timber was just a portion of a tree they had cut down to make a tripod so they could have a chain hoist overhead to move their drill around or pull a stuck rod or whatever they needed to do. So we tried it, and it worked okay. I moved two legs over and went back to hook up the third leg.

The first thing you did when moving those heavy loads was pick up one end of it and go into a high hover, and then you would increase your power so you could pick up the weight very gently. If you could get the weight off the ground and still have a little power left by your manifold pressure, you could tip forward and start flying with the load. It was a delicate situation on the heavy loads, but you always had the alternative of punching them off if they weren't a high-priced load. You had to be very careful about what you were doing, and you had to be real sure you could do it when you started out with the more valuable parts of the drill.

In this case, I came back to the third leg, and picked it up. It was pretty heavy, but I was able to lift it off the ground so I gave the crew a nod signaling that I was going to go with it. I pulled all the power I could pull, tipped forward, and started to move ahead. I felt the helicopter come up tight. By instinct I instantly punched off the cargo hook, and the helicopter lurched forward. I flew back up to camp, set the helicopter down, and walked back down to the drill site to see what went wrong. The drill crew were Canadians who were really good guys and very helicopter-oriented. But when they cut the last leg of the tripod loose, it had fallen in such a way that you couldn't see a cable they had fastened to a root in the ground. When I lifted up I had a little slack so I could start to move, but if I had gotten to the end of the slack, it would have been curtains. Being tied to the ground like that, the helicopter would be a pendulum after it got beyond about 15 degrees. There'd be no stopping it—it would just dive right into the ground. That's about as close as you ever want to come. So we had a little chat, and they were very apologetic, and I wasn't too tough on them.

Moving Smokestacks

We got the first new Hughes 500, and it had a new cargo hook on it—a little electric thing. The tongue on it was fairly small, and the throat was very small.

One of the maintenance people down at Beagle Packing, one of Ketchikan's old canneries, called me and wanted to know if I could lift the smokestack off the building. The smokestack was rusty, no longer in use, and he was afraid it was going to tumble down on the building. I said, "Well, sure, I can do that."

He had a sling hooked on to the smokestack that was long enough to reach the roof where he was standing and far enough away from the stack so my blades would not hit it. I positioned my long line so the caretaker could get hold of it. He hooked it into the eye of his slings, and I lifted up. The stack wouldn't come—it was still secured. I lifted and pulled just as hard as I could pull. I just could not lift it so I punched the electric release and nothing happened. I punched it again four or five times—nothing. I squeezed the manual release and nothing happened. By now the watchman was off of the roof because he had done his job. I had no radio communications with him, and I couldn't get rid of the load.

With low fuel and no place to land, I looked around to see if I had any options. I was tethered and the line was long enough that I could straddle the roof peak, but it would put the tail rotor into the peak of the roof, and I would probably lose control of the helicopter. I could see myself crashing into the old wooden building and burning the whole block up.

I desperately started pulling back and forth on the stack. I saw pieces of rusty metal starting to shed off of the base of it, and I actually was able to break the smokestack off and fly away with it. When I got out to the TEMSCO pullout, I set the smokestack down and landed alongside it.

This was a brand-new Hughes with the factory cargo hook. I hadn't realized that when we put the long line in the small cargo hook, it filled the throat up so full that there was no way it could release. The only way you could use that small cargo hook was to put a small steel ring into the throat of it. Now we had learned our lesson.

I had one other interesting smokestack experience. The owners of Miners and Merchants Bank building wanted a smokestack removed from their building. The smokestack was only about 20 feet high, so it wasn't too difficult to get a line on it. I was able to lift it off, but as I started to move forward, I started losing power—the load was too heavy. We knew it shouldn't be

Here I am pulling the stack off the old Ingersoll building. Unlike my other two smokestack trips, this one was relatively uneventful. (Photo courtesy of Schallerer's.)

too heavy because the brand-new stack only weighed about 700 pounds. It turned out that the old stack had been set on top of a brick chimney, and half the brick chimney came off with the metal stack. Together, the bricks and stack had me way over my gross. I had to land. The weight was more than I could hold, and it was literally pulling me out of the air. I had some control over the direction and speed of my descent, but I was going down, no matter what.

It was a good thing they had the parking area cleared so I could head to it. I managed to get the load down safely into the National Bank of Alaska parking area. The minute the load touched the ground, the weight was off, and the helicopter was under control. I breathed a huge sigh of relief.

Chapter 13,
Turbine Helicopters

In the spring of 1971 we acquired our first turbine helicopter, 9064F, a Hughes 500. Mike Salazar and I went down to Palomar, California, picked up the helicopter, and flew it to the Hughes International Airport in Los Angeles where we got the helicopter checked out. Bill LaMotta, the Hughes salesman who sold it to us, got us both certified in the Alison 317-HP engine and the Hughes 500 before we flew it home.

We soon got a job with a German company, Urangesellschaft, to tour all of the mining sites in Alaska. With "TEMSCO" painted on the side of the helicopter, our company got lots of good exposure when Mike flew it all over the state. When Mike and the

64 Fox, pride of the fleet in 1971. The new Hughes 500A's extended power and range gave TEMSCO new capabilities and set the stage for growth.

German miners got to Chignik in the Bristol Bay area, he parked the helicopter on the beach. A storm came up so he decided to move the helicopter.

In the process of moving it, he hooked onto the cannery's antenna wire, damaging the blades and the driveline. Our mechanic, Bill Hornbaker, took parts to Chignik and got the helicopter flying again.

We all got to fly 64 Fox a bit before its sad ending. Mike Salazar had another trip with 64 Fox—this time to Hole In The Wall on Noyes Island. He had a couple of surveyors with him, one in the front and one in the back, when he attempted to land on a little narrow float that wasn't wide enough for the helicopter. As he sat down on it, one side of the float would sink. He tried various ways to land, and eventually tried putting the helicopter's toes inside the little 4x4 rails on both sides of the float. When the float started to sink, he pulled up rapidly. With the skids hooked under the float rails, he flipped over upside down in the water. Everyone got out of it all right, but that was the end of 64 Fox.

Search for Tony Kilchefski

Leon Snodderly and I got to know Tony Kilchefski when he was flying for Ed Todd so when we heard he was overdue on a trip to Hyder, we joined the search. It was one of the coldest, roughest days we had that winter. Leon knew Tony thought the airplane was tougher than he was because on occasions when Leon flew with him, Tony didn't slow down for rough air when Leon thought he should. There was a possibility on this rough day that his airplane could have had a structural failure.

Leon and I were in TEMSCO's little Jiminy Cricket helicopter, Hughes 269, searching the Rudyard Bay area where Dogleg Pass goes through to Hyder. We had stuffed extra sleeping bags and emergency gear in the cockpit of the helicopter along with extra fuel in the external baggage box.

When it was time to refuel, I landed in an open spot high in the mountains of the pass and turned the engine off. We got out in the deep snow and poured the extra gas into the helicopter. We were in a hurry to get out of the bitter cold so we jumped back in the helicopter and attempted a start. Much to our surprise, the battery was so low it wouldn't turn the engine over. We discovered that the extra gear we had stuffed in the cockpit had tripped the generator switch off. Now we were in trouble. I had just enough battery to make one radio call to TEMSCO to advise them of our situation.

I told Leon, "We must get a fire going," so we wallowed around in the snow trying to find something to start a fire with. Nothing but a few alder limbs were sticking out of the snow. We couldn't find a place to start a fire or sufficient wood to fuel one. Then we realized we really were in deep trouble. I told Leon, "I'm going to try one more start," so I primed the engine and hit the starter button. There was a slight groan and then Bang! The engine started. Leon said, "That was the happiest sound I ever heard." I agreed.

We never did find Tony or a trace of his airplane. One day when I was flying to Hyder, I saw an object that looked like an airplane wing. I landed in the river bottom and hiked up to the object only to find out some helicopter had lost a sling load of painted portable building materials. We have never stopped looking for Tony whenever we fly through Dogleg Pass.

Jennings Graham Accident

One day we got the word that Jennings Graham was overdue, and that he had his young son Jeff and Max Dawkins, a local teacher, with him. A search quickly got underway, and somebody located Jennings on a small lake and brought him to town. Jennings had crashed, but he wasn't hurt too badly so he had walked out to the lake. He told us his son was still up in the Hugh Smith Lake area, and Max was injured—possibly a broken back.

The weather was not good. I flew down to Hugh Smith Lake under the weather, going in through the river valley. There were several small valleys to the north, and in the poor visibility, hitting the right one was very difficult. The Coast Guard's big Sikorsky was en route and was having trouble finding the valley. I was flying the little Hughes 269 at the time. I found the wreck and was able to land up above it and hike down. This was a steep area, and getting down involved a bit of rock work, but I

Cold and scared, this little boy desperately wanted to get home to see his father, Jennings Graham. Thankfully we were able to oblige him, post haste, with a little help from TEMSCO's Hughes 269, Number 41 Fox.

was able to make it down to the wreck okay. I found Jenning's son unhurt, but the passenger, Max, was still immobile and was going to require a lift out of there. I called in, and the rescue squad went into action. Some of them had already landed in the lake below us and more were on their way out, but even with all that help, we were still going to need a helicopter lift for Max.

In the meantime I took Jeff by the hand and led him up the hill until we finally got to the place where we had to climb the rocks. I put him on my back and told him to hang on because I was going to have to use my hands to climb up, and I couldn't hang onto him while I was climbing. He put his arms around my neck and hung on to me for dear life. We crawled up the rock cliff to the helicopter, and I flew him out to Hugh Smith Lake where the rest of the rescue people were waiting.

Dick Borch tried to talk the Coast Guard into going into the area, but they were very reluctant to do it. I got a hold of them on the radio and told them if they didn't do it, I was going to have to do it with the Hughes. It would be a high-risk maneuver for me to long-line Max out with the little Hughes because that was about the maximum load it could lift. It wouldn't be the preferred operation by any means.

Finally I convinced them to come in if I watched their blade clearance for them. Our rescue crews moved Max into a little slide area, which gave the helicopter enough room to get in. With my help, they lowered their line down and hauled him out. The Coast Guard transported him to the hospital where they found out he had no serious injuries—just bruises. He'd bruised his back bad enough that he couldn't move his feet for a while, and he thought he had a permanent back injury, but it all turned out okay.

My First Accident

I didn't record my first accident in my logbook. I guess I was ashamed of it or something. On July 5, 1973, I was home eating lunch when we got a call from Pat LeMay's logging camp out at Francis Cove, which is about a 15-minute flight from Ketchikan. A logger was injured, and they needed a helicopter to evacuate him. The weather had a cloud ceiling at about 800 or 900 feet but had good visibility underneath it.

I flew out to Francis Cove in our newly leased Hughes 500C and landed at the camp. Mrs. Pat LeMay was running the logging camp at the time, and she told me to follow the logging road up to an elevation of about 800 feet to find the accident site. It was

Although we were best known for flying Hiller 12s and Hughes 500s, TEMSCO had one little Hughes 269, "Jiminy Cricket."

kind of foggy up there, but I found the site. A logger had been injured when the winch he was using to pull logs shifted on its base and slammed into him, knocking him unconscious. Everyone was pretty worried about him because it had been a couple of hours, and he was still out cold. They had him in a stretcher and ready to go, but I didn't have stretcher capabilities with that helicopter. Instead we put the stretcher inside the helicopter, and I tied it down so it was secure. I had to leave one door open with part of the stretcher sticking out, but it would work well enough. I asked one of the fellows to ride along with me in the back end to help with the injured man.

I lifted off right on the edge of the fog and started to make a slow flight down the road. I was looking at my gauges and doing 60 knots coming down the hill—just over the treetops at maybe 50 to100 feet. All of a sudden I heard a whack! and the helicopter yawed to the left. I unconsciously dropped the collective a little and got directional control back, but I knew something was broken. I very carefully called a Mayday to our TEMSCO office, and apparently the gal on the radio, Lisa, got a little excited when she first heard me, and she blocked me off so she never heard the Mayday. She knew I'd called, but she didn't know I'd called Mayday. The next thing I knew I was down awful low so I pulled up a little pitch, and immediately the helicopter yawed left again. I dropped the pitch back down, and now I had to start dodging trees. I was over a little Cat road (bulldozed path) that was not big enough to land on. My instinct told me to get that thing down as close to the ground as I could. I figured I'd go into a hover in a clear spot and determine what I had to do at that point. When I came around the corner, I was getting close to the ground so I flared—pulled the nose up—which slows the helicopter down. I headed right for a little point of land with a bunch of stumps on it and pulled pitch. When I pulled pitch, the helicopter spun hard. What I didn't realize was the driveline had failed so I had lost the tail rotor. With the tail rotor out of commission, there was nothing to counteract the torque of the engine. When I pulled pitch, the engine applied torque to the blades and without the tail rotor to hold the helicopter straight, the torque spun the helicopter like a top.

When it happened, the helicopter spun so fast I lost all

vision. I was not even aware of the fact that I was spinning. Instead, all of a sudden I could hear various noises as the engine and the transmission unwound together. No doubt the engine was screaming up uncontrolled. Finally the blades hit the ground, and the helicopter fell on its side. I hit the ground pretty hard, but I was okay. I'd hit on my left side, but I could move all right. The windshield had broken out so all I had to do was turn the master switch off, unbuckle my belt, and step out into the open.

As I got out, I heard some strange noises in the back end—somebody was gurgling.

When I came around the broken bubble, the injured man was okay and climbing out of the helicopter. Apparently the spin had done something to bring him back around. The other fellow who had been looking after him was jill-poked by the stretcher and was choking. I managed to get the stretcher off of him and helped him out of the helicopter.

We weren't too far from the logging camp's bunkhouse, but we were all sort of stunned. As I stood there looking at the helicopter trying to figure out what had happened, I was hurting a bit. I looked up and saw the two loggers walking down the Cat road toward the bunkhouse. They looked back at me, and the thought went through my mind, I bet those guys are saying, "I'll never ride with that S.O.B. again!"

I walked back to the camp, and the airplane they had called to pick up the injured man was sitting at the float. The pilot, Carl Jackson of Revilla Flying Service, came running up to me, and he was just aghast. He said, "You spun! You spun! I never saw anything spin like that in my life!" Mrs. LeMay said to me, "I know you're hurt, but I called this airplane out for my people, and they're going to have to use it." I said, "That's okay with me if you could notify TEMSCO that I need a ride." A helicopter soon arrived to pick me up and take me into town.

My wife Peggy and son Dan met us at the hangar when we arrived and took me off to the hospital. The doctor looked me over and found a couple of broken ribs. Outside of that he said I was okay; however, a couple of years later when I had a chest X-ray, the doctor said, "When did you break your back?" I didn't know I had broken my back, but it must have happened at that time. It never bothered me a bit.

Looking back on the incident today, I realize that I had learned to fly the helicopter with no formal training. In an emergency, I would get as close to the ground as quick as I could. This maneuver saved me in this case, but wrecked the helicopter. The book says to shut the engine off and autorotate to the ground when the tail rotor fails. I was too low for that, but I should have shut the engine off. With no tail rotor failure training, I didn't have the tools to diagnose the problem in the three seconds I had to react. Since then Bill Gale has come up with a very good tail rotor failure procedure for the TEMSCO pilots.

The next morning I got out of the hospital, and we got a report that Carl Jackson was overdue on a flight between Ketchikan and Metlakatla. I didn't feel like flying yet so Al Jones took me out as his extra set of eyes, and we flew until dark in the area between Mountain Point and Annette Island. The next day somebody finally found the plane. One survivor, a young lady, walked to the beach and managed to flag down a boat. She told us what happened.

It was one of those days when you could fly 3000 or 4000 feet high. You could see down, but you couldn't see ahead. Apparently Carl had gone a little out of the way to show his passengers a boat that was having trouble on the beach. Then he decided to take a shortcut through the mountains to Metlakatla. Apparently he was pretty high when he lost control of the airplane. It spun in, crashed, and burned. The young lady was thrown out, but she wasn't injured—just bruised. She was able to walk to the beach for help.

I had hoped to talk to Carl that week because he had seen my accident and had passed on just the two words, "You spun." I wanted to talk to him to find out what else he could tell me about my accident. Instead, I lost a good friend.

The next day the FAA investigator was in town and wanted to go up to Carl Jackson's accident site. I flew him up in the little Hughes 269B. I probably should not have done it because I was all taped up and hurting pretty bad. I didn't dare take a deep breath or make a sudden move with those broken ribs.

There was not much left of the Carl's Cessna.

Tail Rotors

In our early days, the first Hughes 500s and Hughes 300s had tail rotors and main rotors made of anodized aluminum. Anodizing made the blades a little harder but not hard enough to cope with the rain we have in Ketchikan. As a protective measure, we put a heavy grade of plastic tape over the leading edge of the tail rotor and the main rotors. This worked great for a while, and when you threw a tape off the main rotor of the little Hughes 300, it would just hump along for a little bit. You immediately knew what it was so you'd land and replace it or remove the tape from the other blade. But when the tape came off the high-speed tail rotor, it was another story.

The first time it happened to me John Valentine, a Fish and Game biologist, was with me in the little 300. We'd been doing stream surveys and were on our way home. When the tape came off, the ship started shaking badly so I made an autorotation to the beach and landed with power. I removed the tape from the other side so the tail rotors were in balance and flew home. The bad part was that it scared John more than it did me, and you don't like to scare your customers.

The first time it happened to me with the 500, I had Jackie Stevens, the head geologist for U.S. Borax, with me. We were over Kendrick Bay when I lost the tail rotor tape, and it started a severe vibration. When you're flying along with a nice smooth helicopter and all of a sudden it starts to vibrate, you know that something's going to happen pretty soon. I immediately shot an autorotation to the nearest beach and recovered with power. I landed on the beach, got out, and checked. Sure enough I'd lost the tape off of the tail rotor. That wasn't so bad. I pulled the other piece off and flew home.

We had a pilot who was flying up in the Salmon Bay area when he lost his tail rotor tape. His passenger thought he'd lost his tail rotor and went ape and was giving the pilot a real bad time. The pilot was shooting for a landing in a little open spot in the muskeg. He forgot he'd rolled his power throttle off, and the helicopter landed short of the flat spot and was wrecked. The passenger got his leg stuck in the pedals and was screaming and hollering. He ended up with no real serious injuries, just some lacerations and bruises on one ankle, but it was a real traumatic experience for both of them. It really put the pilot in a predicament to have a passenger lose his head and go wild on him. It made it very difficult for him to think clearly and do what he should have done.

We had plenty of trouble with rain erosion on the main rotor blades so we kept tape on them. We almost never shed the tape on the main rotors. Instead, the tape would wear out and start humping, and then we'd have to either remove it or replace it. Working Quartz Hill in the wintertime in the heavy rain, we had one brand-new set of blades last only 300 hours, and $25,000 for a set of blades at that time was a lot of bucks for us.

Nineteen seventy-four was our bad year for accidents. It seemed like every time we turned around, somebody was wrecking a helicopter, and generally for the same reason—running out of power. Jerry Taylor was one who came in too steep on a landing approach and didn't give himself enough time to slow down. Jerry tried to abort, but his floats hit the edge of the helipad

Larry Kemp's helicopter burns after being swatted out of the air by a falling tree. Miraculously, neither Larry, nor the ground crew were hurt.

and bounced him upside down. Nobody was hurt, just another wrecked helicopter.

Falling Tree

Even when we did everything right, fortune dealt us a bad hand. In the middle of the summer in 1974, we were working with Clyde Weatherall who had a drill camp in the Ingraham Bay-Johnson Cove area of Prince of Wales Island. Our pilot, Larry Kemp, was moving their drill. They were working quite close to the trees, but there was plenty of room, and Larry was doing a fine job.

The drilling company had an ex-convict working for them who wasn't too smart. He decided that it was too dangerous for the helicopter to land close to the trees so when the helicopter was gone, he went out with a chainsaw that he didn't know how to use and cut a tree halfway through. When the helicopter came back, he quit sawing and tried to keep the tree from falling over. The tree was just too close to going, and the wind from the helicopter blew it around until it fell over. The tree fell right on the helicopter while it was hovering with a man underneath it hooking up a load.

When the tree struck, Larry didn't know what had happened. The helicopter crashed on its side, the bubble broke, and Larry jumped out. It caught fire and burned up right in front of everybody. What a miracle nobody was hurt!

Alaska Airlines Crash

April 15, 1976 was a typical spring day with northwest winds of 10 knots and wet snow. As usual TEMSCO mechanics and pilots hit the coffee room for a cup of coffee and BS before 8 a.m. work. This day was normal; no flights scheduled for me. About 10 minutes to 8 the phone rang, and I answered it. It was Jack Swaim of Webber Air calling to say, "In case nobody has called you, Alaska Airlines Flight 60 just ran off the end of Runway 11."

I told the crew to get everything out of the hangar. We had five ships to put on line, two Hughes 500Cs and three Hillers. Kelly Shunke and Ralph Yetka were on the 500s; Al Jones, Stan Maplesden, and I on the Hillers. We loaded everyone who could

Alaska Airlines Flight 60 burns in the distance, as seen from Ketchikan. (Photo courtesy of Sam Durell.)

help and took off with no warm up.

Stan Maplesden was the first helicopter out of the hangar with a turbine Hiller. He took Allen Zink with him. Allen said when they arrived, they wondered where all the people were—not realizing most of them had walked off the wing and were walking toward the terminal. He saw people working on the flight engineer who had crawled or been pushed out of the cockpit. The pilot and copilot were still in the cockpit. The copilot was out of his head and fighting everyone. Allen remembers Gene Franks, Steve Matter, Chuck Slagle, and Kevin Hack in particular helping to get everyone out.

The pilot was screaming and thrashing around. His foot was pinned by the foot pedal and wires. Gene Franks had big fire ax and tried to chop the center section of the windshield out, but couldn't. The fire was burning at the bulkhead of the cabin, and looked like it would envelop the cockpit at any minute. Gene Franks said to Allen, "The fire is awful close. If we can't get the pilot out, I am going to knock him out with the ax so he won't suffer." Allen was a big, strong man. He took hold of the pilot, and with all his strength he pulled him loose and got him out of the cockpit just before the flames consumed it.

Flight 60 ran off the runway following a bungled foul-weather landing, and broke into pieces. The plane caught fire, but its fuel load did not. (Photo courtesy of Sam Durell.)

I was the last to leave the pullout and had no passengers. When I arrived on the scene, the airplane was burning in the middle. It was not a fuel fire. As luck would have it, the ruptured fuel tank drained into the creek the plane was straddling. I landed about 150 feet from the plane where I saw people bringing up a stretcher with a flight officer in it. Phyllis Yetka—a nurse, Kevin Hack, Wendell Jones, and a stewardess were heading for my helicopter carrying a stretcher. The person in the stretcher was the second officer, and he was still out of his head, trying to escape. Phyllis had given him a shot and said she had to accompany him to the hospital so she got in the right seat of the helicopter. We put the stretcher on the right cargo rack, and started strapping it in. The second officer wasn't having it, and we were afraid he would break loose in the short flight to the hospital and fall in the bay. Kevin Hack volunteered to sit on the rack and hold him down, come hell or high water. The flight would only last a few minutes, but we had to fly over the chan-

Kevin Hack, nurse Phyllis Yetka, and I lift off, carrying the injured Alaska Airlines copilot across the channel to Ketchikan General Hospital. The copilot was out of his head, fighting to get loose, that's why Kevin is sitting on him. (Photo courtesy of Chip Porter.)

nel and into the Wilson Clinic parking lot. I had to get some altitude. Later Kevin told me, "I hung on for dear life with the copilot punching me in the face!"

I was flying the helicopter from the left seat, so I ran my RPM to the standard 3200 and started to the left. I was so far out of trim that the rotor head started to stop-bang. That meant I had reached the limit of left cyclic, and any further movement meant serious trouble. I asked Phyllis to get out, but she said, "I have to go with the patient because I've given him a shot." The next best thing I could do was to move Phyllis to the center seat. Then I was able to lift off, but I was on the edge of the extreme limit of lateral cyclic. I flew gently across the channel and landed in the Wilson Clinic parking lot, which is adjacent to Ketchikan General Hospital.

On the way back I saw a 500 had landed in the ferry terminal parking lot with a stretcher. I returned to the accident site, and a stretcher with the first pilot was ready. This was a better-balanced load, one passenger and one stretcher. I took them to the Wilson Clinic parking lot straight away.

When I arrived back at the accident site, someone said the Coast Guard had landed some five-gallon cans of Light Water firefighting foam for the fire department on the beach below the wreck. I flew down to the beach and loaded both side racks with five-gallon cans of Light Water and supplies and hovered up close to the wreck. The creek that the plane straddled had a little bridge across it with 2x4 railings that were quite close together. I touched down on the railings being careful not to put any weight on them, but steadying the helicopter so I could be unloaded. The firemen unloaded the right side and stepped back. With the left side still loaded, I was completely out of balance. I couldn't move, couldn't land, couldn't hover, I was stuck. I started jerking my head trying to indicate that I needed the other side unloaded. I sat there for what seemed like minutes before one of the fellows finally got the message and walked on the bridge under the helicopter to the other side and unloaded the left hand rack. Now I was free to go.

The wreck was pretty well consumed by fire. One lady in a wheelchair died on impact, but most of the people got off on the wing and walked down to the terminal. I radioed Flight Service to call TEMSCO if I could be of any more help.

Back at TEMSCO the phones were ringing off the hook with news media trying to get information. I answered one call from an Anchorage news media. They said they heard there were helicopters all over the place, and that I had been taking people to the hospital. I guess I wasn't nice. I told them to call Alaska Airlines for information. I felt it was not my place to give out that information.

We later learned the cause of the accident. The pilot told Flight Service that he was making a missed approach then called back and said, "I can see the runway. I am going to land." He had touched down in the middle of the runway, put the plane in reverse thrust, and then tried to abort the landing. He could not get out of reverse thrust, nor could he get the power to take off

Trapped on the bridge. I can't take off because the weight of the Light Water on the left skid has me way out of balance. I can't land because the railings of the bridge I'm on will collapse. (Photo courtesy of Chip Porter.)

again. He was going too fast to get stopped before the end of the runway, ran off the end, and crashed.

Vallenar Point Rescue

One day in October of 1977, we got a call from the Coast Guard that an airplane had spotted the trolling boat *Arminta* turned over on the Vallenar Bay side of Vallenar Point, and there was a man hanging onto the keel of the boat. The Coast Guard sent a 40-footer out, but it was still en route.

I dashed out with the helicopter, N4415, and located the fellow right away. He was mostly in the water, and the waves were slapping over him, but he had hold of the keel of the boat. The waves were two or three feet high, too rough to land on. I had the Hiller 12E with the big bag floats, so between waves I was able to put one float down right next to the guy on the keel of the boat, and he just looked up at me. He couldn't move. I was shocked for a minute and didn't know what to do. I couldn't do anything by myself, and this guy obviously was not able to move himself. He was probably getting pretty cold by now. I didn't know how long he'd been in the water.

The only communications I had were with our base at Peninsula Point so I called them and told them I was coming back. I'd meet the Coast Guard boat, but I had to have one man get aboard to help me. I was able to intercept the 40-footer and hover, balancing one float on a railing of the boat. I got a man off the boat into the helicopter and took him out to where the fellow was still hanging on the keel of his trolling boat.

The Coast Guard man got out on the pontoon as I hovered with one pontoon on the bottom of the boat. I had taken the door off to make easy access. He reached down, got hold of the fisherman, and helped him crawl up on the float. Together we managed to get the fisherman into the seat next to me.

The fisherman, who turned out to be Eldrid Guthrie, was sopping wet and half frozen to death. He put his arm around me and tried to thank me. We got him back to town and into the hospital where he was treated for hypothermia.

We had to take all the seats out of the helicopter and wash it down inside because salt water is dynamite on magnesium parts. We were able to get it cleaned up and ready for service the next day.

Fourth of July Air Show

Every Fourth of July I flew the American flag with the Alaska flag underneath it to start the parade. We even put on a little air show until the FAA started breathing down our necks. In our first air show, we had five Hillers flying in formation, which was a very noisy little operation. One year we had three 500s do a fly-by and split right, left, and up. It was pretty impressive. We did dip-net pickups of people in the water and cargo hauling demonstrations. Members of the rescue squad rappelled down ropes from the helicopter into a boat. We would do all the things we were capable of doing. The show became a tradition. Now all we are allowed to do is fly the flag, and I still do that.

Red Dog

In July of 1978, I took 20 Fox from Ketchikan up to the Red Dog area to service some really hot prospecting and drilling operations. Red Dog is way up above Kotzebue. They had brought in great big inflatable bladders to handle the fuel, which made a nice fueling setup for everyone. They also had a good camp with a cook and everything. Gangs of people were running around there with several core drills going at once, creating plenty of work for all.

I helped a crew survey the road from Kivalina to Red Dog camp. The plan was to build a road to Kivalina on the Chukchi Sea and stockpile the concentrates until the ice went out. Then large loads of concentrate would be shipped south to the smelter.

One day we had finished work at Kivalina, and I was headed back to camp. On the map the company had marked a large fuel cache that had been taken in by ski planes in the winter. I needed some fuel to get back to camp. The fuel gauge was at the no-fly point, and I was sweating blood. Nowhere could I see any fuel barrels in the wide tundra area. Then all of a sudden, right below me were 200 blue barrels of fuel. What a relief! I quickly refueled and headed for camp.

Red Dog proved to be one of the largest finds of zinc and other minerals in the world and is still being mined today.

On my way back from Red Dog, I stopped in Fairbanks because Pat Stack, one of the pilots there, wanted to talk to me. He had been working for a mining company out of Big Delta. The mountain range around Big Delta runs around 7000 to 8000 feet high with jagged little peaks. They were prospecting in this area and had a camp set up on a little airstrip above the river at Big Delta. Pat said what they were asking him to do was too dangerous. He knew he was going to have a terrible accident, and he couldn't handle it. I stayed and worked the job for a couple of weeks until we got Jerry Taylor up there to finish it out. We had to make some one-skid landings up at the 7500-foot level so we had to be careful, and we had to know what our loads were. It worked out real well for everyone—we did the job for the people, and they were happy with it.

On the Beach in Khaz Bay

We sent Jack McKernan to Cordova for a fish-unloading job with Hiller N5352V stripped down to short skids to allow it to carry heavier loads. The job did not work out well because the small boats he had to work with were not really suited for the operation, and the fishermen didn't like the helicopter hovering so close to their boats. We needed Jack elsewhere so I told him to tie down 52 Victor at the airport eleven miles out of Cordova and catch Alaska Airlines to his new job.

About a week later I found time to go to Cordova and pick up 52 Victor. It was a good time for Dan Eichner to get more time in the helicopter too. We gathered up the dual controls and emergency gear and caught a ride with Alaska Airlines to Cordova. Five-Two Victor had an auxiliary tank so we had plenty of fuel for each leg of the trip. Dan and I had been looking forward to doing a little beach combing along those 100-mile sandy beaches. They're littered with everything from ships to glass balls. It was an enjoyable trip to Yakutat where we fueled up with our old friend Arnie Israelson and took off for Sitka allowing a couple hours extra on our flight plan for beach combing.

We didn't see any place that looked good for beach combing until we were within 30 minutes of Sitka. We were early on our flight plan and needed to stretch a little so we picked a beach in Khaz Bay to land on. It was an exposed beach and a rocky one. There was a flat spot at midtide, but it was solid with round boulders about the size of a man's head. We landed very carefully, sat still for the engine cool-down, and shut the engine off. The blades were barely turning when both of us opened our doors and stepped out. The helicopter started to slowly tip back. I immediately jumped back on the front of the skids only to hear a click-click before the helicopter responded to my weight. We moved a rock under the back of each skid to hold it from tipping back. We didn't fly the short skids very often so I had been a little lax. We took a good look at the tail rotor, and Dan, who was an A&E mechanic, soon found a little kink in the critical area of the rotor. We couldn't fly the helicopter.

Five-Two Victor was stuck at mid-tide, and the tide was coming in. In three hours salt water would cover the helicopter, destroying all the electronics and corroding all the magnesium parts. It would be a total wreck. We got a bit frantic and started to beach comb for something to help us. We found a fisherman's buoy line and tried to rig up a windlass to drag the helicopter, but it was futile.

All of a sudden a bright light came on in my brain. We removed the damaged blades and tied the buoy line to the tail of 52 Victor. We strung the line out about 40 feet to the left side of the tail and at 90 degrees to the helicopter. Then I had Danny tie the rope around his waist and prepare to brace himself against the torque of the engine when I tried to lift off. I made one short up and down. Danny said it drug him a little as I first lifted off, but he could hold it. Now we knew we could move the helicopter about 20 feet on one move so we got busy preparing five landing spots twenty feet apart headed up the beach to a spot high above the tide. It worked. We had 52 Victor safe.

Now we could relax and figure out the next move. I figured the time was about right for an Alaska Airlines plane to be overhead in the area so I made a call on the VHF using Alaska's company frequency and made contact right away. I asked them to cancel my flight plan and to have their company in Ketchikan notify TEMSCO that I was on the beach in Khaz Bay. I was in no trouble, but I needed two tail rotor blades brought to me.

In about three hours, our Cessna amphibian was overhead. I got on the radio and talked to Kelly Shunke and Ed Davis. They said the bay was too rough to land on, but there was a lake close by. In about thirty minutes Kelly and Ed appeared out of the woods and looked the situation over. Ed said, "I can't even reach the tail rotor gear box. How could you have damaged it?" After an explanation, we got busy and tipped the tail down and changed the tail rotor blades. We still had a couple of hours of daylight left so we all took off for Sitka where we fueled up and headed for Ketchikan arriving at home base about an hour after dark. Thank goodness for those long summer days.

Harry the Snake Charmer

When I was president of the Alaska Air Carriers, we were having a board of directors meeting in Nome, and I had taken an Alaska Airlines jet to Anchorage and then to Nome. Before we landed in Anchorage, the stewardess told me the pilot wanted to see me. I went up into the cockpit, and the pilot told me they just got a call from Ketchikan saying that our little Hughes 269 (Jiminy Cricket) was overdue. The wreck had been found on the Soule Glacier, but no people were in it.

I immediately made arrangements to hop on a southbound flight back to Ketchikan. As soon as I got to Ketchikan I took off in a helicopter for the crash site. When I got there I saw that the 269 had wrecked right on the ice, and next to the ice was a big pool of blue water. The pilot's glasses were there along with all the emergency gear, but still no people. I thought they may have fallen into the pool of water and drowned. It had been 24 hours since the initial crash. I flew down the river to salt water, and on the way down I spotted the two survivors—the pilot and his passenger—who were physically unharmed.

Our little 269 was cheaper for customers to hire, but it was more difficult to fly and needed an expert pilot to fly it. Ralph Yetka had flown the job the year before, but he was needed to fly one of our turbine helicopters so I asked my crew where we could find a high-time Hughes 269 pilot, and they recommended a fellow in California, Harry the Snake Charmer (snake charming was his hobby). They said he had several thousand hours instructing beginners in the 269, and they thought he might like to spend a summer working in Alaska.

So we hired Harry, and he had been working off the stern of the boat the prospectors were living aboard. He and the skipper of the boat (who was also a geologist) had taken off to take a picture of an interesting rock formation on the mountain. It appeared that a little alcohol was involved. The two of them went up to the top of the mountain in the 269 and started a slow flight down the mountain, snapping pictures as they went. The glacier being along side the mountain always creates a downwind condition so Harry was actually slow flying and sometimes going into a hover as he flew down the mountain. Harry's explanation was, "It felt just like I was settling with power," and the sad story is that he was. He was settling rapidly as he went down the mountain, and as he pulled more power to level off, the helicopter was already out of control, and they crashed. Obviously, there is a big difference between instructing people to fly a helicopter and working a helicopter so Harry went back to snake charming in California.

Medical Evacuation

In August of 1978, we had a medevac call after dark. A fisherman had dislocated his shoulder and broken an arm. He was ambulatory, but they needed to get him to the hospital right away. The boat was in Tolstoi Bay.

It was a clear night with patches of fog. Looked like a pretty simple flight. I flew over to the Caamano shore, down to Ship Island, and across to Tolstoi Bay. The injured man had been taken to the beach where I landed and picked him up.

On the way back I flew out to Clarence Straits at Tolstoi Point and started down the Tolstoi shore towards Ketchikan. I thought I was being very careful, maintaining altitude and keeping the clouds quite a ways ahead of me. All of a sudden I was in one of them, and I was IFR. It was one of the most horrible sensations I ever had on a night flight. I turned left because I knew that way was clear, and I watched my RPM and my air speed. In a matter of probably thirty seconds, I broke out into the open again, but I'd lived a thousand deaths in that short period of time. Your vision changes when you fly at night, and it is hard to judge distances. In this case I'd been very wrong about how far away those clouds were. I was able to get back to town all right after that, and I took the fisherman to the hospital.

Twin Crashes

In August of 1978, we had a day with some real heavy squalls. There wasn't a lot of air traffic that day, but there was some.

That evening I heard through the grapevine that a 182 Cessna was reported overdue from Ketchikan. A doctor, who was a new IFR pilot, and his nurse had taken off IFR from Ketchikan to Sitka. Flight Service had no report of him after he took off, and they had no idea where he had gone. They did not alert the Ketchikan Volunteer Rescue Squad, but in fairness, Flight Service did not have to notify us. Their job was to report it to the Coast Guard, and the Coast Guard had initiated some kind of a search, but nobody else had been contacted. (Later we had a lot of cooperation from Flight Service that went beyond their call of duty. Together we helped a lot of people.)

Later that evening a Twin Aero Commander was reported overdue with a pilot and four children on board. He had been reported in the Metlakatla area, attempting to go from Metlakatla to Ketchikan when he ran into a heavy squall and disappeared. We'd gotten no word about what happened, but there were rumors that somebody heard an airplane crash up on Deer Mountain.

Now we had a Twin Aero Commander overdue in bad circumstances, and a 182 Cessna missing from Ketchikan. It was kind of strange. Nobody had notified the rescue squad of either of these two overdue planes; we heard about both of them through the grapevine.

In the meantime the Coast Guard was making preparations to go looking. They came down from Sitka real early in the morning on a nice sunny day and started a search looking for the Twin Aero Commander. They located the 182 Cessna that had crashed on Deer Mountain and also the Twin that had crashed and burned a short distance from the 182. The Coast Guard couldn't get to the wrecks and requested me to go check for survivors.

Steve Brown and I took off. I let Steve fly, and he let me off at the site of the 182. I went down and checked to see what had happened. Both the pilot and his nurse were definitely dead. Steve had to hover on one skid to land me there, and he did the same thing to pick me up and move me over to the old cabin site on Deer Mountain, which is the only level bare patch of ground within 500 feet of the top of Deer Mountain. I walked around the trail and over to the wreck site of the Aero Commander. Probably one of the most unpleasant things I ever had to do was to look into a wreck and see children in there. One child is bad enough. Here there were four, all dead and broken. It's something that stays with you for a lifetime.

It appeared that the 182 Cessna pilot sat on the runway at Ketchikan Airport looking at a big black cloud. He didn't want to go. Flight Service told him if he didn't want to leave now his time was up, and he should return to the ramp. He took off and made the wrong turn when he was IFR, which put him into Deer Mountain

The Twin Aero Commander pilot apparently got into bad weather between Annette Island and Ketchikan and attempted to go IFR. He climbed up 2000 feet, took a heading for the Ketchikan Airport, and intersected Deer Mountain.

Floyd Miller

These were the days when we had lots of helicopters on charter up north, and we generally had a roving mechanic and a pilot for our 206 Cessna stationed up there. Occasionally they needed parts from Ketchikan, and I would take our Cessna with amphibious gear on it to deliver them. On one trip in August of '79 I went to Cordova with some parts, then up to Fairbanks, out to Big Delta, and out to Northway.

At Northway we met Floyd Miller who owned the motel at Northway and had a little air taxi operation. He flew a 206 Cessna on wheels, and he'd just bought a 206 with amphibious gear on it. We had a helicopter up in the boonies with a bad engine, and I'd brought an engine up to Floyd to be taken out to the helicopter. Floyd said, "Why don't you ride along?" So I got in the 206 with Floyd and our engine, and we took off to make the delivery. The landing strip was a little uphill strip with barely enough room to land. What a wild operation! He put her down with no trouble at all. We got up to the top of the hill, turned the airplane around, unloaded the new engine, and took the old engine out. Floyd barreled down that hill and off we went.

When we got back to Northway, Floyd said, "You fly seaplanes all the time. I'd like you to try out this new 206 with amphibious gear."

I said I would like to fly his airplane, and told him, "You go ahead and make a takeoff and landing, and I'll do one after you." Floyd took off from the airport and headed out to a lake close by. I said, "Go ahead and take off from the lake."

Well, he made a takeoff, and he wasn't very good at it. He turned around and landed, and he said, "Now you do it." I made a takeoff, and the airplane really performed pretty well. It had a supercharged engine, and it worked great.

After I took off, he said, "How'd you do that?" I said, "How'd I do what?" He said, "Well, you got off of the water half again as fast as I did." I didn't think I did anything unusual so we decided to try it again with him watching to see if I did anything different.

I proceeded to make a normal takeoff, but Floyd noticed something. When you start a takeoff, the pilot holds the aircraft at the angle where the floats will accelerate best. When I start getting up speed, I generally lift one float off the water, which speeds the acceleration up a little bit. Floyd, having never flown pontoons, was holding the airplane down on the water (in effect, dragging his heels) and then trying to get off too soon. Holding the plane down made the floats drag and slowed his takeoff. He appreciated the tip. Floyd was a character we dealt with a lot, and he was a legend in Northway.

Capsized Ship

On December 2, 1979 the Japanese freighter *Lee Wang Zin* was reported rolled over, and the entire crew missing. The *Lee Wang Zin* was hauling ore out of Prince Rupert Harbor headed for Japan when it got a little off course, struck a rock, and rolled over. It had a lot of fuel on board, and it was floating upside down. When we got the emergency call, it was to look for survivors.

Still upside down, the *Lee Wang Zin* started drifting. It got hung up on the beach near Kendrick Bay so we all went out there. The salvage boat was there, and the rescuers were trying to go through the inside of the boat to find any bodies. Finally they got the boat off the beach and were going to tow it out to deep water.

While it was on the beach, a really big storm came up. The *Lee Wang Zin* was a big news item so all the TV people were in town wanting a helicopter ride out to look at the ship. It was kind of a fun thing for me. I took these guys out, and we landed in behind a little break point and walked through the brush to the other side to see the *Lee Wang Zin*. Mountainous waves probably 20 to 25 feet high were going right up over it. The reporters said, "What a Godforsaken place! No one could survive here!" It was miserable.

We went back to the helicopter and one guy said, "Do you think we could get some pictures? I'd like to get some video pictures of the wreck out there." We flew out, and I got down between the swells so he could take some pictures. We were looking up at the waves coming at us. It wasn't a dangerous thing to do as long as everything was running. We got some really spectacular pictures.

The day after the boat capsized was a fairly nice day. Danny and I went out with 42 Mike looking for pieces, and we located a life raft. We landed out in the middle of the straits and checked the life raft out, but there was no sign that anybody had been in it. It must have had an automatic inflator. It was about a 10-man life raft and in good shape. Later on somebody else found another one. We took them into TEMSCO where the Japanese investigators came to see if anybody had ever been in them or not. It appeared nobody ever got off of the ship.

The tug people from Portland, Oregon, who were the official salvage people for firms all over the Pacific Ocean, came up to get the boat off the beach. They were experts and knew what they were doing. We had repeated trips to go out and help them, and there were a number of helicopters in the area. On several occasions we transported stuff from the Coast Guard Base to the Coast Guard Cutter *Monroe*. When you land on the *Monroe*, they signal you down and motion you around. We didn't know what all the motion was for; it was a great big deck. I didn't need any help to land there, but it was their procedure.

We landed men on the bottom of the *Lee Wang Zin* to determine where they could put dynamite to finish the sinking of it or where they were going to have to shoot it with the Coast Guard ship's guns. They weren't sure yet. There were a lot of experts from Southeast Alaska helping on the job.

Later I had to land on the tugboat that was pulling the still-floating *Lee Wang Zin*. The crew on the tugboat really knew what they were doing. The minute I touched down they had me tied down at four points because the water was very rough. I did what I had to do and took off again.

Shortly after I left the tugboat, the *Lee Wang Zin* sank. As the ship fell to the bottom, its weight overpowered the tug's winch and started peeling off tow cable—peeling it off clear to the end. The sinking ship was pulling the tugboat backwards,

My experiences at Caamano Point and elsewhere pointed to the need for a device for rescuing people out of the water without the help of another person. With that in mind, we invented the "people netter," which is little more than a giant-sized crab ring that snaps into the cargo hook. In this demo, I "rescued" my son Dan, dressed in a marine survival suit.

and it was a very dangerous situation for a little bit. Boats have been pulled under by their sunken tows. Somehow they got the line either cut or freed at the end. These guys were experienced, and they knew the predicament they were in and how to handle it, but it was a close call. The ship sank midway between Cape Muzon and Langara Island.

After the *Lee Wang Zin* sank, oil spilled and washed up on the beaches. We had a big fiasco with a cost-plus thing where ten of our chainsaws would go out in the morning to cut up and burn the logs on the beaches that were covered with oil. At the end of the day only five chainsaws came back. We didn't know where they were going. It was really a bummer, but the project did clean up the mess to some degree.

Later on some of the oil drifted into Forse Cove over by Thorne Bay on Prince of Wales Island, and the environmental people used Forse Cove as kind of a study to see what happened to the marine life around the area where the oil ended up. We had repeated trips up there to check on Mother Nature.

Sabine, Texas

In April of 1980, we secured two positions on brand-new Sikorsky S76 helicopters that were coming out of the factory. We put some pretty good-sized money down on them and were anxious to get the ships. We got a call from Bristol Helicopters in England wanting to buy our two positions because they needed those two helicopters right away. We made a deal with them to pay us back what we'd invested, and in addition they gave us two Hughes 500D helicopters that were based in Sabine, Texas.

Later that month Danny and I, Dick Borch and Chuck McGee went to Sabine to pick up the helicopters. Sabine was an interesting place because there was a lot of helicopter activity connected with serving the oilrigs. Sabine has a lot of frontier history, and this was my first visit. The Bristol people got our helicopters ready to go, and we took off for the long trip all the way from Sabine, Texas to Alaska's North Slope, which was nearly 5000 miles.

The trip was uneventful except for one serious snowstorm where Dan and I got separated from Dick and Chuck. Dan and I had a lot of trouble with the weather and eventually had to land at a small-town service station to buy some kerosene to get us to the next airport. The next day Flight Service helped us get back together.

I enjoyed the cross-country trip; it was fun. In those days we didn't have the GPS. You had to look at your maps and run compass courses, but it didn't seem any harder. The GPS that we have nowadays certainly simplifies those long trips and straightens out a lot of curves.

The People Netter

In October of 1980, three men were on their way back from their cabin and oyster farm in Sunny Cove during rough weather when something happened, and their boat sank. They got in a little life raft and apparently drifted for quite a few hours that night. They couldn't all get into the life raft because it was pretty small, and one of the older fellows died.

We got the call from Allen Zink who was in an airplane and spotted them drifting in Clarence Straits near Caamano Point. Martin Jetton and Ralph Yetka immediately rolled a helicopter out of the hangar, grabbed two survival suits, and dashed out there. I wasn't at the office at the moment, and when I arrived I was told that Martin and Ralph had taken off. They dropped one survival suit, and it missed the life raft so Ralph got out on the skid of the helicopter and was able to grab the survival suit and drop it into the sinking life raft—quite a feat in that rough water.

I called them on the radio and said, "Hey, do you guys need the dip net out there?" I had devised a dip net that was a big circular hoop about ten feet in diameter with a net on it. I could sling it underneath the helicopter on a long line and scoop people out of the water with it. We called it the People Netter. I'd demonstrated it a number of times on the Fourth of July, but we had never had an occasion to use it. They didn't know if they could use it or not, but I took off anyway with the dip net underneath me. I could only do about 50 miles an hour with the dip net dragging underneath. As I approached the scene, I could see debris from the boat. I finally got to the two survivors as their life raft was sinking on them. One guy had gotten into a survival suit completely, and one of them was halfway in a survival suit. The tugboat *Edith Olsen* was there bouncing around like a cork. They didn't know how they were going to get those boys aboard the boat without injuring them.

I had Bill Gale riding with me in the back seat so he could observe what was going on and help me with clearance from the mast of the tugboat. The dip net worked like a champion. I dipped down and scooped the first guy out of the water and set him on the deck of the boat. Within a couple of minutes, I had both guys aboard the boat. The tugboat dashed over to Clover Pass while the men were being treated for hypothermia. The two fellows emerged very well from the accident, but they'd lost one person as well as their boat and gear which was a tragedy.

The dip net was a good thing in the right areas, but you couldn't carry someone very far in it unless they had a survival suit on because hypothermia would finish them off. Sergeant Morris Rogers arranged for me to demonstrate the dip net to oil people at Nikiski in the Kenai area. They were quite impressed and wanted to buy some, but at that time all I could do was to send them the plans. I tried to convince people in Hawaii that it would be a good thing, but they do their own thing over there—they like to go out and demonstrate their swimming skills more than anything else. The Ketchikan Volunteer Rescue Squad, with the help of the State, built a dozen rescue nets that were collapsible so they could be transported faster. We sent them to several places—one to the troopers in Anchorage and one to a helicopter company in Cook Inlet.

One of my pilots, Doc Gomert, was working up at Kaktovik, a little Eskimo village on the Arctic Ocean, where they have a short period of time when the ice is rotten. When their people go out in their boats and get into trouble, there was no way to rescue them. Doc told the mayor of Kaktovik about our dip net, and he asked us to send one up.

So far I haven't heard of anybody else using them. We've used them here in Ketchikan several times. I've done it, and I know Bill Gale has dipped people a couple of times with it when they were in the water close to our hangar. At the right time in the right place, it's a valuable little tool.

Dale Clark Overdue

I'd just come home from work one October day in 1980 and was listening to the scanner when I heard about an overdue airplane. I called Flight Service to find out what was going on, and they told me Dale Clark was overdue. The Jackson boy and a passenger had gone out to Leduc Lake and found the crash site. Dale had a broken arm, one passenger was dead, and one had a possible broken back.

The weather was so bad in Leduc Lake that the Jackson boy left his passenger and took off by himself to try to arrange for help. Darkness was setting in, and obviously the man with the broken back was going to have a very difficult time making it through the night. With the sketchy information we had, it looked like a very bad situation so I organized a rescue operation right away. I figured it would take two helicopters, one to transport the injured man and one to take a crew in. We hustled up a crew as quickly as we could. I elected to take four medical people instead of taking a woodsman along to help—a decision I would later regret as this turned out to be one of the most difficult rescue operations I ever participated in.

Bill Gale loaded Jerry Martin, a medevac team member from Pond Reef, and Caroline Hall, a nurse from the hospital in his Hughes 500. I had Steve Rydeen, a medevac team member from the Fire Department, and a first aid person from Ketchikan Fire Department in mine. We finally got organized and took off from Peninsula Point.

It was dark, and the wind was strong and gusty with hard rain. Leduc Lake is roughly 35 to 40 minutes away in the Hughes 500 at normal cruising speed. Bill Gale had not flown in the area before so he had to follow me. Following another helicopter when you don't know where you're going is probably the hardest thing in the world to do, especially when it's dark and you're flying in the mountains. You don't dare lose sight of the helicopter you are following. As we went along, I warned him of the rough air spots, when I was slowing down, and when I was resuming speed.

As we flew up the Chickamin River, we could barely see the outline of the hills in the dark. It was gusty and rainy, just not a good night to fly. Leduc Lake is cradled in the mountains, and at the entrance of the lake is a big waterfall. As I came in over the front of the lake, the darkness was impenetrable. It was just a big black hole. I could see the entrance and the white water of the waterfall, but that's all. I told Bill I was turning around. I just could not penetrate the rain and darkness.

We were only a couple of miles from the accident site, and I decided that I just couldn't give up. I would make one more desperate effort. I told Bill I was going to descend closer to the falls. The white water of the falls was very vivid, and I was concentrating hard.

I guess I didn't explain what I was doing very well because as I made a descending turn down to the top of the waterfalls, all of a sudden there were lights coming right at me. I was looking straight at Bill Gale. It startled us both, but we reacted properly—both of us broke right and proceeded on.

I was able to slow-fly past the waterfall. I could barely pick up a dim shoreline to follow to the head of the lake where there is a big, flat swampy area. Turning my landing light on, I moved up into the flats far enough to leave a landing area for Bill behind me. About that time I saw somebody up the hill a few hundred feet waving a burning rag. It was a help to me at the time, but it was a foolish thing for him to be doing with the gasoline from the crashed airplane all around him. When I got down, I called Bill on the radio and said, "Bill, I think we can move up a little closer." Bill responded, "I'm not moving." It had been a horribly strenuous flight for him.

I sent the first aid people up to the wreck while I secured the helicopter. Then I grabbed some emergency gear I had aboard and went up to the wreck. We had originally planned to pick up the injured people and take them to Old Man Wolfe's cabin at the head of the Chickamin River, but the weather was such that we weren't going to be able to do anything until daylight. It was raining so hard it was unbelievable.

When I got up to the crash site, two of my crew were dragging a man up the bank, and I said, "Hey, that guy is supposed to have a broken back, don't move him." They replied, "Oh, this guy's dead. We're just getting him out of the way." That was kind of a shock.

Then we went over to a fellow who was lying in the creek. He thought he had a broken back and didn't want to be touched. We very carefully maneuvered him onto a backboard and lifted him out of the creek. We moved him up the bank ten or fifteen feet to a level area where we had made a shelter out of tarps. We put the injured man in the shelter, and the two medevac people and the nurse looked after him. They'd given him a shot, and that was all the painkiller they had.

Trying to decide how the rest of us were going to spend the night, I sent Bill Gale and Steve Rydeen back to sleep in the helicopters. Then I had to do something with the young fellow that Jackson had brought in. He'd been futiley trying to get a fire going, and was really in a state of shock himself. He finally realized he wasn't going to get a fire going so we told him to go get some sleep. He crawled into the tail cone on the airplane and huddled up to spend the night.

That left the injured Dale Clark and I. We found a spot near the damaged airplane where we could get out of the wind and rain. Dale was suffering with a broken arm, and he asked me if I had any painkillers. I told him they had just used the last of it on the man with the broken back. He said, "Isn't there aspirin or something like that?" I found a box of aspirin in the first aid kit so I put a couple in my hand and started back to Dale. I looked at my hand, and it was raining so hard the two aspirin had already melted in my hand. I went back and got the whole box and finally got Dale some aspirin. The rain provided plenty of water to drink.

I don't think we slept. We just talked. Dale explained to me that he'd taken off and made a turn at the head of the lake when all of a sudden a gust of wind hit him and slammed him on the ground. He had no control whatsoever. He was feeling very bad. He loved to fly so much that he was afraid this was going to end his flying career, but I assured him that it would not. There was no reason for him to quit flying. He would be an even safer pilot after this accident. Dale is still flying and doing a great job of it. He's one of the better pilots in the country.

We'd weathered the night, and the next morning TEMSCO

tried to send another helicopter out, but the weather was so bad he didn't get very far. Things didn't look that bad from where we were, so I decided to go down and get Bill Gale to bring his helicopter up to the accident site. If he made a one-skid hover landing, we could load the man with the broken back into Bill's helicopter, and I could take everyone else. When I arrived, there was a foot and a half of water over the skids of both helicopters. It had rained so much the lake had come up out of its banks. Bill and Steve were still asleep in the helicopters when I walked up. They hadn't gotten much rest. They were still in a daze when I told Bill what I planned to do.

Bill took the helicopter up, hovered, and got the injured man in plus two other people. The helicopter had a special door with a sack on it so we could put a stretcher in the back end, and the person's feet would stick out the right-hand side in the canvas sack and be protected from any exposure to the wind.

I loaded up the other three passengers, and we started sneaking our way out of there. The weather was terrible, but we were able to work our way out and around it. It took some careful flying, but we made it back to town around midday.

Dale's arm would heal, and after a short stay in the hospital, the fellow we rescued from the creek recovered in good shape. His injuries were serious, but his back wasn't broken after all. Looking back, we knew we had saved his neck. Lying in that creek, injured and unable to move, he wouldn't have survived the long night out.

Award

I was nominated for the Alaska State Troopers' Civilian Man of the Year Award, and in March of 1981 I went to Juneau with the troopers and received this award. It is probably the one I am most proud of. The plaque is inscribed with the words "In recognition of your unfailing courage and selfless devotion to search and rescue."

I was particularly impressed by the official letter by Colonel Anderson, which appears at right.

STATE OF ALASKA
DEPARTMENT OF PUBLIC SAFETY
DIVISION OF STATE TROOPERS

JAY S. HAMMOND, GOVERNOR

P.O. BOX 6188 ANNEX
ANCHORAGE, ALASKA 99502

March 7, 1981

Mr. Ken Eichner
TEMSCO Helicopters, Inc.
Box 5057
Ketchikan, Alaska 99901

Dear Mr. Eichner:

I am pleased to have this opportunity to recognize you for the courageous assistance you have provided to many people in this state through your personal involvement in search and rescue in Southeast Alaska.

In particular, I would like to point to your efforts on October 6th, 1980, involving a downed Cessna 185, and again on October 17, 1980, involving a boat sinking in Clarence Strait. These rescues leave little reason for anyone to question why you are often referred to as a "living legend."

On behalf of the Division of State Troopers, thank you very much. Your efforts have assisted greatly in successfully concluding search and rescue missions.

Sincerely,

Colonel T.R. Anderson
Director

TRA:cw

Chapter 14,
TEMSCO's Growth Years

TEMSCO's growth in the 1970s and 1980s was steady. It seemed like we were buying at least four helicopters a year. We finally made the step into medium-sized helicopters by buying a Bell Super 204 to help with the heavier work at Quartz Hill. That was kind of a painful start, with maintenance problems, and a blade failure accident involving Dave Spokely. We learned from that and finally got a Bell 212 which put us on a better track. Later we added another 212, and a couple of the French ASTAR AS-350s which worked well with our tourist business in Juneau and Skagway. They worked so well, we bought several more. We were running 30 to 40 helicopters total, but the bulk of our work was seasonal. In the wintertime it seemed like we were too idle, and when a good deal came along to buy Tyee Airlines, we went for it. With a great lot of effort over several years we got the airline in pretty good shape, but the competition was pretty stiff battling with Westflight Aviation. Finally

What started with one Hiller was growing quickly. Eventually TEMSCO had 26 Hughes 500s, plus a bevy of other helicopters and fixed-wing aircraft.

they gave up and sold out to us. We had things going pretty well with 23 airplanes. I flew a few airplane trips, which I liked, but really my heart was still in the helicopter business or should I say in flying helicopters. The business part I really didn't like. But working with all of the great people who worked for me and with me made it all worthwhile.

Berserk Shooter

As TEMSCO grew, we started getting some really strange calls. In April of 1981, I got a call from the Alaska State Troopers requesting a helicopter to go over to the Chickamin River. Somebody had gone berserk over there. We flew over and surveyed the situation from a fair distance in the air. This fellow was in a boat out in front of a cabin and had been shooting at the cabin. Inside were a watchman and his wife or girlfriend. The man in the boat was the other watchman. Apparently they were all on booze or something, and the one watchman went berserk and started shooting at the couple. At their first chance the couple called on the radio to get help.

I landed in a place where we were safe from the shooter. Then Sergeant Rogers and I hid behind some trees and hollered at the guy. Now I'm a pilot, supposed to be running a flying service for a living, and here I am hiding behind a log, yelling at a crazy person with a gun. We finally convinced him to give up. When he came into the shore, Sergeant Rogers put handcuffs on him, took his gun away from him, and told him we were going to take him back to town in the helicopter. The guy said, "I'm not riding in that helicopter with my hands handcuffed. If it crashes I couldn't even get out." Rogers said, "I'm sorry, boy, that's the way it is. You're riding in the helicopter."

It wasn't exactly your average day on the job.

Jim Zorn

Jim Zorn, the Seattle Seahawks' quarterback, used to come to town pretty regularly. I'd given him and his girlfriend a ride so every time he arrived in town, he'd give me a call hoping I'd give him another ride, and I was always happy to accommodate him. I would finish the ride by landing up on Deer Mountain and taking off the mountain over a cliff with a drop off of 1500 feet. It was always a thrill for his girlfriends—and him, too, I believe.

He was a very nice fellow. I enjoyed Jim a lot.

Quartz Hill Accident

In June of 1981, I took the National Transportation Safety Board to Quartz Hill where we'd had an accident with our Bell 204 helicopter. The pilot, Dave Spokely, had the job of moving about ten miners from the camp up on the hill to the mine where they were working. His mechanic was riding in the right front seat. When he landed, the mechanic got out and unloaded the passengers. As the mechanic started to get back in, Dave hollered at him that he was going to pull it off because the helicopter was starting to shake. He didn't think he was on solid enough ground to complete a landing. The helicopter was shaking very badly, and Dave lifted it up and started to move backwards. The helicopter flared up, and everything came apart. It spun around and crashed.

In the meantime the passengers were running up a little gravel road away from the helicopter. One of the passengers fell down when he was running away and claimed he had injured his back.

Dave was injured pretty badly. A medevac team was there and took immediate care of him. He had a back injury—it looked like he was going to be a paraplegic. Dave was a very determined boy. He worked and worked and worked and finally got to where he was five percent or less handicapped because of the accident. He made an amazing recovery due to his own strength of will, and his determination that he was going to fly again. He accomplished that.

However, the passenger who claimed he had a broken back brought a lawsuit against us. He told his buddies in camp that he was going to retire off of TEMSCO, and believe it or not, he did. After his injury, he was driving Cats down in Florida and able to do everything physically, but when it came to the trial, he could hardly walk. It was an obvious sham that cost the insurance company $1.4 million and didn't make us feel very good.

After the accident we decided that the blades were all messed up and there was no use saving them. We took the basic

While most of our work was done with the smaller Hiller 12s and Hughes 500s, we used larger helicopters like this Bell UH1B on fires and heavy lift jobs.

helicopter back to town, but we bulldozed those blades under the muskeg at Quartz Hill. Later on, to our sorrow, it became obvious in the testimony at the trial that the blades had failed. It was something that happened to those older 204 blades. They called it blade separation—the blade starts to separate, goes out of track and balance, and you lose control of the helicopter. We were reasonably sure that is what happened, but the NTSB missed it entirely, and the Bell representative wasn't about to tell anybody so it was passed on as unexplainable. We learned a lesson. After that whenever we had an accident, we hired expert investigators out of Vancouver, B.C. who saved us a lot of money over the years.

Goat Tagging

The Alaska Fish and Game Department wanted to do some goat tagging, and also put radio collars on some of the goats around Southeast. No one had done this very successfully in our part of the world yet so among the bunch of us, we had to figure out how to do it. This was a fun operation. We tried several things. First, they used a dart gun. We put the shooter in the back seat on my side of the helicopter. With his door off and a seat belt on, he could handle the shooting very well. Sometimes I had an observer with me in the front seat, but most of the time it was just the two of us. They liked to shoot the goat in the hip. It takes about five minutes before the tranquilizer knocks him out, so once we darted a goat we would back off real quick and maneuver around at a greater distance trying to keep him from going into a cliffy area. The risk with mountain goats is that when you dart one, he immediately runs to a place where he thinks you can't reach him—the side of some incredibly steep cliff. Unless you work to keep him off the cliff, the goat runs up on the side of the cliff, gets drunk from the drugs, and falls off. We never picked on a goat unless he was in a safe area where he wasn't going to fall off of a cliff. We were pretty successful, and we never lost a goat.

The Fish and Game people had another contraption—sort of like a shotgun—that fired a net to entangle the animal. Four weighted points spread the net out. We tried this little net out on a little billy goat. The net covered him nicely, but the goat headed for a cliff and went over it. The net hung up in the bushes, and the goat's horns hung up in the net. To our amazement, here was the goat just hanging there, suspended by his horns like something out of a comic book. He didn't struggle; he just lay there limp. I landed, shut the helicopter off and went over to help the Fish and Game man. We pulled the goat back up, and there wasn't anything wrong with him. He was as alive as could be. They gave him a shot so they could do their physical exam, put a collar on him, and let him go. That was the last time we used the net. It wasn't very practical in that steep mountainous country.

Later on we worked a very nice goat transplant operation moving goats from Quartz Hill to Revillagigedo Island (where Ketchikan is located). We used four helicopters, two of them as shooters and two of them as transporters.

We would shoot a goat and get him tranquilized and stopped. Then the pickup team would arrive and load him in the other helicopter and take him to Pete Amundson's barge where they did a physical exam, put a collar on him, and transported him to upper Mahoney Lake. In one day we transported 16 goats.

In gathering those 16, we had one misfortune. We darted a nice big billy and watched him closely, but he worked himself close to a steep area. I hovered in close to him and got him stopped, then headed him uphill. I told my observer that he had better get out and keep the goat from turning around. I put one skid down on a clear sloping area and let the observer out, but before he got to the goat, it passed out. The goat fell over backwards and slid off the cliff. It was a sight I will never forget—it seemed like a human falling in space all spread out.

Recently I looked at the goat herd around the Mahoney area, and it is doing very well—producing more goats every year. I'm sure the Fish and Game people are going to open a season on them one of these days, at least on a permit basis.

Fish and Game man with one of their net guns.

Engine Failure

I went to work one August morning in 1981 and was to fly 71 Fox, a C model Hughes 500, to take some Fish and Game biologists out to survey several streams on the Unuk River. When I arrived the helicopter wasn't where it was supposed to be—it was out on the back lot all fueled up.

I was scheduled to be back for another flight at 8 a.m. and it was after 7:15 before my passengers showed up. I figured their proposed flight would take too long because they were late. They said, "Okay, we'll change our destination. We'll make it Carroll Creek," which was just half as far as the Unuk. That way I could get back in time to make my eight o'clock trip. So I took off with Gwendolyn Emil, Candia Coombs, and Lane Johnson—all Fish and Game people. I had noticed on the flight sheet that 71 Fox had been written up for over-revs on the governor. Every time you'd slow down and reduce the power, the governor would let the engine overspeed a bit. I kept that in mind throughout the trip.

Flying helicopters offers many special moments. I snapped this picture one day while taking the chance to examine some icebergs from the LeConte Glacier.

When we got down to Carroll Creek, my passengers asked if I thought I could land in a tall tree area. I looked the river over and saw nothing but 200-foot spruce trees, but I spotted a place where it looked like there was room enough to go between the trees and get onto a little sandbar. I turned away from the trees doing a 180-degree turn to set me up on my downwind leg. When I got close to the river, I turned 90 degrees. As I reduced the power, I watched the RPM very closely, and I didn't get an overspeed. It didn't dawn on me for a split second that the engine had quit. As I completed my turn, I realized that I had no power. My training for autorotation came into play instinctively—the minute the power goes off, you bottom the collective and shove the nose down. The turbine engine is subtle—when it quits there is no warning. All of a sudden your power starts to fade and the engine spools down. At that time the new turbine engine installations were having trouble with the warning systems, and we often pulled a circuit breaker to turn the false warning off.

I was in a horrible position. I was about 250 feet high, and I only had about 25 miles an hour air speed. The RPM was on the low side, and I had no place to go. The only choice I had was to go through the trees down into the creek bottom. Acting on instinct only, I bottomed the collective and shoved the nose down and headed for the trees. I made my first turn inside the trees and actually got into the creek bottom area.

Up ahead I could see a nice little sandbar, but a great big log was lying across the river between the sandbar and me. It looked like I could make the sandbar, but it was all happening so fast I didn't have a chance to look at my RPM to see how much I'd recovered and how much I hadn't. I started to flare, which builds RPM and slows you down for the landing, and ker-whang! The skids hit the big log. We were just inches short of clearing the log and hitting the sandbar. But when you hit with a down force like that, the blades flex down and immediately chop the tail off. When that happens it also turns the helicopter around sideways. We turned around sideways and fell off of the log with the helicopter landing within inches of the creek. Lane Johnson was in the right-hand seat so he was at the bottom. The helicopter was still propped up a bit, so he opened his door, took his belt off, and went down into the creek. Candia Coombs was right behind Lane, and she did the same thing. I was on the high side and still belted in, waiting for them to get out. Stepping on the side of the console, I opened my door and stepped out through the top side. Then I opened the back door and helped Gwendolyn out. We stood on the sandbar looking around. I asked, "Is everybody okay? Anybody got any injuries?" All of a sudden Gwendolyn said, "I have a funny tingling feeling. I don't know what it is. It's right here." She pointed to her throat area. Then I realized she'd gotten a little jet fuel on her. We washed her off real quick, and she was okay.

The next order of business was to try to get help. I knew the VHF radio wouldn't do any good, but we also had the Forest Service radio in the helicopter. I thought it might work pretty well because there was a mountaintop repeater not too far away from our area, and I might be able to hit it. I went through all the channels, no answer. I wasn't calling an emergency—I was just calling to make contact. (Later on one of the Forest Service guys said, "I heard your voice on the radio in the FS radio shack, but I thought you were trying to get a hold of the office. I wasn't really working the radio. I just was listening.")

We figured somebody would be out pretty soon because I had a trip at eight o'clock, and if I wasn't back by eight, they would be looking for me. We sat around and nine o'clock came, ten o'clock came, and nothing happened. I didn't know what was going on. They know I'm supposed to take a trip at eight o'clock, and I'm not back. Surely they would have things figured out by now. So I thought, "Okay, we'll do a little Boy Scout lesson."

I told my passengers: "We need to get a fire going, that's the first thing you do, and I'll show you how to do it."

So I showed them how to get some pitch off of the spruce trees, and some dry bark and dry limbs. We started a nice little fire in no time at all. We stood around a while longer, then I went back and tried the radios again. No response.

Five hours later, I heard a helicopter coming so I jumped back in the helicopter and got on the radio again. This time I used the VHF because I knew the helicopter would be on our company VHF frequency. I gave him a call, and sure enough Al Jones answered.

I said, "Al, you just passed right over us. We're in the bottom of Carroll Creek." Al turned around and spotted us, and he asked if we were all okay. I said we were okay, but we needed a ride out of there. Al came in making his approach the same way I had. He came down through the trees and landed on the little sandbar. We all got in, and Al took off and headed home.

I was a little unhappy with the office force, and I went to find out what happened. When I didn't show up, the two girls in the office panicked, of course. They pulled all the blinds in the office so nobody could see them. Then they started calling on the radio, and I don't know what else they did, but apparently they thought they were doing everything just right. End result was that Al Jones was in the coffee shop, and when he told the girls in the office he was going to town to pick up the mail, they let him go. He was the only pilot available. Finally when he came back, Bill Gale was on the radio talking to the girls in the office and wanted to know where I was. They said I hadn't come back from my first a trip. And he said, "Have you sent anybody out?" No, they hadn't. So he said, "Send somebody out! Right now!" So Al Jones hopped in his helicopter and started out looking for us. Al had passed me in the morning going up Carroll Inlet so he knew the route I was taking. This put him right on our course. Otherwise, without the radio, it would have taken a lot longer to find us.

Funny things happen—people panic and do the wrong thing. This time the girls in the office were the ones who panicked. Everything else went okay.

After the accident Gwendolyn realized that life is pretty fragile, and never certain. She had been putting off getting married to her boyfriend, but a very short time after the accident, they were married. She'd thought, "Well, I'd better do it while I can."

I saw Lane Johnson recently, and he told me, "Thanks to your skill we survived the Carroll River accident. You know when you started diving through the trees? I first thought you were just hot-dogging it!"

We were lucky. One of the things you find out in an emergency is that you only do what you've trained yourself to do. You don't have time to really think—you just react. All your thinking is automatic. Some people get into those predicaments and can't think and can't act automatically, and that's deep trouble.

Long-Line Rescue

Not long after the accident on Carroll Creek, I had a trip to Swan Lake. It was just a trip out and back to drop somebody off and pick them up later. I took off from our pullout area at Peninsula Point and turned in to Ward Cove. It was a funny hazy condition—you could see down from any altitude, but you couldn't see ahead. So I turned around and came back and circled and climbed to about 3500 feet. I could see right over the top of the haze. I sailed on through and went out and did my job, dropped the guy off, turned around and came back.

Just as I was approaching the hazy area, there was a Beaver circling, and he was talking to Flight Service. He said, "Hey, I think that's an airplane burning down there in the trees." He circled around again and said, "I'm sure it is." I said, "Well, I'm coming right up on you, so I'll go take a look." I flew over it, and sure enough there was a Beaver down there, and it was consumed in flames. The flames were really shooting out of there. After the experiences I'd had already with Beaver accidents that burned, I didn't look forward to seeing that again.

The wreckage was in very tall timber. I found a landing place about 1000 feet above the crash area. It was a pretty small area, but I was able to get into it. I shut the helicopter off and ran down the hill. I guess I was a little panicky. I thought I knew exactly where it was, and with that big cone of smoke, I didn't think I could miss it. I was a little too far to the left, and all of a sudden I realized I'd gone too far so I turned back to my right, crossed over 100 feet and then came back up right on the wreck. I was looking at the wreck and I could see nothing but flames. All of a sudden I raised my eye level, and there around the perimeter were six people. It was just hard to believe. One of the survivors said she would never forget the expression on my face when I finally spotted the people. They were mostly lying down, I think one guy was standing up, but all the rest of them were lying down. They'd been injured, but they'd all gotten out of the wreck. The pilot was off to the left, and he wasn't very well at all. I checked the best I could to find what was wrong with everybody and if there was anything I could do right away that would help. I sort of catalogued the injury situation and started running up the hill.

On the way back up the hill, I ran into Morris Rogers, the head Alaska State Trooper who was in charge of the Ketchikan Division. I told him what the situation was, and he had a radio so he was able to call down and get our rescue program going. We needed people on the ground. We needed a chainsaw to clear some area to get the helicopters in close enough, and we needed medevac people and stretchers. He got the orders off in good time, and I dashed up to get to my helicopter. As I arrived at my helicopter, Allen Zink had just dropped Bill Hornbaker off to move my helicopter because it was the only good area to land in. Bill and I went back to TEMSCO to start bringing in help.

We decided we were going to have to long-line all of the people out. Allen Zink had left some equipment off by hovering on a stump, but it was really too close. Hauling a person on a stretcher on a 200-foot rope is kind of an eerie feeling for the person, but it was a slick way to do it. We put the stretcher inside of a net just as a safety precaution, and hooked on. We also had a safety line on our long line so in case the cargo hook failed, your line was still hooked on to a seat belt. If you had a problem, you would have to undo the seat belt to get rid of your long line. We managed to long-line all of the people out and down to Ward Lake where ambulances were waiting to haul them to Ketchikan General Hospital. They all survived the accident.

One older man went home on the airplane a few days later, but died in a month or two. Whether he died from the accident or from some other causes, I never was sure. However, his wife was very appreciative of the help we had given her husband. She sent the rescue squad money, and she came up to visit. She brought her children up and had us show them where the crash was, and what we'd done to rescue them. For quite a few years after that she sent money to the rescue squad. Those were the kind of people who made us feel appreciated, that made us feel right about what we did.

The pilot had flown into the hazy area, but he was too far in when he attempted a 180-degree turn on instruments and flew into the trees. The plane caught fire. There was one door the passengers could crawl through, and all of them made it out. Really it's amazing they all got clear and with relatively few injuries.

Cessna Crash

On September 5, 1981, we had a search for a Cessna 340 that crashed somewhere close to the airport. We could hear the ELT putting out a good signal, and we were very frustrated trying to locate it. We had a ceiling of 300 or 400 feet in fog, and we were flying below the ceiling. We could go south of the airport and the signal got louder and louder, but the closer we got to the airport the dimmer it was. We'd go back in, flying sort of southwest of the airport, and the signal would get louder and louder again. We couldn't get any definite position. We struggled around trying to figure out how we were going to locate it. Finally we got a break in the weather, and one of the helicopters was able to get up higher. Chris John from the rescue squad had his radio gear out and was able to find the wreck very quickly from 3000 feet.

Nobody had landed there yet so I took a state trooper, Jerry Castle, and my son Dan, and made a landing. When we arrived up there we quickly realized that there wasn't anything we could do—they were all dead. It looked like the guy had started a missed approach and apparently had turned too soon. You could see that he had attempted to dodge the mountain. He must have seen it at the last second because he had turned real sharp. A wing caught the ground, and the plane cartwheeled. It hit the ground once and actually bounced another hundred feet before it slammed into the ground again. I made a couple of trips up, and we took the bodies out that we could get out of the airplane. The pilot was impaled on the wheel, and we couldn't get him loose, so we had to leave him for the night.

In the meantime the fog had rolled back in, and we were stuck on the mountain. I didn't feel comfortable hovering off the mountain with that many people. After all, I had two troopers and Earl Mossberg with me. I said, "We're better off to tie the helicopter down and walk off the mountain. I'll call TEMSCO and tell them were going to hike off the mountain, and they can send a helicopter over and pick us up in the muskeg." Darkness was approaching so we hurried. Earl and I were in pretty good shape—both of us were pretty active hunters. We went sailing off that mountain leaving everybody else behind. We had to slow down to let them catch up with us. When we got down into the muskeg, it was dark. The helicopter pilot was able to find us with his landing light. He picked up two of us and came back a few minutes later and got the rest of us.

The next day the weather cleared up so I had a helicopter take me up so I could retrieve my helicopter. We also took a crew up to recover the pilot's body and the FAA to check the wreck. It was one of the most unpleasant jobs we had to do. Later the FAA called me from Anchorage and asked me to go back up and get the readings off of the plane's instruments which they had not done when we were on the ground.

Rescue in Failing Light

It seems during the 1980's there were rescues left and right. This time we got a call that said some Fish and Game men were out on their own goat hunting, and someone got hurt. Terry Wills had taken them into Paradise Lake in an airplane, but the weather was such that the airplane couldn't get back in there. So I got a call from Terry Wills who told me where they were, and what a predicament these guys were in. They figured they had to get the injured man out of there right away to save his life. I said, "Okay, we will have to take two helicopters to do it. One will take a crew up and land and try to prepare a site to pick up the injured man, or at least be able to control the ground operations for the second helicopter."

We took off for Paradise Lake, and it was already getting dark on us. I was the lead ship. I took the people in to prepare the patient and crew. When the other helicopter came in, we had a place for him to get one skid down and load the injured person. I was hovering off a little ways directing the operation the best I could. Both of us had our landing lights on, which was a help when loading from a hover. Once the injured man was taken out, I hovered in, and the Fish and Game boys threw their guns and packs into my helicopter, and we headed out. As soon as we got into flight, I turned the landing lights off so my eyes could adjust for the night flight home.

The Fish and Game fellow who was rescued was very appreciative. He came around several times with thanks, and his wife made a point to come around and thank us because she said we'd saved her husband. It was questionable whether he'd have made it through the night. It was rewarding to perform a rescue like that and do it the way we planned to do it. The main thing was we beat darkness by finding them in the failing light—a narrow margin to get all those people out of there.

Rough Water Rescue

A few days later I got a call from the Coast Guard. They said, "We've got a trolling boat sinking up at Ratz Harbor with one guy aboard. We have a Coast Guard ship in the area, but he's about six miles from there. He's going to proceed over there and try to help, but the visibility is very poor. Is there anything you can do?" I said I didn't know if I could do anything. It sounded like the Coast Guard would be there before I would. After I hung up I got thinking, "If the guy got out of his boat and didn't have a skiff or anything, I could drop him a life raft, and that might save his neck." We weren't told if he was in a wet suit or anything. The boat was named *The Spring*, and it had belonged to an old friend of mine, Fred Olsen, at one time. I called the Coast Guard back and said, "I'm going to go up there and see what I can do to help."

I got a helicopter ready and got a life raft and a long line. Charlie McLeod was working for us at the time, and I said, "Charlie, let's see what we can do. You get in the back. If we have to drop the life raft, I'll hover low, and you drop it but hang onto the inflation cord. Jerk the inflation cord as soon as it gets out of the helicopter so it will be inflated by the time it hits the water. Just don't do it inside the helicopter." The wind was blowing roughly 35 to 45 miles per hour, and the ceiling was very low. I was able to get across the straits by zigzagging. We finally hit the Prince of Wales shore and followed it on up to Ratz Harbor. I thought I knew where the guy was, but all I had was a description—he was coming to Ketchikan and was in the Ratz Harbor area. I headed out from shore. All of a sudden I saw a gas slick on the water. I knew if the slick was coming from his sunken boat, the guy was going to be downwind. The wind was blowing strong southeast. We turned downwind and in a matter of a mile or two, we came on a man. Charlie said, "Hey, there's a guy in a survival suit!" We turned around and saw him waving at us. I hovered upwind from him, and Charlie got the life raft out, punched it off, and dropped it right in front of him. It was inflated by the time it hit the water, and he grabbed the life raft and climbed in it.

I couldn't use a long line because I'd be up in the clouds, and we didn't have a hoist. The water was too rough to pick him up so there was no way we could do anything right then. I got on the radio and told the Coast Guard we'd located the fellow, and I didn't dare leave him, or we'd lose him again. The Coast Guard said they were going to head that way.

Pretty soon another voice came on the radio. It was a 90-foot workboat called the *Sea Raker* with two men aboard—a skipper and a deckhand. The skipper said, "I have you on radar. I'm not too far away. If you just keep hovering there, I'll come over and see if I can pick the guy up." We hovered for what seemed like a long time, and finally the boat came out of the fog, right in to us. We stood by to see what happened. I told the skipper if he wanted to stay with the raft, I would go to the beach and put a short line on. Then I would be able to lift the guy onto the deck of the boat. The skipper said, "No, I think I can pick him up all right." He came along broadside with the guy upwind from him, and a big wave rolled the boat and squashed the raft, poking a hole in it and pushing it away from the boat. They were in a terrible spot now because with just two men on the boat, the skipper couldn't leave the wheel long enough to help the deckhand, and the deckhand couldn't get the man aboard by himself. They turned around and put the man downwind from them on the lee side. This time the skipper left the wheel for a minute, and they managed to haul the man aboard. I realized what a tough deal it is to pick a man out of a rough sea in a boat. It's a good way to either help or hurt someone. Our rough water is a short choppy sea that doesn't give you much time between waves.

We proceeded to town and realized we'd saved the guy's life. It was very rewarding to get back to the pullout and say, "Hey, we found him, and we saved him," when to begin with I didn't think I could do anything for him.

Funny thing how people appreciate things—the guy called me on the phone the next morning and said, "The Coast Guard says I have to bring this life raft back out to you, and there's a

Eichner saves one more

Jay Gelman, Anacortes, Wash., abandoned his 40-foot wooden troller Monday as his vessel sank near Ratz Harbor on Prince of Wales Island.
Gelman was rescued when a Temsco helicopter, piloted by Ken Eichner, dropped a life raft to Gelman. Eichner then stood by and directed rescue craft to Gelman.
The Coast Guard received a call from Gelman at 1:25 p.m. that his boat was taking on water faster than he could pump it out. The Coast Guard cutter Planetree was diverted to the area, on the northeast end of Prince of Wales Island, to assist.
At 1:52 the Alaska State Troopers sent a helicopter to the area. The Planetree arrived in the area at 2:06.
Gelman was already in the water by the time Eichner arrived. Eichner spotted Gelman, who was in a survival suit, and was able to drop a liferaft to him.
Eichner then stood by until the vessel Sea Raker was able to pick up Gelman and the raft at 3:16 p.m.
In its news release, Alaska State Troopers commended Eichner "for efficient work in saving another life."

hole in one section of it." He was calling from Service Electric so I said, "Just leave it at Service Electric. I will pick it up." He offered no thanks, nothing. I suppose down inside he would thank me many times, but on the outside he didn't bother. He was on his way.

Barrow to Ketchikan

In December of 1981 a D model Hughes helicopter with only about 300 hours on it came up for sale. It belonged to the North

Slope Borough at Barrow, and some guy in New York was taking bids on it. It looked like a good deal to us, and it had some extra stuff with it so we put in a bid. We got the bid. We didn't know anything about the North Slope or the city of Barrow, but we now had this helicopter up there, and we needed to go get it because we didn't want to leave it there all winter. We didn't know whether it was out in the deep freeze or not. We checked and the weather wasn't too bad up there—it was 30 below zero with winds blowing 30 miles per hour. I rustled up all the winter gear I thought we were going to need along with some emergency gear, and I took Norman Peratrovich along with me as a mechanic to check things out before we started back. Barrow is the most northern point in North America, and it's about as far as you can get from Ketchikan and still be in Alaska—a distance of around 1500 miles. We took commercial airlines to Fairbanks and took progressively smaller aircraft until we finally reached Barrow.

Barrow in December is in total darkness. Instead of having a sunrise, a little pink glow comes in the sky and stays there for three or four hours, so you can see in twilight. We arrived at Barrow, and it was the first time either of us had been there. Barrow is strictly an Eskimo village, but there is a Navy petroleum reserve there. It's never been drilled, but some way or other they extract gas from it, and the city of Barrow uses gas for heat and power. The military hangars there were heated, nice and warm, and were used by the city of Barrow. Instead of the deep freeze we were worried about, they kept their helicopter in this nice warm hangar.

One of the interesting things in Barrow was their natural gas pipeline. When it came to a road, the pipeline went up over the road, not under it, because of permafrost. Not only would it be too expensive to dig into the ice, this way they didn't have to worry about broken pipes.

The day after we arrived, we went over to the Rescue Center and talked with the rescue crew: Randy Nelson and Don Gamble. We had a nice little talk, and they said, "Let's go out to the hangar and look things over." They showed us what we had purchased. We got all kinds of stuff—extra parts, stretchers, even pontoons. They had all the extras they could possibly buy for this helicopter so it turned out to be a real bargain for us. The helicopter had very low time and was very clean. It had two ADFs in it (automatic direction finders), and everything they could get crowded into the instrument panel. It had an auxiliary tank that gave us a good 3-hour cruise with 15 minutes reserve, which was really nice, especially for this particular trip.

We got everything figured out and thought we would leave about ten o'clock in the morning because there was a little pink in the sky at that time. They opened the hangar doors and let that cold air in. It was blowing 30 miles an hour and was 30 below zero. That's horribly cold and came as a terrible shock after spending the previous hour in the nice warm hangar. We almost froze to death just trying to get the helicopter fueled up. As soon as we got it fueled up, Norman and I got in the helicopter and fired it up. It was cold as sin there on the ground, and we sat in our seats shivering as we tried to get the engine wound up. After a few cold minutes we got the engine warmed up and waved goodbye as we took off. I was going to head for Anaktuvuk Pass, but as I got altitude I figured it would be better to go directly to Bettles above most of mountains in the Brooks Range. I flew from Point Barrow in as much of a direct line as I

This is one of those mountaintop helipads I was talking about. Here I'm unloading 52V on a trip to Spiel River.

could. We had the ADFs so we could tune in on the direction of Bettles and also of Prudhoe Bay. We were told if we had to detour to Prudhoe Bay, we could put the helicopter in the hangar there—it would just cost us a thousand dollars to open the hangar doors! We weren't planning on doing that, but we still needed to have a second option.

That land is so desolate in the wintertime. It was blowing snow, and in the twilight, it was not very pleasant to think that you might have to land and spend the night out there. We thought we were prepared, but we weren't acclimatized, and that makes a difference. If we had to land, it would be a very serious survival situation. Randy thought we might stop at Anaktuvuk and have a cup of coffee with the radio man there. He liked company, but with the extra tank I figured I could make Bettles, get fuel, and make it to Fairbanks the first day. I decided to push it.

As we passed one mountain after another, Norman was getting kind of nervous because the fuel was going down. Then Norman hollered out, "There is the Anaktuvuk haul road. I can see it over there." We were right on course. We went into Bettles and landed close to the fuel pumps. It wasn't as cold there—it was about 10 below and the wind wasn't blowing. The fuel man was right on the job so he fueled us up quickly, and we lit out. We still had twilight in the sky so I figured we could make Fairbanks. We got into Fairbanks that night and spent the night in a hotel.

The next morning we fueled up and got ready to go. The boy who had fueled us up didn't seem to know what he was doing, and I hadn't stayed to watch him do it. We got in the helicopter and got ready to go. We turned on the fuel gauge, and it didn't come up to full. The auxiliary tank was full, all right, but the main tank fuel gauge didn't show full up. We took off anyway and fueled up again at Northway and made sure those tanks were topped off.

Now we were squeezing daylight again to get to Juneau. We took our regular route down through Canada, flying over Kluane Lake in the Yukon Territories. It's a lake that just seems to go forever. It's actually about 100 miles long. We got down the lake and followed the road down into Haines where we hit salt water and headed for Juneau. It had started to snow, and it was getting dark on us. We got to Burners Bay which is almost to the end of the road in Juneau, and I could go no further. I circled around and found a house and a barn. There was a light in the house so we thought, "Boy, this is for us." We had sleeping bags and everything, but we weren't figuring on using them if we could avoid it. With the landing light, we were able to pick out a spot where we could land safely. Wires were my biggest worry. We landed not too far from the house. The people there, Will and Rose Oack, were the guardians of this summer camp. They gave us one of the cabins to stay in, and we survived the night very well. In the morning they gave us breakfast and sent us off to Juneau. We appreciated their hospitality, and later on we did some favors for them to show our appreciation. We ended up at home after a little more than two days flying with N51337. The ship served us well, and later, because of the big fuel tank, I was able to take it all the way up to St. Lawrence Island.

Hillers Sold

In late 1981 we finally sold all of our Hillers to Porterville, California. They wanted them delivered so three of us took off with the helicopters. Danny was flying at that time, so he and I flew one ship down. Just prior to that I had been in the hangar where the boys were moving a helicopter, and for some reason I was hanging on to the tail when they did the wrong thing and I dinged my back up. I was still hobbling around when this trip came up and riding an old Hiller clear down to California is a long, slow trip. Once I got in the helicopter I was okay, I could fly all right, but I had to be helped out of it and helped back in again. This trip didn't do my back a bit of good, and after the trip, I went to the doctor. They took pictures and said, "You're never going to get over this. You've got some bone spurs that are going to create a problem for you, but in the meantime you could take some orthopedic exercises and that might help." I did that for a little bit and then went home. I just kept my exercises up and proved they were wrong. I got rid of the back problem, and I realized you've got to be a little more careful with the body as you get older.

Yes Bay's aircraft piled in near Misty Fjords. While many of the passengers were rescued, the suffering and loss of Mary Orr in particular touched everyone.

Unheeded ELT

Around 9:30 p.m. on July 26, 1984 Bill Gale called me and said TEMSCO had heard by the grapevine that there was an ELT (Emergency Locator Transmitter) going off in the Wilson Lake area. They had confirmed it through Flight Service, and he wanted to know if he and Chris John, a Forest Service radio technician, should go look. Here it was after sunset, and the weather was starting to blow up. I felt the night search would be next to impossible along with the fact that there were no reported overdue aircraft. With Wilson Lake being one of the most popular fishing lakes, the possibility of an airplane on the lake overnight with an accidentally tripped ELT was very real. I recommended a 4 a.m. takeoff instead. At 5 a.m. my phone rang. It was Bill Gale. They had started out at 4 a.m., and he was calling from Quartz Hill Mining Camp. They had located a Beaver floatplane, which had crashed in a little drainage up from the outlet of Wilson Lake. One person was dead, and four women were seriously injured. The pilot and one girl were walking around.

The fog was thick everywhere except on the lake and in Smeaton Bay. Bill had been unable to land but had left Chris

John off with a one-skid landing. He would meet me at the head of Smeaton Bay to lead me to the site. I alerted everyone I thought we needed which included George Chipman, our 212 Bell helicopter pilot who would alert the Pond Reef medevac crew. Then I got Jerry Castle and my son Dan. I also called the state troopers and told them what I was going to do. If they had a trooper there before we left, he could go with us, but we were not waiting. A new trooper arrived on time, and I took off with Dan, Jerry and the trooper.

Arriving in Smeaton Bay, I found Bill waiting for me. Bill got on the radio and said to follow him up the river. We had to hover up to Wilson Lake and then hover up a little drainage to the very end of it. Bill said they had tracked the radio signal to that point and had not seen anything, but as they turned around to the left, there was the wreck right in front of them.

When we arrived at the scene, I finally found a spot to land a little over 100 yards from the plane. As soon as I could shut down and unload my people, I looked around and was able to find a safe spot for Bill to land. Bill had gone over to the Quartz Hill Camp, where Chuck McGee was watchman and made the phone call to me. He brought Chuck back with him. Chuck had brought a little chainsaw and a first aid kit with him. The chainsaw turned out to be so dull we couldn't do much with it. Chris took the chainsaw and started to cut one bull pine tree, which was most in the way. He finally got it down. In the meantime Dan and Jerry had prepared a spot to pick up the injured women. Mary Orr was riding in the copilot's seat and seemed to be the worst off. She seemed to be only slightly injured but was slipping further into shock and hypothermia. She was the first one to be taken out. By the time they arrived at Smeaton Bay, the medevac helicopter was there, but she died en route.

I checked on the other two women who were lying down on the floor of the plane. They had feeling in their legs and were talking sensibly. They told me that the bugs had been unbearable. That was a good sign. I could not figure out who the uninjured girl was. She kept calling me by name. I just could not put it together. All these ladies from where? All in a plane wreck in this area?

The trooper wasn't much help. He said he had never seen anything like this before. I think it was his first time on a trip like this, but we worked around him. Dan and Chris saved him from walking into the tail rotor by inches. Hovering all the way to and from, it was slow moving everyone to salt water. I arrived back at our base, and my good friend Carl Klein was there thanking us for the rescue of his daughter, Cherie. Now it all came together. It was Carl's daughter who had been talking to me. She was so out of place for me on that mountainside—a 15-year-old girl—I didn't recognize her.

Checking into the accident, we learned the pilot for the lodge, Steve Dewey, was bringing the crew into town for a weekend before the next group of sportsmen arrived at the Yes Bay Lodge. He decided to give the ladies a treat by taking them sightseeing to Misty Fjords. He had not told anyone of his change in plans. During the flight he tried to out-climb the mountain and stalled the plane. He came down flat and sheared the floats off, ending up straddling a little creek. The ruptured fuel tank drained down the creek so there was no fire. The pilot and Mary Orr were thrown out of the plane. Betty Sonerland hit her head on the pilot's seat and died instantly. Young Cherie Klein was lucky with only bruises and scratches. The other three women, Renita Peres, Diane Brown, and Melissa Madsen, had possible back, internal, and leg injures.

We were disturbed by the loss of the Mary Orr from shock and hypothermia because of the late arrival of help. We learned that the Coast Guard had one good satellite hit around 2 p.m., then a questionable one, and then another good one. They finally notified Flight Service, which in turn notified the state troopers in Ketchikan around 7 p.m.

No rescue was ever officially started. At the time the Coast Guard was trying to get used to the satellite locator warning system and was having lots of false alarms—mostly from around towns, airports, and harbors. When they got this hit in a remote area, they should have sounded the alarm, but without an overdue aircraft I suppose they were reluctant. I found it very hard to get anything done with the Coast Guard from my level, but with the help of my friend, Senator Frank Murkowski, we did at least get the Coast Guard to do an in-depth review of their procedures.

The Ketchikan Volunteer Rescue Squad was never officially recognized so unless a federal employee took it upon himself to notify us, we were not notified about emergencies. Dick Borch and other members of KVRS listened to the emergency frequencies regularly and alerted us. We had some great troopers who worked with us and some wonderful Flight Service people. It seemed like with every change of command, we had to reintroduce and prove ourselves to them, but we continued to perform our self-appointed duties and bail people out of trouble.

Umiaks awaiting walrus hides at Savoonga. It took three cured walrus hides to cover one umiak.

Several Southwestern Alaskan islands have crumbling fortifications that date from WWII. I photographed this pillbox while working in Dutch Harbor.

Chapter 15,
Savoonga

In 1966 we figured out a way to fly from Nome to Savoonga with the old Hiller. A government contract had come up for a helicopter out at St. Lawrence Island. We looked at the maps and saw that St. Lawrence Island was about 190 to 200 miles across the Bering Sea from Nome. We could take the old Hiller, put extra fuel and some survival floatation on it, and fly from Nome to Savoonga. First we tried to get the government to take the helicopter over in a C-130, but that didn't fly so we bid what we thought it would take to do it. I planned on making the trip myself, but it fell through because our price was too high, and no one else bid it. After completing the trip with the Hughes 500 some years later, I realized that I really would have been stretching things a whole bunch with the old Hiller 12E.

Trip to Savoonga

In July of 1983 we got a job for two weeks work on St. Lawrence Island for the State of Alaska. We planned to use 337, the Hughes helicopter with the extra fuel tank. It was the only one that would have the range to fly across the Bering Sea safely. It was going to be a nice trip, and I thought, "Boy, that's the trip for me." Peggy decided she would be happy to go with me on the first leg of the trip. She didn't want to go to St. Lawrence Island, but she would fly up to Nome with me. We flew through Fairbanks and then down the Yukon River, and I stopped at Ruby to see my old friends Harold and Florence Esmelka, whom I'd worked with at the Alaska Air Carriers Association. Harold was a well-known figure in that area. He owned an airline of his own at that time. His main headquarters was down at Galena where there was a nice airport and a fighter base.

We landed in Harold's back yard, and one of his neighbors came over and told me I couldn't land there. I had difficulty convincing him that Harold had told me it was all right. After a nice visit Florence gave Peggy a couple jars of their smoked salmon. Peggy put them in our food locker when we got home, and a few years later we discovered the jars. The salmon was so good. Now I know why Florence had the reputation of making the best smoked salmon on the Yukon River.

We stopped in to see John Billings at Galena, and then from Galena we proceeded down the Yukon River till we got to the little village of Nulato, and then we cut across the mountain ranges and headed for Norton Bay, which is a little indent in Norton Sound, and from there we followed the coast to Nome.

We passed Moses Point along the way. I always remembered Moses Point because during World War II all of the National Guard boys from Ketchikan were sent up to Moses Point to train for the Battle of the Aleutians. Also this was the last 100 miles of the Iditerod Trail to Nome. Along the trail were some remnants of the Gold Rush Days of '98. One thing that stood out was a portion of railroad track with an ancient engine and a few cars scattered by itself with nothing around it—no railroad track going anywhere.

Dick Gallagher, the new owner of Munz Northern Airlines, was running the main operation in Nome, and he was my main source of information. Just as we arrived in Nome, my ADF went out. The ADF was probably the most valuable tool you had to go across the ocean to St. Lawrence Island. Dick said, "That's no problem. I have some friends in Anchorage. We can send the ADF out on the next airplane, and they'll have it back in a day." We sent it out, and a month later we got it back in Ketchikan. So I was faced with a problem: When I take off from Nome to cross 200 miles of Bering Sea, I'm going to have to do it with the old "whiskey" compass as they say—just the old alcohol compass.

Compass Course

Peggy wasn't going to go to St. Lawrence Island with me so I had to go that leg of the trip by myself. I tried to get all the information I could about St. Lawrence Island, but it wasn't too much help. I laid out a couple of different courses trying to hit St. Lawrence Island from Nome. Finally the day came for me to go. I had a life raft and a survival suit aboard, and I was wearing a float coat. As I headed out that day, the wind was blowing 30 to 35 miles an hour. I had a head wind, and the Bering Sea was full of whitecaps and didn't look very friendly. I filed my flight plan with Nome, and they told me I could close it by telephone when I got over there. Their radio would only work about half way there.

I headed out on the compass course, and I couldn't see anything. There were clouds around 3000 feet, and there was no sign of any land out where I was heading. I kept on course, and I got about 100 miles out when I noticed my pressure differential light come on. This startled me because it could mean I had contaminated fuel. I reduced the collective a little bit, dropped my torque from 70 down to 65, and the light went off. So that made me think, well, maybe it's just the gauge acting up. Nevertheless I gave it some serious thought while looking down at the ocean. I had pop-out floats on, but I knew if I popped the floats and landed in the ocean, I was going to tip over almost immediately so my life raft was handy. I had that figured out, but I didn't have my survival suit on. I just had on the float coat which would be better than nothing. The pressure differential light came back on so I reduced the power to 60 on the torque gauge and the light went off again.

Now I had lost communications because I was out of reach of Nome and hadn't been able to pick anybody up in St. Lawrence. In fact I didn't even have anybody out there to call. I kept boring on my course as near as I could, and all of a sudden I saw three mountains coming out of the ocean in the distance. I thought, "Oh boy. That's good. It's St. Lawrence Island all right. It has three mountains, and I am heading right for the middle of it. That's just perfect." Well, I went along a little farther, and I didn't see three mountains, I saw about seven mountains. I thought, "Oh-oh. That's Siberia!" Siberia is only about 35 miles from the end of St. Lawrence Island. I turned a little left on my course to avoid ending up in Russia and kept plugging away.

All of a sudden I looked down, and my oil pressure gauge just went to zip—to 0. This was a frantic moment. I started looking around watching my oil temperature because as soon as the oil temperature goes up, that's it. All of a sudden the oil pressure went back up. My heart slowed down a little bit and started beating kind of regular again.

Now I was heading for St. Lawrence for sure. There were mountains everywhere, and snow on all the mountains. Finally I got to St. Lawrence Island, but I was nowhere near Savoonga. I was probably 30 miles down the coast of St. Lawrence Island. I'd jogged that much trying to miss Siberia. I followed the coast in to Savoonga and landed at the airport. People were out there to meet me. I said, "How'd you know I was coming?" And they said, "CB tells us! CB tells us!" The Eskimos all have CB radios, and they keep everybody posted about what's going on around their island.

Accommodations

Dan Renshaw and J. Clough, the two state geologists I was working for, were already there. The purpose of the trip was to see if we could find coal on St. Lawrence Island. We were to examine every part of the island that we could to find a source of coal to replace the oil that was being used to heat the homes on the island.

I was to stay with the Gologeren family who had what they called a little motel. It was a plain little building with four or five wooden bunks and very few of the comforts of home. The government was trying to build a sanitary system for the village, but they hadn't succeeded as yet so the people still used honey buckets. We were served murre eggs for breakfast; otherwise, we sort of took care of ourselves. We got rides out to the airport in lots of different snowmobiles and other weird six-wheelers.

The word was out. When we were in our room, we had many visitors with ivory carvings to sell. I bought a number of nice ivory pieces and other local crafts. One young boy sold me his sister's mukluks. He assured me she was going to get a new pair. I still have the mukluks.

Winter Travel

One of the characteristic things about St. Lawrence is that each family has an outpost or hunting grounds they use in the summertime. They traveled out and spent their summers gathering food. Fish, berries, and seals were the things they liked the best, and of course earlier in the season they got walrus and

Having a helicopter in Savoonga made me quite a celebrity, particularly with the local kids.

reindeer. They would travel to these various points, some of them by boat, some over land. It was just the way they lived.

The Gologeren family lost their father the winter before. The basketball team had gone to Gambell about 70 miles away for a game and was supposed to come home the next day. A snowstorm started, and Mr. Gologeren was afraid they would have trouble so he took off to intercept the party. About half way to Gambell his snowmobile broke down, and he froze to death. If he had been traveling with a dog team, it never would have happened—the modern machine got him into trouble he wasn't prepared for. The ball team had stayed over in Gambell because of the storm.

Entertainment

One night I was told they were having a dance at the schoolhouse, and we were welcome to come. Renshaw and I thought we had better go. We arrived at the building and were shown to a seat on the floor. The orchestra consisted of four older men with little hand-held skin drums they used to beat out the rhythm. On a motion, a dancer would get up and perform. It was generally a younger female, sometimes a little on the heavy side but extremely light on her feet. The dance portrayed an arctic animal with all the audio sounds made to perfection. They enjoyed doing this for us.

Search for Coal

We chartered Munz Northern Airlines to haul fuel over for us so we had plenty of barrels of fuel stashed on the airport. We had a little trouble with the Eskimo kids who weren't very well disciplined. I was nice to them and kept them from crawling all over the helicopter and causing problems. They were always out there to see me when I took off and when I landed. They were a happy bunch of kids, but some of them were full of beans.

We would take off and hit every place on the island trying to discover coal. We did find coal in several of the creek bottoms, but it had been reported before. St. Lawrence is a very low island. It has a couple of volcanic mountains that crop up 2200 feet, and the rest of them are about 1200 to 1800 feet high. We found lignite coal, but it was such a low-grade form that it would take more heat to burn it than you could get out of it so it was of no value. It showed us that at one time this area must have had a tropical climate with a lot of vegetation.

Gambell

We continued our search, and the geologists did other geological work while they were at it. On our trips we always had to have one of the Eskimo guides with us so I had two geologists and a guide wherever we went. Most of the time I stayed with them, but sometimes I left for fuel and came back. On this one

This cold war casualty sat largely undisturbed for years.

occasion we ended up in Gambell. Our native guide had to go in because one of his elderly aunts had cancer and was on her last days. He had to go say some prayers, and Dan Renshaw was a very religious man, and he also said some prayers for the woman.

Gambell sits on a point about 35 miles from Russia. Its beaches and lowlands were all pea gravel. If you stepped on the beach, you sank in up to your ankles in pea gravel. Whereas Savoonga was more or less a muskeg and everything was built up on stilts so you could walk around in the summertime. In the wintertime it was frozen solid so it was no problem to get around.

Working our way out of Gambell heading south, I came across something that looked like a great big barn out in the tundra. As we got closer I realized it was the tail of an airplane. You could see the airplane had crash-landed in the low tundra country and had partially burned up. It was a Navy PV-2.

Then our guide told us the story. Eskimos wouldn't go near the wreck because it didn't belong to them. During one of the cold war episodes, Russian planes attacked the PV-2. It was doing reconnaissance work, and of course they thought it was doing spy work so they shot it down. It was on fire when it made a crash landing, and the center part burned up. Machine guns and other parts that did not burn were lying around. As I understood it, most of the guys got out of it. A couple of them were pretty badly burned. The big tail looked like a five-story building sticking up out there in the absolutely flat tundra. It was quite a sight to behold.

Eskimo Camps

As we worked around the island, we stopped at most of the little Eskimo camps. As I have said, they had camps all the way around the island where people stayed to gather their food. We found every personality you could think of in the camps. We found the sharpies, the dumb ones, the mean ones, the good ones—you name it. Most of the natives out there were glad to have company, especially a helicopter. There had been very few helicopters on their island. They were isolated except for airplanes and the CB radio.

Many of the campsites had a buildup of soil and earth that had turned to permafrost. As a result all kinds of artifacts from the ages could be found in these old sites. All the people I saw were digging in their own sites. In the summertime the permafrost melts a couple inches a day so they could dig a couple inches a day and try to uncover various artifacts. One family up around Kongkok dug some nice little tiny artifacts. They were beautiful, and of course the family tried to waggle a good price out of me. They finally did, and I bought a half dozen of their artifacts which turned out to be quite precious little things.

At the next place, Puguviliak, there'd been gold reported, and the geologists wanted to pan for it. We were panning for gold in the creek when this old timer came out of his cabin waving a gun. The guide said, "That nice fellow doesn't want us here, so let's go." The Eskimos never said anything bad about anybody. He said "that nice fellow," but he really didn't mean that. We got out of there before the nice fellow got rambunctious with us.

Umiak

Back in Savoonga that night I was looking at some umiak (skin boat) frames and one of the fellows told me it took three walrus hides to cover the umiak. I asked him, "How do they sew them together so they don't leak?" He said, "Oh, women do that." One of the Eskimos asked me if I could move their umiak from the south shore across the island to Savoonga. They had gotten stuck with it on the other side of the island when they were hunting whales, and it was going to be a tough job for them to bring it back. They told me how much it weighed. It was right up to my maximum—about 1100 pounds. I said, "You know, if it's too heavy I won't be able to lift it." They thought very seriously about it and finally backed off and said, "No, we'll figure out a way to do it ourselves." "But," they said, "you can do one thing for us. We need to locate the reindeer herd because we need a little reindeer meat. If you'd take one of our men out, he could locate the herd." We never did see the main herd, but we found small herds here and there. The Eskimos live off of the reindeer. They kill a certain number each year. The herd is just a free-roaming meat locker for them.

Later on when I got back into town, they said, "Now, you

could do one more thing for us. Would you take two barrels of fuel out and leave them at our camp at Fossil Creek?" They wanted the fuel out there because they were stretching the gas limit of their snowmobiles when they ran to and from the camp. This would give them some reserve so they could safely work farther out. Fossil Creek turned out to be a roundup area for their reindeer herd.

Eskimo Huts

As we worked around the island, we found some of the old diggings where Eskimos originally lived in either stone or sod huts that were just about level with the surface. They were covered over with mud and grass. Generally rocks were piled up, and then whalebones sometimes were the bridge across the roof. Inside were small round living areas with little tunnels between them. In the old days body heat did a lot to keep them warm in there, but I guess it was kind of an odiferous place. Now the government had them living in regular houses that weren't very good. It took oil to heat them, and the government had to furnish it so we were looking for coal to replace that need for oil.

Kookoolik Mountain

The geologists wanted to go up on what they called Kookoolik Mountain, and the Eskimo guide, Brad Gologeren, shook his head and said, "No. Bad. Bad up there." But they wanted to go up anyway and asked, "Would you go with us?" Brad said, "It's bad, you know. One helicopter crashed up there, and they almost froze to death so it must be real bad up there." I said, "I think we'll be all right, Brad. I'll be very careful." I took one geologist and Brad in the front seat and went up into Kookoolik Mountain. It was a volcanic mountain; we landed up in the core of the volcano. They took samples and looked around. There was nothing bad about it, but when they had the crash up there, I guess the weather hadn't been too good, and it was questionable whether they could get the guys out in time to save their lives.

Southeast Cape

When the job ended, the geologists didn't want to ride back in the helicopter so they took the airplane to Nome, and I was to meet them there. I spent a couple extra days in Savoonga. The

Gologerens, whom I still keep in contact with, had their summer camp out on Southeast Cape—Cape Kialegak—and they wanted to go out there. I took Ora and her daughter Erma Smith. Erma was a deaf-mute; they called her the Dumb One. Erma was married and had a family. Her boys talked to her in sign language, and they were so clever with it. I told her, "You know, your sons ought to be pilots because they are so clever with their hands. They would be able to handle all kinds of

Murphy's Rock

One of the places we stopped was called Murphy's Rock. It was a very spectacular place, and I took some pictures of it. Little pinnacles came out of the ocean there, and the ocean waves slapping around them were very spectacular. The story was that Murphy, a Coast Guard man, had tried to blast the rock off, and something happened. The charge went off too soon, and Murphy was the one who got blasted off the rock.

electronic and manual things." Anyway we went out to Southeast Cape, and I spent the night out there with the

Eskimos. They had a little house out there, but of course there were too many people for the house so we slept in a tent.

Brad was with us, and we went out where they dig for artifacts. We looked things over, and I could see a few fossilized tusks sticking out here and there. I noticed some of the things they'd dug up were buckets made out of walrus hide. They had been frozen in for many, many years. Later, they even found a body there, and it was sent into Fairbanks to the university to be analyzed. Then they sent it back for a normal burial. All of the various artifacts they were digging were out of their old campsite which had a buildup of maybe 15 feet. They were digging here and there, and each person had his place where he'd dig and nobody else could dig there. Brad went out and dug all day long and gave me everything he got. His other brother, who died of cancer a little later, was the one who cooked breakfast for us in the morning. He had a bunch of artifacts, and he said, "Take all you want." I took a few of his artifacts and ended up with quite a nice collection of things from St. Lawrence Island.

The next morning the Gologerens informed me that their neighbors would like to have me come over for a cup of coffee. It was a very formal thing. We went over and sat in their house and talked a bit. When we got ready to go, they presented me with a little spearhead artifact out of their collection. It still had part of the native copper blade left on the ivory spearhead. I don't know where they ever got it, but it was really an old piece.

Northeast Cape

Back in Savoonga the next day, another Eskimo Jonathan Annogovac asked me if I would take them out to their summer campground. He said, "My wife and I are too old to travel out there any more in the skin boat. The young folks are already out there." I said, "Sure, Ill do that."

Their camp was located on Punuk Island out by Northeast Cape. I had forgotten my sleeping bag at Southeast Cape so we stopped there and picked it up on the way. Punuk Island is 25 miles off of Southeast Cape across the Bering Sea. We could hardly see it. The weather was not really great that day. There were clouds here and there, and it looked kind of ominous. When we arrived the people were thrilled to have their parents come out and see them. They showed me a little artifact they had dug up. It was like a little doll. They said it was worth $10,000. They told me that every winter after the freeze up comes, buyers came from New York and bought artifacts from them. The older the artifacts were the better. The fine work that was done on them—the inscriptions and the carving—were decorative and really nice. They gave me several pieces of ivory, and the senior of the group who had asked me to take them out there said, "When we get back to town, I'll show you some walrus tusks, and you can have whichever one you want."

Back in town they had a pile of fairly fresh walrus tusks—about 25 or 30 of them. There were five or six boys in the family, and I don't know whether they were killing walrus just for the tusks or what. I asked no questions. He said, "Take whichever one you want." I didn't want to be piggish and take the very biggest one so I took one that was a couple notches down from the biggest one. He said, "Fine, I'll send it to you, but first I have to put my name on it. It takes a little time." After I got back home, every once in a while he'd call me on the phone—they now have satellite phones—and say, "I have to boil it and get the meat off of it. Then I have to dry it, and then I have to put my name on it. It's coming along pretty good." Finally it arrived, and here was this nice set of walrus tusks mounted on a board and scrimshawed with all the animals of the Arctic on both horns. It was really a spectacular thing. I kept it in my office for a long time, and when I sold TEMSCO I gave it to my son Dan who has more room to display it than I have.

Leaving Savoonga

Come time to leave St. Lawrence Island, I went over and knocked on the door of Ora Gologeren's house and told her I was leaving. She already knew, and she said, "I have a lunch for you." There was a little peach in the lunch sack. I can imagine what it cost her to give me that peach. She said she knew I was going to take a long trip, and she wanted to be sure I had something to eat.

She gave me another sack too, and said, " Erma wanted to give you this, but she was too shy to give it to you. She enjoyed the helicopter ride so much." I didn't look in it until later when I got to Nome. Here was this beautiful little Eskimo doll made

out of all the furs—lemming, fetal seal, reindeer hide and things like that. The face, eyes, mouth, and ears were stitched in, and the stitches were so fine you almost had to have a magnifying glass to see them. It is one of my prize possessions—a little Eskimo doll—one you could never find in a curio store.

Ora, Erma, and another family member posed for this photo with me.

When I was fueling up the helicopter, one of the Eskimo fellows I had seen around Savoonga came up to me and said, "What are you going to do with the empty barrels?" I said, "You can have them if you want. Why don't you take those other barrels too? They have been here quite a while." "Oh," he said, "they don't belong to anyone here. I can't take them." Those people are extremely honest. What a great virtue.

Now I was ready to head for Nome, and an Eskimo came up to me and said, "You're going to Nome?" I said, "Yeah, I'm going to Nome." He said, "You got nobody with you." I said, "That's right." He said, "Do you mind if I ride with you?" I said, "No, that's fine with me." He got in the helicopter not knowing what he was getting into. I was chuck up with fuel which gave me plenty of extra fuel. I could go halfway out and come back easily. As usual I had to run a compass course to Nome because I had no ADF.

I took off on my compass course and ran into some low clouds. I started going underneath the low clouds, and they got lower. Finally they became a low fog, and here I was halfway across the Bering Sea. It was not rough that day. That was the only good thing. The clouds were squeezing me. I was getting down to where I was getting uncomfortable under a 100-foot ceiling. I got on the radio and nothing. I thought I had better get on top of this stuff. Here I was out in the middle of the Bering Sea scud running like I was at home in Southeast Alaska.

I decided to do something different. I found a hole, crawled up on top, and stayed over the hole for a minute. When I got up to a couple thousand feet, I got on the radio and contacted Nome. I told Nome that I was running into a lot of fog, and they said Nome was all fogged in. I said, "How about Anvil Mountain?" Anvil Mountain was open so I decided to go for it. Anvil Mountain is behind Nome and there was a road that went all the way up to it. It was the old gold mine area, and Dick Gallagher had taken me up there and showed me around. He had a cabin up there. So I got on top of those clouds and headed for Nome. I finally got to Nome and called them on the radio and told them I was over Nome and headed for the Anvil Mountain Road. I was going to hover down the road to Nome. About halfway down, Flight Service called again, "Well, where are you now?" I said, "I don't know. I can't tell for sure, but I'm still on the road, and I'm still working my way toward the airport." I finally got to town, scudded over the water out to the airport, and safely down.

The Eskimo guy got out of the helicopter and said, "Thanks a lot, bye," and away he went. One bad thing happens to a lot of the Eskimos. No liquor was allowed on St. Lawrence Island so when they hit Nome with their low tolerance for liquor, they have a lot of trouble. And this guy did; I saw him later.

I stayed in Nome an extra day waiting for Clough to try to retain my services a little longer to do a job for his agency up by Teller and Wales. No such luck so I bid goodbye to my friends in Nome and started my trip home. I would rather have had company on the trip back, but I enjoyed the trip because it was now more familiar ground.

When I got home I sent Bradley Gologeren an ELT so if he broke down and drifted away when they were whaling, the Coast Guard could find him. They had very recently had a boat break down, and the people drifted around for a week before they were found—they barely survived.

Chapter 16,
Last Years with TEMSCO

As TEMSCO matured and grew, I found myself stuck behind a desk a lot more than I might have liked. I still flew a lot, but my main concern had to be keeping the business running. Bringing on my manager Bill Gale helped a lot, and let me worry less about the day-to-day affairs. That let me look at more strategic concerns and spend more time in the field. I saw what jobs were coming in so every time a good long trip came up, I took it.

Umnak Island

Some mining engineers wanted to go to Umnak Island out on the Aleutian chain, which was right down my alley. That's what I liked to do, long cross-country trips.

It was August 1986, and I was flying 1107G. We put the long-range tank in it, and started off for Kodiak. My daughter Suzy and her husband Russ Lybecker were visiting us at the time, and they wanted to go to Seward and on in to Anchorage to visit some friends, so Suzy and Russ got to ride up the coast with me.

Those big long beaches between Cape Spencer and Cordova are fantastic. There are always glass balls to be picked up and a bear or two to be seen out on the sandy beaches. You can read all kinds of stories of shipwrecks just by watching the coastline; the masts of some of the boats are there sticking out of the sand where they've been totally sanded in. It's always an interesting trip. You can see for miles, but fog conditions occur quite often. When they do, oftentimes you're flying under a 50-foot ceiling.

We got up the coast to Yakutat and took a little detour over the Hubbard Glacier, which had been advancing. The Hubbard Glacier had come ahead so far that it cut off a small bay, transforming it into a lake. A bunch of seals were trapped in the area.

It was on national TV, but we had to take a look for ourselves. Some environmentalists were there trying to capture the seals and move them to salt water. It was quite a show.

Then we headed into Yakutat Bay and up the coast to Cordova. We fueled up in Cordova, and flew up the coast to Seward at the head of Resurrection Bay. Seward was the town that suffered the horrible experience of the 1964 earthquake where parts of the town disappeared. It was really devastated.

I managed to buy a barrel of fuel at Seward and fueled up the helicopter with my hand pump and headed off by myself for Kodiak Island. I flew down the coast from Seward, and from there across a chain of islands to Kodiak. The first islands are the Chugach Islands, and then the Barren Islands. From there you hop over to Afognak Island, and across Afognak Island into Kodiak.

Kodiak's airport goes right into a mountain. The airplanes all seem to work it, but it sure doesn't look like a very hospitable place to me. There was a very friendly boy hanging around the fuel pump, and one of the important things on trips like this one is to have a supply of company hats. I gave the boy one, which made him pretty proud. After I got home I got a letter from one of my former office gals, Linda, who saw the boy wearing a TEMSCO hat and quizzed him about where he got it. She was sorry she had missed me.

After fueling up at Kodiak, I flew across the island to Karluk, which is on the Shelikof Straits side of Kodiak Island, and from there I could cross the straits to the far side where I was heading for Wide Bay. The crossing is about 30 miles, and you always feel kind of naked. It's one of the roughest stretches of water in the country—the wind just whistles down through the straits.

I went up the river at the head of Wide Bay until I came out onto the big wide flats on the peninsula. I saw the big duck flats, lakes and muskeg, bears and caribou—interesting country. The Aleutian Range is on the east side of the peninsula, and there are numerous big volcanoes that are active once in a while. I stayed out in the flats and followed the coast over to Port Heiden where, much to my surprise, I found a guy wearing an

One of the treasures of those long flights is a chance to beachcomb for glass balls. Here Bill Hornbaker and I have gathered some real beauties near Cape Sukling.

old Ellis Air hat. He was running the airport and the fueling for Northern Air Cargo, which runs all those stations out there. It was Ray Chamberlain, the son of an old mechanic I knew from Ellis Air.

After I fueled up, I headed on down the beach toward Cold Bay which was another two hours away. All the legs of my trip lasted about two hours, so flying at 110 knots, I would cover in the neighborhood of 220 miles. I saw some amazing things flying up the coast to Cold Bay. I passed one area where there were thousands of glass balls. I made a point to remember where that was, and on the way back I picked up about 100 glass balls and gave them to the crew in Juneau.

Another interesting thing I saw along the coast was stacks and stacks of crab traps that looked like huge buildings. In some places there were piles of the floats that are tied onto the crab traps, some stacked up like a mountain. I had no idea of the immensity of the crab fishing operation that had gone on here in the past. It is shut down now.

I flew by Point Molar and then on down the coast into Cold Bay which is a little windswept spot with an airport and a runway 11,000 feet long. It was one of the more important runways built during World War II, and it could handle anything. I guess it could even handle a spacecraft now.

I took off from Cold Bay and headed down the Alaska Peninsula. Near the end of the peninsula you cross a place they call False Pass to reach Unimak Island. There is a big bay on both sides and a little narrow gut where the water flows between the Bering Sea and the Pacific Ocean. I followed along the outside north shore, and when I got to Cape Sarichef at the end of Unimak Island, I heard the voice of another helicopter pilot crackling in my headset. It happened to be Tim Enabrad, one of my former pilots, who was flying for one of the fish companies in the area. He told me, "If you get into trouble, there is a barrel of fuel at Cape Sarichef." When I first came to Alaska, there were two men on Cape Sarichef Light Station and the whole works, people and all, was wiped off by a tidal wave from an earthquake in the area.

With that in mind I crossed a stretch of about 40 miles across the ocean, what they call Unimak Pass, to hit Akun and Akutan, the first two islands in the next series of island chains. Akutan had a little mine on it as well as a cannery and a nice little harbor. Akutan was also in the history books in World War II. A Japanese airplane raiding Dutch Harbor took a bullet from the ground troops that affected one of his gauges. He thought he was going to have an engine failure so he declared an emergency and told his buddies that he was going to land in the spot they had selected ahead of time to use if they were damaged and had to make a forced landing. It was a great big flat area, but the Japanese did not realize it was a wet, soggy muskeg. The pilot attempted to land with his wheels down, and the plane flipped over and landed on the cockpit, breaking his neck. The plan was for a Japanese submarine to come and pick up any of the survivors from the airplane. In this case the two airplanes that were with him circled over and saw he was upside down. Orders were to destroy the airplane, but they thought he might still be alive, and they couldn't bring themselves to destroy him too, so they left the airplane. Later the wreck was discovered, and the U.S. Army and civilians disassembled the airplane, carried it out, and sent it to California. It was rebuilt, and its flight performance was measured so the Americans could hone their tactics and build an airplane that would out perform it in every way. And that's what they did with the Grumman F6F—the airplane that was built to beat all the specs of the Zero they had captured at Akutan Island.

Dutch Harbor is located on the Island of Unalaska and opens up into the Bering Sea area. Their airstrip was built on a little peninsula right in the bay. It's a fairly small airstrip, and a lot of airplanes have had trouble there. The Japanese bombed Dutch Harbor a couple times during the war. An old ship had been sunk in the harbor in those raids, and it was still there when I got there 40 years later. The people here were all prepared for war. It was interesting to see all the pillboxes and caves for their ammunition in the mountains. They even had a barbed-wire fence area where they kept a few prisoners from Attu after the Americans took it back. Attu was the last island out, and one of the ones the Japanese occupied for a while. The Americans also invaded Kiska, but the Japanese had sneaked out during the foggy night and saved their lives. Otherwise, the Japanese would have fought to the death.

Dutch Harbor was a real busy place. It was kind of a rough place when I was there because all the fishing boats were in port. The public bars were a good place to stay away from. However, I did learn a little bit about flying on this trip.

I met my two geologists from AMAX Inc., John Galley and Dick Hornsnail, who had arrived by commercial airlines, and we started out from Dutch Harbor. Their goal was to go down to Umnak Island. Umnak Island's claim to fame was a secret airfield called Fort Glenn built by the military during World War II. When the Japanese bombed Dutch Harbor, they didn't know that Fort Glenn existed. Somehow on the first raid there was a mix-up in communications, and the Canadian Air Force, which had fighter planes at Fort Glenn, wasn't alerted until it was too late. But on the next occasion when the Japanese attempted to bomb Dutch Harbor, the airplanes from Fort Glenn gave them a bad time, shooting down a number of their airplanes.

Fort Glenn was an extremely interesting place located right at the base a volcano. The airport was built on the level grounds of volcanic ash that covered the area—it made a nice spot for a landing field. There was no harbor at Fort Glenn so all the materials used to build this very nice airstrip had to be landed on the beach and carted up.

Across the bay from Fort Glenn, on the very far end of Unalaska Island, was the harbor of Chernofski which had gone down in history as the homestead of people by the name of Holmes who brought cattle in. The land out there is barren except for grass so it was a natural place for cattle. They built a homestead and had a large herd of cattle roaming around. There have been some interesting stories about the Holmes and their farm. The military built great big dock facilities and warehouses in Chernofski Harbor and abandoned them after the war. Some of the facilities are still standing.

Fort Glenn was abandoned too. I don't know how many troops were stationed there, but there were thousands of them. Some houses were built out on scenic points, which I didn't think was too wise for the military, but I guess they were officers' quarters. Bulldozers were used to dig a hole for the Quonset huts so that if they got bombed it would take a direct hit to get the Quonsets. We saw two large hangars still standing, and it was eerie because the wind was blowing a little and you could hear doors squeaking. Thousands of men had come through and fought a small part of World War II here, leaving these rusting metal memories. There were a lot of animals left behind after the occupational period as well. Wild cows, wild sheep, and wild horses were hanging around the old facilities. They weren't really wild (they didn't seem too afraid of people), but they sure looked strange. A sheep that has never been sheared is quite a sight. It looked like something out of another world.

Our job was to do some exploring down on the southern end of the island. The mining company had ten barrels of fuel brought in by airplane to the old airstrip, which was still usable. The airstrip had steel mats on it at one time, but the military removed all the steel matting for some reason. The buildings were left intact and contained parts and tools and everything else. I understand the tool shops were left completely equipped.

We worked on the south end of the island where there are

volcanoes and glaciers side by side. The engineers were looking at a bunch of water geysers. Hot water action from the volcanic area had revealed some traces of gold. The scenery was really something. Here we were prospecting a few miles from a geyser like Old Faithful that went off every ten minutes.

In prospecting around, we had one narrow escape—we got trapped on top of the mountain and had to hover off the mountain to get underneath the fog and get out of there. The geologists wanted to take a look at Okmok Cauldron so we flew up in there, and I landed on the upper ridge looking into the cauldron. It must have been ten miles across. There were steam vents here and there, and it was a real spooky-looking place. The geologists got out and picked up a few rocks. I wasn't too anxious to go down into the lower part of the cauldron because it looked like an active place to me so we took a few pictures and that was enough of Okmok.

Fog was quite prevalent in the area, and I finally learned one important thing after the first trip back from Umnak to Dutch Harbor. On the first trip out the fog rolled in just as we started back. We had to fly up the Unalaska shore, which has many little bays, and since we couldn't see but a quarter of a mile ahead, I had to go into the head of every bay and come back out. It made a very long trip back to Dutch Harbor. One of the geologists was on the map for me to help me find my way around. It was just a matter of following the shore, but at least he could tell us where he thought we were.

After we got back to Dutch Harbor, I got acquainted with a Goose pilot named Tom Madsen who told me that when the fog is on the Bering Ocean side, you go on the Pacific Ocean side and it won't be foggy. We learned our lesson. The next time the fog rolled in, we came down the Pacific side, and it was great. The fog was only on the Bering side.

We stopped at the Holmes Ranch just to let them know we were in the area and had a little talk with them. The Holmes had gone into town, but their boy was home. I think he was about 13 or 14 years old. A young lady who was his tutor was also there. It was interesting to go into their house. They had a real cowboy operation. In talking to them, the tutor said they had gone out with a metal detector and found some old Russian coins so she was enjoying her stay immensely.

Apparently after an inspection, the Holmes couldn't sell their cows on the meat market because of new meat care laws. Lucky for them, there was a great big rush to sell beef to the crab fishermen for bait. This seems kind of ridiculous, but at that time it was the heyday of the king crab fishery, and there were so many boats out there that the Holmes did really well. Even after that a lot of the fishing boats would call them up and have them prepare beef for them, disregarding the sanitation rules so they would have beef for their trips. Some of those fishermen stayed out at sea quite a while when they had a mother ship to take care of their catch for them so fresh beef would be quite a treat.

Finally the trip was over. The mining people took the scheduled airline back, and I started flying the helicopter home. It was foggy that morning, and I had a hard time getting out of Dutch Harbor. I wiggled around a whole bunch of islands and finally broke out into the open on the far side of Akutan and headed for Cold Bay. On the way into Cold Bay, I saw a great big brown bear out in the flats so I had to go down and say hello to him. He reared up on his hind legs and swatted at me so that was enough of that. If I had a little engine trouble or something right then, I knew what would happen to me.

I went on in to Cold Bay, fueled up, and traded hats with the pump attendant. I didn't have any trouble finding the spot where I'd seen all those glass balls. I had three survival suits aboard the helicopter so I dumped the survival suits out of their containers, threw the suits into the back seat, and filled up all three sacks with glass balls to distribute to the guys at the Juneau base of TEMSCO.

When I got into Juneau, they were as busy as ever running tourists up to the glacier. There'd been an airplane accident over in the Pelican area, and the state troopers needed a helicopter right away so I volunteered to take it and interrupt my trip back to Ketchikan. On the way to Pelican, we were cruising along fairly low, and we came right over the top of a big humpback whale with his mouth wide open and little tiny fish just flowing out of his mouth. We were looking right down into his mouth.

We proceeded on out to Pelican and found the accident on the mountain. For some reason the Coast Guard couldn't get next to it so they wanted us to remove the bodies. We weren't supposed to bring them in—they would do that—so we had to move them to a place where the Coast Guard could land and pick them up. The plane was a little Luscombe, and apparently they were looking at deer and stalled the airplane. It did a half-spin and crashed straight down. The most unusual thing to me is the fact that the pilot's right hand, which must have been in a direct line to the dashboard, penetrated the whole dashboard. It just doesn't seem possible, but the way things were lined up, that was the way the force acted, and his right fist was shoved clear through the dashboard of the airplane.

It always bothered me to see accidents like that because the one thing you don't do when you're flying around the mountains is get slowed down. Some airplanes are worse than others, but it always seems so needless to come upon a scene like that.

The Blue Team

For a period of six years between 1985 and 1991, I was on the Blue Team—a helicopter development team for McDonald-Douglas comprised of approximately twelve helicopter professionals from different countries. We met twice a year to discuss various aspects of the development of the Explorer, a NTR (no tail rotor) helicopter. Our goal was to develop a helicopter for civilian use that could serve all of our needs without making individual modifications. It was an educational experience for me and a challenge for us to match our needs with the engineering capabilities of the McDonald-Douglas people.

Building the Explorer was an international effort with people in Australia building the body; Japan, the transmission; Canada, the engine and electronics; Israel, the seats; and the United States, the rotor systems. The helicopter was assembled in the United States.

I got to fly one of the Explorers, and I purchased a production number (a purchase option) for myself and two for TEMSCO. The Explorer was a success in my mind, but the price of each helicopter was going to be $2.6 million—apparently about $1 million over the targeted price range. The Explorer was not able to compete in the helicopter market at that time, and only a few of them were built.

Helicopter Logging

In April of 1988 I took Jack Erickson from Erickson Sky Crane and a couple of Japanese men into the Iskut River area to look at some timber they thought the Canadian government was going to turn loose and make into a helicopter logging show.

I went into a pretty small spot in an isolated area so I just about had to do all the trips myself from then on so I could find the spot. On the next trip I took the fallers in to do what they call fall, buck, and scale, where they fall several trees, buck them into the right lengths, and then check them for quality and determine the value of the timber.

Another pilot would have much difficulty finding a small logging area because the fallers didn't even know where the place was, and there was nobody but the pilot who knew exactly where they had to go. This was quite often the case in helicopter work. You had the necessary knowledge to do what they wanted, so it was very important to put the right pilot on the right job. Oftentimes when you didn't, you had very poor PR.

Helicopter logging can be tricky business. This is a Bell UH-1 working near Metlakatla.

Bell Jet Ranger

In our business we had always stuck with Hillers and the Hughes, but we finally ended up with the bigger Bells, the 204s and the 212s. We had

The Ketchikan Gateway Borough did me a great honor in 1973 by naming one of the airport ferries the *Ken Eichner*. To this day I'm humbled every time I see my name on the side of that boat.

a need for a 206 Jet Ranger so we bought one from Scappoose, Oregon. Peggy loved to ride in the helicopter so we picked up the helicopter in Scappoose and brought it back to Ketchikan. We came up the coast on the way back, and stopped at Port Hardy for fuel. Old John Boranek was the fuel man. He was well into his 80s, and he had been there for many years. This was probably going to be the last stop I'd make to see old John.

John had been so good to us when we were ferrying airplanes and helicopters through there. When we hit Port Hardy, our next jump was Prince Rupert about 260 miles away, which was stretching the fuel limit of the Hughes 500s. John was not allowed to fuel up cans so he would say, "Well, I'm going to turn my back for a few minutes, and then I'll come back and read the meter." That was the way we were able to get enough fuel to make the next leg of our trip. We'd have to stop somewhere to pour fuel from the extra cans. With the Jet Ranger, however, and only two people, you could fill a tank up full and make the leg to Prince Rupert easily.

Forrester Island

The Alaska Department of Fish and Game counted sea lions,

and it was my job as long as I was available to take the Fish and Game people out to count. They counted the baby sea lions on Forrester Island about 25 miles off Dall Island on the west coast of Prince of Wales Island so they could determine if the sea lion population was increasing or decreasing. I would take the Fish and Game guys out there and land on a rock while they made their count. The rocks were pretty odiferous thanks to the birds and sea life, and there were large numbers of seagull eggs all over the rocks. I thought it would be a nice thing to bring a few eggs in for the office girls. The eggs are about the size of a chicken egg and are two-tone brown in color. I gave one to each of the girls in the office. Juanita was Bill Hornbaker's secretary, and she put her egg in a desk drawer and forgot it. She arrived in her office one day about two weeks later, and the egg had exploded and really smelled bad. All the other girls dashed home and threw their eggs away.

Another thing we did on Forrester Island was to take the Army out to catch young osprey. The first trip we caught three beautiful little white puffball osprey. The Army was going to train them to chase the starlings away from some of their airports. The next time they were looking for osprey to be trained to fly in aircraft as spotters to spot downed pilots with orange life vests.

When we went to Forrester after osprey, the young ospreys were ready for their first flight. One of the Army fellows got too aggressive, and the young osprey took off on its first flight and sailed out over the water. Its parents were nearby, and they buzzed the bird and turned him back toward the beach, but he crashed into the water before he made it back. We were able to pick him out of the water and dry him off all right, but he was pretty badly stressed. I was a little more tactful and caught two more, which were all the Army boys wanted.

I also took some foresters out there to dig a big hole in the muskeg to catalogue it. The muskeg or peat moss was very old, like some in Norway. Another company sent their geologist out to be sure they had not missed any mineral deposits.

Kenny Swaim

After TEMSCO bought out Tyee Airlines, we were operating

Army biologist with two of the Osprey at Forrester Island.

quite a fleet of airplanes. Kenny Swaim, son of Jack Swaim, who owned Webber Air for many years, was flying for us. I'd helped Kenny get some hours in the air, and he got his commercial license. When he finally started flying for us, Kenny had 5000 hours in the Otter. He just loved that Otter.

The morning of July 31, 1988, I had again selected a day off. I was going to take the weekend off at our cabin at Survey Point. Early the next morning an airplane kept buzzing the cabin. It was real early, and the airplane kept buzzing and buzzing and buzzing. Finally it landed and taxied up the beach, and I realized he was trying to attract my attention. I thought if TEMSCO wanted me, they would send a helicopter for me. I went down the beach and here was Miles Enright in his little Super Cub. He said that Kenny Swaim was overdue, and they thought they found the wreck so they wanted me immediately. I got in the Super Cub, and Miles gave me a ride into TEMSCO. I got all the information I needed and took a helicopter over to Dall Island.

All of the airplanes that had been searching for Kenny

arrived at Liscome Bay at the very south end of Dall Island. The sad story was that Kenny Swaim, who had been flying the Otter regularly, took a young couple out to Security Cove in a Cessna 185. They wanted to leave a couple of five-gallon cans of gas because they were going to be flown out and dropped off with a rubber boat so they could explore the outside shores of Dall Island. Kenny had taken them on one of these expeditions once before so he said, "I'll take them," and the dispatch girls never gave it a second thought and let him take the trip. Well, that moved him from the Otter to the 185, and the 185 is not a friendly airplane at low speeds and in tight quarters. Kenny took the couple out, and they looked over Security Cove, but there were some boats in there so they were afraid to leave their gas for fear somebody would steal it. The weather was not good; they had to fly under a low ceiling. They flew into Liscome Bay, which is fairly narrow, and at the end of the bay, Kenny attempted too steep a turn. The airplane stalled, crashed, and killed them all. It was a sad day for me, one of the harder things to take in the business.

Ralph Yetka

On August 12, 1987 I took a short vacation to visit my old partner Duey Barber in Sandy, Oregon, and as always seemed to happen when I took a little time off, something terrible happened. The USGS was doing a survey of minerals on Annette Island. Ralph Yetka had taken over flying the geologists when I went down to Oregon. When I got the call telling me we'd had a midair accident and Ralph had been killed, it was a real shock. Ralph was such a brain—he was so much help with everything around TEMSCO. He did everything plus his job. He taught celestial navigation at the college, and he was just one of those guys who could do anything you wanted him to, and do an excellent job of it.

Ralph was flying back in from Annette Island with one of the geologists who had a medical appointment. Ralph was going to take him into town during the noon hour. Ralph passed Corky Swaim in the back channel between Pennock Island and Gravina Island just before he came by the airport. From Ketchikan Air on the airport, Mike Salazar had taken off on the taxiway instead of the runway. Of course, Ralph would have been looking for somebody to come off the runway. Mike made a left turn and flew right into the top of Ralph's rotor system. One of Mike's passengers saw the helicopter coming, but he thought Mike knew it was there. The rotor blades cut the floats out from under the airplane, but Mike managed to make a belly landing at the airport with no serious injuries

Ralph Yetka at a TEMSCO function.

as a result. It was a total disaster, however, for the helicopter. Ralph was wearing a required helmet for government work which would have increased the blind spot in the upper left corner of the Hughes 500D. It's not likely that Ralph ever saw the airplane.

Customer Service

We got a call at the office that Dale Clark had taken Cliff Taro and his son and daughter-in-law out fishing at Freely Lake, and they hadn't come back in. There had been no contact with him so somebody had to go look. Immediately I went down there with the helicopter and found foggy conditions in the area.

There was some confusion about which lake was Freely Lake. I went first to the lake I had always thought was Freely Lake. Then someone called me on the radio to let me know that Reef Lake (which is another three or four miles up Portland Canal) was actually called Freely Lake.

When I got there, the ceiling was right down; but I was able to hover up the hill and follow the lakeshore to the head of the lake where I found Dale. He'd made the wise decision—it was too foggy for him to take off with the airplane. The Taros needed to get back to town right away so I took them back in the helicopter as far as Hidden Inlet Cannery. In the meantime I called TEMSCO on the radio and had Ernie Robb bring an Otter down with a load of jet fuel. Because I had extended my search so long, I needed more fuel to get back to town. Ernie left the fuel on the dock and took the Taros back to Ketchikan. I went back in to the lake to see if Dale could get out. There was no way he could get out so Dale spent the night on the lake, and I spent the night on the dock at Hidden Inlet, but our passengers got home to nice warm beds. This is just the way things go in the bush operation in Alaska.

Dave Doyon owns a nice little cabin on the beach at Hidden Inlet, and I figured there must be a key somewhere. I looked all around, but I never did find it, and I didn't want to break the door down just to get in to spend the night out of the weather so I slept in the helicopter for the night. Later Dave told me where the key was, but it was a little too late for that particular trip. Next time I'll remember.

Green Monster Mountain

One of the nice things about flying a helicopter is you get to do a lot of things that other people pay to do. In July 1989, my last year with TEMSCO, I took Jerry Booth, the Cominco chief geologist, and his boss, over to Jumbo Basin. They wanted to go underground to explore the old mine there. When we landed, they invited me to go along.

As a rockhound and prospector, I thought that was great. Green Monster Mountain is noted for epidote crystals, which are green, semi-opaque crystals, and they have a beautiful shape. The Cominco people were prepared with hard hats and lights and everything else, and we walked into the underground mining addit. Starting in we were wading in water about a foot deep, but then as we got back in the cave, it dried up. We went back in quite a ways and saw the extensive workings inside, big caverns where they'd taken out the high-grade ore.

Low-Side Governor Failure

After moving those people in and looking the site over, they had to move a couple of loads off of the mountain. In the process I had my first experience with a governor failure on the low side on an Allison C20B engine. When you talk about a high-side failure, it's pretty obvious. The engine runs away with itself, and you've got to shut it down. But a low-side failure—nobody really ever explained what a low-side failure was, and I don't believe very many people really understand it yet. But the low-side failure occurs on the high side of your torque when you're using power. Normally speaking, with a turbine engine, you're supposed to very closely watch the torque and temperature gauges while you fly, and you don't exceed certain levels. You're allowed so many seconds over 80 psi, and things like that. Actually, if you were to pull even 100 psi, you'd probably get an over-temp. The engine would keep running, but the low-side governor would supply extra fuel to keep the rotors turning, and the engine will quickly overheat. So on a low-side governor failure, you pull too much torque and that extra fuel never gets there. The engine just goes flat.

I was lifting a pretty big load off of Green Monster Mountain. It took me 80 psi just to clear the ground with it. I had to move just two feet forward and over the cliff, and dive down into the valley. I'd just started to move forward, and when you do that, you quite often pull just a couple more pounds of torque to do it, and the minute I pulled over 80 torque, the engine went flat, just as if you'd shut it off. I had just cleared the edge so I was able to dive out and reduce the collective. Now the engine was running fine, and I went down the hill and landed the load. I thought it was my technique.

Later on this occurred several times, and the fact is, Jack McKernan had the same thing happen up at Petersburg. He had a load of people in 88 November, and he was overloaded. He was used to nursing the helicopter out with the maximum load. In fact, he was known for going over the max quite a bit, and we were working on him real hard to keep him from doing that. But in this case he lifted up, and it was just 50-foot trees he had to clear, and he was going into a vertical hover. He had three people and their baggage with him, and he lifted up but couldn't quite clear the trees. The engine went flat, and he set it back down. He went through the procedure three more times, and finally he got to the top of the trees. He thought he could go, but when he started pulling more power, it faded, and he crashed. I believe he had a low-side governor failure. The factory people came up, and a representative said, "No, he just took off downwind." Knowing what I know now about low-side governor failures, I think his problem was low-side governor failure.

Later on 29 November, the helicopter I was flying that day, was still giving us trouble. And the failure kept getting worse. It got to the point where you couldn't pull 75 psi without it going flat. If you just pulled right up to 75 and never pulled another bit more, you could fly off with it, and it would fly fairly normally. You almost never used that much torque to land, so it was no problem.

One day Danny started out with it, and it started to fade at an even lower speed so we parked the helicopter and had them change the governor. All the problems were cured. Low-side governor failure should be stressed more with pilots flying turbine engines—it should be made clear.

Hunters, Helicopters, and Bureaucrats

Normally we were not allowed to pick up hunters with a helicopter, but occasionally hunters would get into trouble, and the state troopers would give us authority to go pick them up and bring them out. To begin with, we were not allowed to bring their guns or anything. Later on that law was relaxed. But we quite often just called the troopers and told them what the problem was, and they'd say, "Well, go do it." Some of our airline people had taken a group of hunters up to Tyee Lake. They were lawyers and other professionals. The Otter was unable to get into the lake, and the hunters were several days overdue. The wives were getting quite concerned. An airplane had gone up there every day for three days but couldn't get up on the mountain.

This particular day Ernie Robb called me on the radio and said he thought a helicopter could get those guys out of there today. I said, "Okay, I'll be up." I called the troopers, and there was no trooper in for the day so I told the gal in charge what I was going to do. There wasn't anything she could do about it, but I reported it and figured I'd done my duty. If we waited we wouldn't get them out of there. I went up to Tyee Lake and was able to get in. Ernie was waiting on the lake below. I was able to sneak up the ridge and get up into the lake and pick them up. They loaded up real quick, and I took a couple loads down to Ernie and the Otter. In the last load I had three fellows, and I said, "Well, there's no point in leaving you off at the Otter, I'll just take you to town because I'm going to town anyway." So I took them on into town. Well, all was well except later some of the people I had rescued off of the mountain got to bragging in a bar about getting picked up on a goat hunting trip with a helicopter. Word got out to Fish and Game, and they got hot on our trail. It was never pursued any further, but they sure had us nervous for a while. I thought I had done everything I needed to do to clear for that operation, and I had done everything by the book—the way I thought it should be done. But the Fish and Game was not too sure I had. However, they never made a formal case of it. Thank goodness.

Sold TEMSCO

We sold out all the stock in TEMSCO Helicopters, Inc. to Southeast Stevedoring in December of 1989. The three other stockholders who stuck with me were well rewarded.

Now my flying and rescue business is down to a bare minimum because I'm not sitting there listening to the radio for everything that happens. I've managed to help out in a handful of cases (including rescuing my grandson Eric after clogged fuel filters forced his, and another TEMSCO pilot's helicopter down near Ketchikan), but most of my flying is fairly uninteresting — except when the weather kicks in.

Re-Learning Old Lessons

In October of 1996, Lyn Campbell and two hunters crashed while looking for goats in the mountains. The rescue squad had gone up and taken the bodies out, but they left their survival gear behind. It was pretty important gear—enough gear for them to spend several nights on the mountain—so Jerry Kiffer and I flew up to get it.

It was snowing and not nice. I was unable to land, but I hovered with one skid down and let Jerry out. There was about two feet of snow on the gear, but he was able to locate it. I was still in a hover, and all the snow and the wind from the helicopter was making it extremely cold for Jerry, but he was able to get the gear and put it in the helicopter. We lifted off and got out of there.

Moments like this made you realize that you were really not prepared for this kind of weather. Strangely enough, this seemed to happen every winter. In the fall when it first turns to snow in the high country, and it is still pretty nice in the low country, you would find yourself up on the mountain improperly dressed without the proper gear, and you realized how cold it was and how easily you could get into trouble. After the first trip, why you were jacked up, and from then on the rest of the winter you were in pretty good shape to look after yourself.

Green Island Overnight

I kept one helicopter for personal use out of the TEMSCO sale, and I make occasional trips to Prince Rupert, B.C. with it to play a round of golf. On the way back from one of our golf trips with Gary Boles and his son Greg, we got into a condition where the ceiling was down to 100 feet. I left Rupert and started dodging around the little rocks between Rupert and Tree Point, and we finally ended up at Green Island light station, which is still manned. We landed and talked to the people, and I said, "We're going to try it once more, but if we don't make it, we're going to come back here because Prince Rupert is fogged in." I took off, and we went up the shore of Dundas Island.

We couldn't see across to Tree Point so we went back and spent the night at the light station. The two couples there were very hospitable. They cooked up a big dinner for us, and we spent a nice evening with them. They had made some home brew, and we each had a couple of bottles before we went to bed. Next morning the weather was good so we were home in 30 minutes. Later on we dropped by Green Island and left some goodies off for a thank you.

Flying Old Glory

People are funny. Three days after the terrorist attacks on September 11, 2001, I got permission to fly the flag over Ketchikan. It was a bluebird day, and I just thought it was a patriotic thing to do. Our country was having some real problems, and I wanted our countrymen to know we back them.

Quite a few people waved at me, including passengers on the cruise ships—some of them very enthusiastically. Many people left appreciative messages on my answering machine thanking me for the gesture. The *Ketchikan Daily News* carried a color picture of the helicopter with the flag on its front page.

Much to my surprise the city of Metlakatla invited me to fly the flag over their town the next day. The whole town was outside when I arrived. Children were released from school just to wave at the flag as it flew by.

I've been flying the flag during the Fourth of July parade for many years, and people seem to just take it in stride. It's strange how terrible events like that can bring what's important back into sharp focus.

In Retrospect

When TEMSCO sold, it took me off the front lines of aviation, particularly search and rescue. While I still help out here and there, the main responsibility now falls to my grandson Eric, who recently took the reins as chief pilot at the company my partners and I founded.

Over those years I made many trips along the coast of Canada, ferrying aircraft up the coast to Ketchikan from Bellingham, Washington or back down for modifications. Those trips have often marked major turning points in my life, and stand out in my mind. I remember the 12 hours of flight time it took to bring one of our first Piper PA-12s down for modifications, fighting headwinds all the way. I remember the 9-hour nonstop trip I made to Bellingham using autopulse gear to pull fuel up from the floats. I remember bringing the slow-flying Hillers all the way north carrying extra gas on the pontoon racks so we could make the longest leg of the trip—244 miles.

In May of 2002, Peggy and I made the trip from Ketchikan down to Bellingham once again to work on finalizing this book. This trip, taken in my personal Hughes 500D took only 4 hours and 54 minutes flight time. Things have certainly changed. The helicopters are vastly more powerful, and much, much faster. The navigation aids and radios are so much better than what we had. Even so, many of the critical skills of being a pilot: judgement, understanding your aircraft, understanding the weather, and learning everything you can about flying still ring true today. Pilots and outdoorsmen learn from each other's experiences, both good and bad. This book records many of those experiences and records a bit of Alaska's history along the way.

As I said at the beginning of this book, I've been extremely lucky in my time as a pilot. I've also been very fortunate that my wife Peggy was always supportive of whatever I wanted to do. Only on a couple of occasions did she ask me not to attempt a night rescue, but I felt I had to go anyway.

I've made full use of all my "nine lives" and probably used up several more. On many, many occasions if I had gone left instead of right, I wouldn't be here to write this book. It is my hope that by writing those experiences down, future generations of pilots will not have to learn those lessons and use up their "nine lives" the way I did.

About The Author

Father, pilot, businessman, sportsman, and rockhound, Ken Eichner spent most of his adult life in the seat of an aircraft. Based in Ketchikan, Eichner's adventurous life profoundly affected helicopter use in Alaska, helicopter design, the course of mineral development in Southeast, and the lives of many — especially those he and his employees plucked from the jaws of death in Alaska's wild country.

Photo courtesy of Cliff Kamm.

Recipient of both the Les Morris Lifetime Achievement Award (for pioneering achievements in helicopter aviation), and the Robert Trimble Memorial Award (given for exemplary mountain flying), Eichner was well-known among pilots in the American Northwest and Western Canada. After retiring from commercial flying, he kept his hand in various business ventures near Ketchikan. An outdoorsman to the core, he and his Hughes 500 were often seen flying from point to point, going prospecting, fishing, or otherwise enjoying Alaska's beauty. He flew the flag at Ketchikan's Fourth of July observances for years, and occasional flights to Prince Rupert to play golf punctuated his summers at home. Winters were spent in Kona, Hawaii, where he and his wife Peggy maintained a small vacation home. It was his hope that this book will share the color and character of his life, provide insight into Alaska's history, as well as pass on lessons learned to future generations of helicopter and seaplane pilots.

Kenneth Charles Eichner passed away Jan. 27, 2007.

TAYLOR Press
Additional Titles Available:

Thank you for reading **"Nine Lives of an Alaska Bush Pilot" by Ken Eichner.** For additional copies, follow the "Ordering Instructions" at the bottom of the next page. 352 pages, illustrated, softcover. ($19.95)

Sporting titles:

The Glock In Competition, Second Edition, by Robin Taylor

If you own a Glock pistol, and want to know more about it, this book will introduce you to the Glock's highs and lows as seen through the eye of veteran practical shooting competitors. Seven years in the making, the second edition of "The Glock in Competition" covers not only how to play the most popular shooting games, it explains reloading for the Glock, curing jam problems, tuning the trigger, and fixing the Glock's "Achilles heels" before they bite. Learn from champions like GSSF whiz Dale Rhea, Cor-Bon's master pin blaster Richard Morgan, and USPSA's top Glock jockey, Armando Valdes. 248 pages, illustrated, softcover. ($19.95)

Coming Soon!

The Practical Shotgun Book, by Patrick Kelley and Robin Taylor

If you want to shoot a combat shotgun well, get this book. Practical shotgun competition (a.k.a. "combat shotgun") is expanding wildly among pistol clubs around the world (yes, pistol clubs!). In this crucible of fast action and intense multi-gun competition, shooters are learning more about how to shoot combat shotguns than ever before.

This book has nothing to do with bird hunting or Skeet. We've picked the brains of the America's top competitors to bring you the "best by test" PRACTICAL shotgun techniques. Learn the strengths and weaknesses of the various popular shotguns, learn speed reloading techniques that ACTUALLY WORK, learn to use barricades and other supports effectively, get advice on stocks, ammo carriers, and other equipment, then learn little-known modifications to improve reliability in the most popular combat shotguns — particularly the Remington 1100.

If you rely on a shotgun in your line of work, you can't do without this book. Order now. Page count TBA, illustrated, softcover. ($19.95)

Ordering information:

Send payment plus $5 for postage and handling to: Taylor Press, 2559 Woodbine Place, Bellingham, WA 98229. You may purchase this and other titles through our website: www.taylorpress.com or www.taylorfreelance.com. Please allow three to four weeks for delivery. Dealers, please contact us at rtaylor@taylorfreelance.com or call us directly at (360) 733-5649.